THE FULL STORY OF THE ISRAELI-EGYPTIAN
PEACE TREATY — BY THREE JOURNALISTS WHO
WERE ON THE SCENE

EITAN HABER is the military correspondent for *Yediot
Aharonot* and author of a biography of Menachem Begin.
ZEEV SCHIFF is the military analyst for *Haaretz* and author
of a history of the Israeli army. EHUD YAARI is the head of
the Arab affairs department for Israeli television.

Their research took them from Jerusalem to Cairo, Wash-
ington, Morocco, as well as to secret meeting places where
Israeli and Egyptian negotiators met to pave the way for
Sadat's visit to Jerusalem. Their unprecedented story—
THE YEAR OF THE DOVE—is based on deep-cover
protocols, documents and interviews with Israeli, Arab and
American officials.

ABOUT THE AUTHORS

EITAN HABER is the military correspondent for *Yediot Aharonot* and author of a biography of Menachem Begin. ZEEV SCHIFF is the military analyst for *Haaretz* and author of a history of the Israeli army. EHUD YAARI is the head of the Arab affairs department for Israeli television.

THE YEAR OF THE DOVE

Eitan Haber,

Zeev Schiff

and Ehud Yaari

THE YEAR OF THE DOVE
A Bantam Book/November 1979

ISBN 0-553-13397-7

Published simultaneously in the United States and Canada

Bantam Books are published by Bantam Books, Inc. Its trade-
mark, consisting of the words "Bantam Books" and the por-
trayal of a bantam, is Registered in U.S. Patent and Trademark
Office and in other countries. Marca Registrada. Bantam
Books, Inc., 666 Fifth Avenue, New York, New York 10019.

CONTENTS

The Egyptian-Israeli Peace Treaty: Six Phases of Withdrawal From Sinai

=== Positions to be taken by U.N. troops as Israelis withdraw in gradual stages during first nine months

:::: North-south U.N. buffer zone during rest of three-year period before final Israeli withdrawal

● Israeli settlement

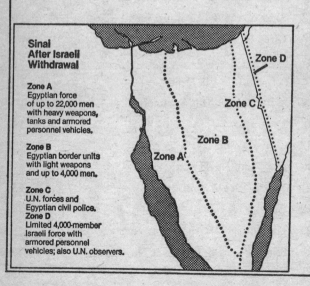

Sinai After Israeli Withdrawal

Zone A
Egyptian force of up to 22,000 men with heavy weapons, tanks and armored personnel vehicles.

Zone B
Egyptian border units with light weapons and up to 4,000 men.

Zone C
U.N. forces and Egyptian civil police.

Zone D
Limited 4,000-member Israeli force with armored personnel vehicles; also U.N. observers.

Zone D

Zone C

Zone B

Zone A

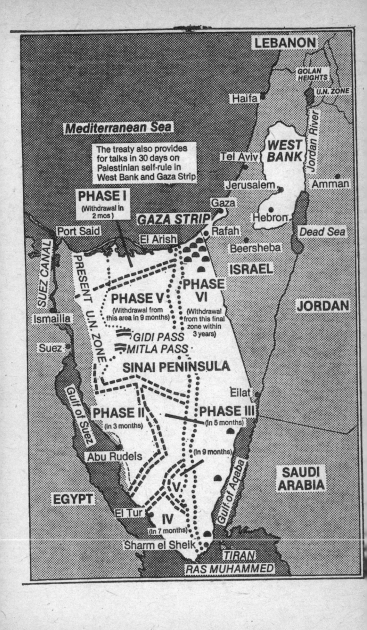

1 "I WILL GO TO JERUSALEM"

In Jerusalem, Prime Minister Menachem Begin and his wife Aliza were watching the movie *Gunga Din* on television, as were many other Israelis.

In Cairo much of the TV-owning population was tuned in to channel 2, which was showing the local film *The Black River*, while others watched Anthony Quinn on channel 1.

But not all of Cairo was watching TV. The Egyptian parliament, called the People's Assembly, was filled to overflowing that night, November 9, 1977. President Anwar al-Sadat had been speaking for two hours. Sadat makes many speeches, and his spokesmen regularly announce that each speech is "important," but so far no one had detected any "important" deviation from what he had said in the past. Now, however, the Egyptian minister of war, Abd-el-Ghani Gamassi, noticed that President Sadat had stopped reading from his prepared text. Gamassi leaned over and whispered to Ismail Fahmi, his country's foreign minister.

"It looks like he's going to drop a bombshell," Gamassi said.

Fahmi demurred: "There isn't going to be any bombshell; we've already used all our ammunition."

Neither one knew what Sadat was going to say.

There was no stirring in parliament as Sadat said, "I am prepared to go to the ends of the earth if this will help to prevent a single one of my sons from being killed or even wounded in battle." He had said this many times before in closed meetings of his national security council. But he went on:

"What I'm saying is that I'm prepared to go to the ends of the earth, and Israel will be surprised to hear me tell you: I am ready to go to their home, to the Knesset itself, and argue with them."

As thunderous applause rocked the large, circular hall, Gamassi leaned over to Fahmi and said: "There's the bombshell!"

"No," Fahmi replied. "It's an old idea which he rejected ages ago."

Begin heard the gist of the speech on the late night newscast, which mentioned the Knesset proposal only in passing. He went to bed. Naftali Lavi, adviser to the Israeli foreign minister, called his chief, Moshe Dayan. "This might be the usual way Sadat talks," he said, "but we must have the right reaction, do it quickly." Dayan said, "We'll examine how serious it is tomorrow and the day after."

Among those applauding in the Assembly Hall in Cairo was Yasir Arafat, chairman of the Palestine Liberation Organization. He apparently thought the words were just rhetoric.

The words were neither rhetoric nor a shot in the dark. Both sides had danced around the idea of a direct meeting for months, ever since the Israelis had put Begin and his Likud party in power in May 1977. The new Israeli government, like others before it, was enamored of the idea of direct negotiations. Sadat, fearing he was confronted with an opponent whose steps would be difficult to predict, felt the new situation in Israel required a change in Egyptian tactics.

Sadat knew that Begin was adamantly opposed to any settlement that was not a final peace treaty. Even as a minister in the National Unity government, Begin had disapproved of partial agreements, regarding them as a means of obtaining Israeli withdrawals without offering anything in return.

Begin had in fact been trying to find a channel of direct contact with Egypt. Shortly after the election, in June, Begin was the guest of Samuel Lewis, the new United States ambassador to Israel.

Begin, not yet sworn in, told Lewis: "My first objective as prime minister will be to open negotiations with Egypt for signing a peace treaty. I'm sure that the U.S. will allow us to use its good offices." Lewis did not know what to say. He knew that the U.S. government was working toward reconvening the Geneva conference with the participation of the major powers.

A month later, at the traditional Fourth of July reception at the American ambassador's spacious villa on the Mediterranean in Herzlia, Begin, now prime minister, mingled with the guests, who followed his every move. Begin seemed to derive great enjoyment from his new position and the deference it brought him. He met the Rumanian ambassador to Israel, John Kovacz, beside the swimming pool. Begin gripped his arm and said in a low voice: "Mr. Ambassador, if President Ceausescu will be so kind as to invite me to Bucharest, I will be happy to go to him." Kovacz was surprised, but said: "I'll deal with it."

Later that month, the Israelis, having uncovered evidence of a Libyan plot to assassinate Sadat, passed word of their findings to Egypt through Morocco, whose ruling family has long had a close relationship with Jews. The plot was frustrated, but no acknowledgment from Egypt reached Israel.

In August, the Rumanian visit became reality. Rumania was the only communist country that did not close its embassy in Tel Aviv following the 1967 Arab-Israeli war. While supporting Arab positions since then, Rumania tried to maintain correct relations with Israel, sparing no effort to contribute to bringing peace to the Middle East. Rumania has a respected Jewish community, and there is a fairly lively commerce and tourism between the two countries.

The president of Rumania, Nicolae Ceausescu, has been doing his best to gain a place in history as a great leader and he has done more than his task would naturally de-

3

mand. Ceausescu has a personal interest in encouraging the parties to the Israel-Arab conflict to reach a settlement. He is afraid of the Russians and believes that in a more stable Middle East they will be pushed aside. Moreover, were another war to break out, the Russians might impose large numbers of troops on Rumania on their way to intervene in the Middle East. In 1972 Ceausescu tried to arrange a meeting between Golda Meir, then prime minister of Israel, and Sadat. Meir responded to the invitation and went to Bucharest, but Sadat did not show up. The Israelis surmised that Rumania had gone too far in its role as intermediary, without having gotten the Egyptian president's consent. The Israelis regretted that an opportunity had been lost.

Begin was given a cool reception on his arrival in Bucharest in August 1977. In a ceremony which was supposed to be festive, the Rumanian prime minister criticized Israel's policy.

Begin was furious. The words of Prime Minister Manea Manescu were not in keeping with the traditions of hospitality. The Israeli leader replied somewhat sharply. Begin's aides considered cutting the official visit short. Its failure seemed assured.

Next day the sun shone. At Snagov, about 150 kilometers from Bucharest, the president of Rumania shook Menachem Begin's hands warmly. He had heard about the incident with his prime minister, and although he supported Manescu to the hilt Ceausescu thought that some attempt should be made to correct the bad impression that had been made on their guest. At the Rumanian president's residence, surrounded by acres of flower beds, lawns, and streams, Ceausescu invited Begin for a trip on the lake. The two leaders boarded the yacht *Zorila* ("Dawn"). A small group of reporters followed the two men from a distance, but could not hear a word of their conversation.

Ceausescu, who is not an easy conversationalist, used an interpreter, and the conversation lasted seven hours, until late in the afternoon. The two men talked at length about their respective years in the resistance, and finally reached political subjects.

Begin said: "I am ready to go anywhere, at any time, to meet the leaders of the neighboring countries. I would like to meet President Sadat. I am convinced that this would

4

be extremely useful in bringing peace to the Middle East."

Ceausescu had heard similar statements in the past from Golda Meir and other Israeli leaders. Begin knew that the Rumanian president was in direct communication with Sadat and had no doubt that he, Begin, had to prove the sincerity of his intentions. Ceausescu questioned him at length about his attitudes. He did not conceal his impression that Begin was in earnest.

"And if Sadat agrees to the meeting you propose," Ceausescu persisted, "will you make concessions?"

"Definitely," Begin replied.

The Rumanian president gave his Israeli visitor no respite. He spoke at length about the need to establish a Palestinian state and a total Israeli withdrawal from the occupied territories, subjects which Begin was least prepared to discuss. He firmly restated his opinion that there was no place for a Palestinian state and that there was no point in discussing a complete Israeli withdrawal. Begin and his host argued, but from time to time Begin said a few words which did not escape the Rumanian president: "Everything is open to discussion in negotiations."

As their long sailing trip came to an end Ceausescu concluded that his guest was a tough customer, but that it was not impossible to talk to him. "As the next stage," he said to Begin, "your representatives can meet Sadat's representatives and possibly in the near future there may be a personal encounter between the two of you."

Begin hoped that his Rumanian host would try to get some message through to Sadat. He decided to wait.

Sadat felt the days slipping by quickly without a solution. At the beginning of September he was talking to Hassan al-Tuhami, his deputy prime minister, a tall, robust man with a pointed beard, silvery hair, and spectacles who had become Sadat's secret confidant.

They were sitting in the guest room of the presidential palace at al-Kanter al-Hiriah, the Baraj, a castle built in the nineteenth century by Mehemet Ali near the old dam on the Nile. The castle, surrounded by a large park, is Sadat's favorite residence.

Sadat and Tuhami discussed the need to break the deadlock in the Middle East in September 1977. Sadat felt that a new, bold measure was required. Tuhami agreed.

5

They were silent for thirty very long seconds. Then Sadat said, almost carelessly it seemed: "Perhaps I'll go straight to Jerusalem." Tuhami was taken aback. Then he considered the possibly tremendous advantages of such shock treatment. Later Sadat put this idea before Vice-President Hosni Mubarak and Foreign Minister Fahmi, but he did not discuss it at length, so neither took the idea very seriously. Another time, Sadat, speaking to the national security council, hinted at the possibility of a journey to Jerusalem, but the members of the council did not take him in earnest, partly because he spoke in general, ambiguous terms.

Sadat was still turning the idea over in his mind, trying to find the right time and place. The process had to be slow and cautious; the idea had to penetrate people's minds gradually. Sadat called for the head of his intelligence services, General Kamel Hassan Ali, and asked him to examine opinions within the Egyptian army and among selected groups of civilian employees. How would they react to the idea of coming to terms with Israel? In the strictest secrecy, General Ali conducted an opinion poll. "The response is positive," he reported.

Gradually Sadat warmed to the idea. The affair had become a personal test. "It is impossible to change reality unless there has been a genuine shift in ideas," he said later. "It was then that I grasped that the responsibility I bore toward my people, this generation, and the generations to come compelled me to do my duty without taking into account the office in which I served . . . If I evaded that obligation I would be erring toward myself and toward my God . . ."

Sadat is a religious man immersed in Islamic tradition. A man of impulse, he visualized peace as a religious as well as a national mission. The journey to Jerusalem began to take on the mystical qualities that had been so much a part of him since his childhood. Sadat found a partner to his belief in Tuhami. Once during the weeks when Sadat was formulating his decision, the two men listened attentively to the dream of one of their colleagues, who declared that the Prophet Muhammad had appeared to him, commanding that peace be brought to the Middle East.

Sadat knew how to get in touch with Israel. When he decided that the time had come for the first exploratory meeting, Sadat chose Morocco as the site, and Tuhami as his representative. The Egyptians told the Moroccans that Israeli Foreign Minister Dayan would be the most suitable person with whom to establish contact.

The choice of Morocco was not accidental or arbitrary. The Moroccan royal family has a long tradition of patronage and warm relationships with the Jews. The Alawi dynasty, of which King Hassan II is the twenty-first ruler, has always been distinguished by its tolerant attitude toward Jews. During World War II, his father, Muhammed V, refused to impose the anti-Semitic Vichy regulations on the Jews of Morocco. Not only were Moroccan Jews never persecuted, but since the beginning of the seventeenth century Jews had held senior positions within the royal court. No persecutions of Moroccan Jews are known. In many respects Moroccan Jewry was a flourishing and protected community whose traditions had been adopted as part of the wider culture. Sites sacred to the Jews had become national holy places. The graves of Jewish saints had become sites of pilgrimage for Muslims and Jews alike.

Thus, unlike other Arab countries, Morocco had a special relationship with Israel. Although it had supported pan-Arab decisions and had sent troops to fight alongside the Syrians on the Golan Heights in the 1973 war, Morocco had taken a moderate political line in the dispute with Israel, and had allowed mass emigration of Jews to Israel in the fifties and sixties. This special relationship was accelerated when the struggle for the Western Sahara began. The foreign press related that Israel had invested efforts in cultivating its ties with Morocco. It had helped Hassan by giving him advice on conducting the war in the Sahara. Israeli advisers briefed Moroccan soldiers on how to fight desert guerrilla forces. Hassan sought international support and increased aid in order to contend with the Algerian forces and the Polisario Front, and decided, among other things, to obtain this from the Jewish community. He began advocating in public the amalgamation of "the Jewish genius with Arab power." He invited Moroccan Jews who had emigrated to Israel to visit and even return to live in Morocco. At the same time he attempted to persuade Sadat and the Saudi Arabian emirs, who often visited him, to try to reach an understanding with Israel.

The friendships of Morocco with Saudi Arabia and Egypt made Hassan an important link between Israel and the moderate Arab states.

With this background, Dayan suggested to Begin that an initiative begun in Morocco by Begin's predecessor, Yitzhak Rabin, be renewed. Begin agreed.

2 THE MOROCCAN CONNECTION

Dayan, on taking up his post at the old huts that house Israel's Foreign Office, had asked for all the documents on peace efforts, particularly from the recent past. Among them was one signed by Yitzhak Rabin detailing his contacts with the Moroccans.

The foreign press reported that in October 1976 Rabin paid a secret visit at the request of King Hassan, who told Rabin that he was afraid of the radical trends in the Arab world. He believed that Sadat would have to return to the Soviet sphere of influence sooner or later if the deadlock in the Arab-Israeli conflict was not broken.

Rabin asked his host why he, an Israeli prime minister, had been invited to the king's palace. Hassan smiled and said: "Back in 1958, when I was still heir to the throne, I proposed at a summit meeting that Israel should be accepted as a member of the Arab League. The Arab leaders almost fell off their chairs in surprise when they heard me. How many Jews are there in the state of Israel? Two and a half million? That's a tiny island in the Arab world, and anyway half of your population is like us."

Hassan proposed that the Israeli prime minister meet Crown Prince Fahd, strong man and heir to the Saudi throne. Rabin agreed. Hassan said he would inform Fahd, who has a house in Morocco where he sometimes spends his vacations. The two men arranged to meet again. Before leaving for Paris on his way back to Israel, Rabin left two questions in writing on the king's desk, directed to Sadat: (1) What does Egypt want in exchange for nonbelligerency? (2) What does Egypt want in exchange for a peace treaty?

Now, in September 1977, Dayan left Israel ostensibly for New York. But the El Al plane stopped off in Paris, where King Hassan's Mystère-20 jet was waiting for Dayan and his aides at the airport. Dayan removed the patch over his eye and wore sunglasses so that he would not be recognized. The Mystère-20 took off for Tangiers. The El Al plane continued to New York without Dayan.

In Tangiers, Dayan was taken to one of Hassan's palaces, where the king and the Israeli foreign minister conversed freely as they waited for another guest. Soon the door to Hassan's offices opened and Hassan al-Tuhami, Sadat's deputy prime minister, came in. The men stood up and the king's adviser Ben-Suda introduced Dayan to Tuhami.

Tuhami smiled. "There's no need to introduce Mr. Dayan," he said. "I know him well."

They shook hands. Dayan got to the point immediately. "Do you really want peace?" he asked.

"At least as much as you do," Tuhami replied.

Dayan said, "I propose that we arrange a meeting between Begin and Sadat, as Begin suggested to Ceausescu in Rumania."

"Sadat will not shake Begin's hand as long as Israeli soldiers are occupying conquered territories," Tuhami answered.

The conversation shifted to recollections of the distant past. Tuhami and Dayan argued over who was to blame for peace not yet having been attained. Tuhami spoke about a withdrawal from the Sinai as a minimum condition for a meeting between Sadat and Begin. When he realized that he had gone too far he asked only for an Israeli commitment to abandon Sinai as a condition for the meeting.

Dayan responded: "Impossible. Everything is open to discussion, without ideology. Maybe Sadat will convince

Begin to withdraw from Sinai. But this can only be the result of an agreement and not a condition for a meeting." Tuhami interpreted this remark as an assurance, and later reported accordingly to Sadat.

It was evening, the atmosphere was good and dinner was served, the members of the king's court participating. The king himself came and went from time to time. During the discussion he had often left the two men alone. Every now and then Tuhami would reminisce about the past.

There were light moments too. During their previous conversation Tuhami had spoken bitterly about Nasser's regime and Nasser himself. But during dinner he chided Dayan: "Do you want to tell me that you weren't hand in glove with Nasser, that you weren't paying him a salary?"

Everyone fell silent.

"Are you crazy?" Dayan retorted.

Tuhami told of Nasser's mental and physical exhaustion after the dissolution of the United Arab Republic in 1961. He mentioned the necessity of stopping the Russians. He hinted that Egypt wanted Israel's help in its conflict with Libya if there was an opportunity to act against its ruler, Muammar al-Qaddafi.

Dayan laid Israel's defense problems before Tuhami: "We have no interest in ruling Nablus or Gaza," he said. "The reason for our presence there is that the Israeli army can defend Israel from there."

Tuhami jumped from one subject to another. He described his religious views to Dayan. He believed that the Middle East had been the cradle of the three great religions but had fallen into a great decline, which was now about to be reversed. "We must remove the obstacles, among them war, which are preventing a tremendous spiritual blossoming and economic prosperity." After these achievements, Tuhami said, the region would take the place predicted for it by the prophets and the way would be paved for the inevitable war of Gog and Magog, when the sons of light would overcome the sons of darkness. Israel would have to decide in which camp it wanted to be.

Dayan was skeptical about the possibility of cooperating against the Russians, and switched the conversation to more immediate topics. He hinted to Tuhami that Israel would be prepared to include the PLO in the peace

11

process, or that at any rate he did not reject that possibility at some time in the future. Tuhami gained the impression that the Israeli veto concerning the PLO could be sidestepped.

After seven hours of discussion, Dayan and Tuhami took leave of one another in the presence of the Moroccan king. Dayan pressed Tuhami for a guarantee that contacts between Israel and Egypt would continue. The Moroccan king supported him in this, advising Tuhami not to be stubborn and to recognize that the main issue was Israel's readiness to engage in a dialogue and Dayan's assurance that "everything was open to negotiation."

Dayan asked: "Shall we meet again? In Washington, Morocco, or Jerusalem?"

"I'm not at all sure that we will see one another again," Tuhami replied.

Later Tuhami claimed he had purposely misled Dayan when they parted because he did not want to hint at President Sadat's proposed peace initiative. Before his journey to Morocco, Tuhami had known that Sadat intended to take a bold step toward peace. He had met the Israeli foreign minister to get an idea if such a step would meet with an appropriate Israeli response. He did not want to discuss the details of the agreement with Dayan. Tuhami gained the impression that there was a basis for a peace initiative, and reported it to President Sadat. He also informed the Saudis of the meeting.

Tuhami found it difficult to assess Dayan's character. During their long meeting he had been impressed by Dayan's familiarity with details, but he was not sure which were real opinions and which were being presented merely for bargaining purposes. Tuhami later said that he felt there had been some kind of understanding between him and Dayan, that it went much deeper than what was concluded during the talks between Israel and Egypt.

Dayan's interpretation of his conversation with Tuhami was much more limited; he expressed highly critical views about his counterpart. He returned to Paris and sent Begin a coded cable. From its contents the prime minister realized that nothing particularly new—except for the meeting itself, which was the first of its kind with the deputy prime minister of Egypt—had arisen during the discussion. Dayan had been on his way to the U.S. but chose to return to Israel to report in person to Begin. His unplanned return attracted the attention of the media. The tension rose, as the mystery remained unresolved; wild guesses were made in the press, on radio, and on television. Had Dayan met an African ruler or an Arab leader? In Cairo Tuhami was angry at the furor aroused by Dayan's return to Israel. Not a word was published in the Egyptian press, even later on, about the meeting, to avoid admitting that the ground had been prepared for Sadat's initiative. There was also annoyance about Dayan's return in Jerusalem. Dayan's opponents, both in the cabinet and outside it, claimed he had done it to gain publicity. Dayan did not say a word. Next day he left for the U.S.

In the second week of October 1977 President Carter sent Sadat a secret message about the deadlock in the efforts to convene the Geneva conference. Carter wrote that the deadlock could be broken only by a bold step. "What can be done in order to reach a compromise between the two sides?" Carter asked.

"From that moment," Sadat later said, "I began thinking in terms of acting quickly. I decided to view the situation from a new angle and to analyze it afresh."

Sadat's closest aides were still unaware of his deep reflections about the forthcoming change. "I reached the conclusion that any change must be in the very nature of our stand. We have grown accustomed to the idea, and an entire generation has been educated to accept it, that Israel is something taboo, something which emotional associations prevent us from approaching. If we really wish to come to grips with the nature of the dispute, in order to attain peace, we just find a new approach which will overcome all official procedures and will break through the barrier of mutual mistrust."

Toward the end of October Sadat, along with his foreign minister, landed in Rumania. He had lengthy talks with President Ceausescu, who told him of the discussions he had had two months previously with Begin. Sadat asked Ceausescu what his impression had been.

"Begin wants a settlement," Ceausescu answered.

Sadat said: "Does Israel's present government, led by Begin, the head of the fanatical Likud party, want peace? Can an extremist like Begin really desire peace?"

"Allow me to say in no uncertain terms that Begin does want peace," Ceausescu replied.

Sadat rejected the Rumanian president's suggestion of arranging a meeting between the foreign ministers of Israel and Egypt or one in which Sadat and Begin would participate. "I have heard all I want to know," Sadat said. As he flew to Cairo, with stops in Iran and Saudi Arabia, he said, ideas came and went.

In Jerusalem Begin guessed that the president of Rumania had talked at length about peace with Sadat. He sent a letter to Ceausescu: "What about the meeting?"

Ceausescu replied: "Activities are continuing."

In Cairo Sadat's ideas were focusing on a personal visit to Jerusalem at about the time of the festival prayer in the Al-Aksa Mosque as the first move in a political process which would bring about a radical change in the rules of the negotiations. "I have said that I would be prepared to go anywhere in my search for peace," Sadat said later. "Could I now rule Israel out?

"I wanted to put the ball in their court."

3 IMPASSE

The immediate channels of communication leading to the peace initiative were Morocco and Rumania, but it was clear from the start that the central role would be played by the United States—not just as a channel but as an active mediator under whose auspices the process would take place. Without the assistance of a great power, no progress would be possible. And even if they bypassed the Americans in the earliest stages, Egypt and Israel generally made sure to secretly inform the U.S. of what was going on. They both needed guarantees from the White House. Both were dependent on the Americans—the inhabitants of both countries ate daily from U.S. financial support—and saw the negotiations as a triangle in which the president of the United States played a key role. Washington could not be ignored. But America had a new president and both sides wanted to get to know him and his aides.

In March 1977, while still prime minister of Israel, Yitzhak Rabin, in Jerusalem, decided it would be worthwhile to have an early meeting with Jimmy Carter, who had been inaugurated in January, Rabin visited Washington and was given full honors and a warm reception. "I propose we go up to my room," said Carter to Rabin even before the coffee arrived. Rabin was surprised. The other guests remained at the dinner table while the president of the United States and the prime minister of Israel went upstairs to one of Carter's private rooms. They sat down by the fire.

"Here we are sitting by the fire, like close friends," said Carter to Rabin. "I'd like you to tell me your real views on the solution to the conflict."

Rabin was surprised again, and suspected that Carter was trying to trap him. Rabin thought the president wanted him to state Israel's withdrawal positions, or other views, so as to be able to say later that Israel had two positions—one for public consumption, and one private. Rabin was somewhat annoyed.

"Mr. President," he said, "I told you my real views just a while ago, downstairs, during dinner! I have no other views." Carter dropped the subject.

During the White House visit, while Rabin was being presented with an honorary doctorate at American University in Washington, Carter met the White House press in a news conference slated to deal with internal matters. But the second question, planted by the White House, was on the Middle East. The president, in reply, said that he was in favor of Israeli withdrawal to the 1967 borders, with slight territorial adjustments, and of a solution of the Palestinian problem.

The American suggestion during Rabin's visit that the talks be kept "inside the family" had been violated by Carter while his guest was still in Washington. Rabin returned from the university to Blair House. He studied the president's words closely, and a little later met Secretary of State Cyrus Vance. "Why did the president have to say all this?" Rabin asked. "I thought it was agreed that we were to keep it inside the family."

"What are you talking about?" said Vance, who added that he knew nothing about the president's statement. Within minutes a transcript was brought to him. Vance read it.

"Oh, no! No!" he cried. He was surprised.

Rabin left Washington an angry man. He saw Carter's act as a personal insult. He thought that this president had preconceived notions, collaboration with him was impossible, his methods were very strange, he broke promises and set up unpleasant surprises. "This president won't be good for Israel," thought Rabin.

In contrast, warm relations between Carter and Sadat arose almost immediately. Carter promised to work for an early settlement, guaranteeing to increase American aid to Egypt and hinting that he would try to bring the PLO closer. Sadat expected good things of Carter. He often spoke of Carter as an "honest man," and saw in him an exceptional president who in the course of two terms could change Washington's traditional policies. Sadat and Carter liked each other from their first meeting. Their religious motivation and their visionary tendencies united them, and—in the Israeli view—immediately created a different atmosphere in the traditional American attitude to Israel.

Sadat was ready to talk peace, though without normalization of relations, and without changing the fundamental Arab approach which refused to recognize Israel's right to exist. He spoke of a comprehensive settlement, and not of a separate peace between the two countries. "Anyone who wants to wipe Israel off the face of the earth—let him go ahead!" Sadat said to his people in response to the criticism of extremists. "Believe me, I'll applaud him. I have said, and I say again, that Israel is a fact." The Egyptian president chose the art of the possible. A series of interim settlements, resulting from Henry Kissinger's "shuttle diplomacy," changed the map. They removed some of the danger of war and created a momentum of negotiation and agreement. Israel got accustomed to the idea that it would gradually have to withdraw from at least part of the occupied territories. The Americans took upon themselves the role of active mediators. But now it became more difficult to achieve further settlements.

At secret talks during 1976, another settlement had been suggested: Israel would withdraw to the Al-'Arish–Ras Muhammad line in exchange for a conclusion to the state of belligerency, thus trading two-thirds of the area for an agreement which was less than peace. Peace would be agreed to in the unspecified future in return for complete withdrawal. Rabin and Kissinger believed this was the path to follow.

When Begin took over as prime minister he sensed that the era of interim agreements was over, and he wanted to check out the Carter administration's positions for himself, and to meet President Carter. He understood from the Rabin-Carter talks that there was no way to continue the method of prior consultations and mutual adaptation of positions, which had operated previously between Israel and the United States, especially with Kissinger.

In late July 1977, before his visit to Rumania, Begin arrived in Washington. Zbigniew Brzezinski, Carter's adviser on security matters, advised the president to avoid any conflict with Begin on this visit. Information from Israel suggested that the Begin government seemed very united, and that an attempt at confrontation now would only unite the Israeli people further. The decision of the White House was just to let Begin feel good during his visit, and Begin knew about this. Nevertheless, the White House did not refrain from presenting its plans and views on a comprehensive solution in the Middle East, through an emissary, a Jewish senator, Abraham Ribicoff of Connecticut. At a meeting at Blair House, Ribicoff told Begin that he had prepared a proposal of his own, containing guidelines for a solution to the conflict. "I've shown it to Secretary of State Vance," he said.

Begin was certain that the State Department was behind this errand.

"The goal of the negotiations is a comprehensive settlement," Ribicoff explained. "And this peace will be total, including diplomatic relations, trade relations, and freedom of movement."

The price Israel had to pay for peace was stated in the fourth and fifth points of Ribicoff's plan: "Israel will withdraw to recognized borders on all fronts." This would be a gradual withdrawal in stages, parallel to which security arrangements would be made in the area. The fifth point dealt solely with the Palestinian problem: the establishment of a Palestinian entity on the West Bank, which could be a demilitarized area that would conduct economic relations with Israel. In the first stage there would be a trust administration on the West Bank, with the participation of Israel and Jordan. After five years a referendum would be held on the West Bank to decide its future and the nature of the relations of the Palestinian entity with Jordan and Israel.

Begin saw clearly that although this program did not rule out the possibility that the Palestinian entity would find its expression in a Jordanian framework, it left the inhabitants of the West Bank the option of establishing a Palestinian state. This was directly opposed to Begin's plans and views.

The same day, July 19, 1977, Begin met President Carter. There was no talk of a Palestinian state. Begin put forward a nine-point proposal of his own, which he called "a framework for the peacemaking process between Israel and her neighbors." The main point was that Israel was willing to renew its participation in the peace conference at Geneva, which was to open on October 10. Begin also quoted to Carter from the paragraph on the Middle East in the Democratic party's 1976 platform, which said there was no substitute for direct negotiations. "I will greatly appreciate any initiative to promote such a meeting," Begin said. He left his meeting with Carter very pleased; on his return to Israel he declared joyfully: "There is no conflict!" The truth was that the conflict between him and Carter had only been postponed.

The White House had already developed a clear position by summer 1977. The proposals were brought to the White House by Brzezinski and Vance, who had drawn their ideas from a report prepared by a team of experts, most of them Democratic party activists, at the Brookings Institution. This brief report, first published in December 1975 and updated a year later, was the ideological basis for the Carter administration in drawing up its proposals for a solution of the Middle East conflict. The Brookings report became a bible for anyone who wanted to understand where President Carter derived his ideas.

Its point of departure was that it was necessary to work urgently for a comprehensive overall settlement, because interim settlements could not resolve the basic conflict. The key problem was defined as the Palestinian question, which had to find a solution in the settlement. The right of the Palestinians to self-determination would ultimately find expression in an independent state (which would take upon itself the obligations ensuing from the peace settlement), or in some kind of federal union with Jordan.

The report set out rules for solving one of the most sensitive issues: the status of Jerusalem. The principle was that the Holy City was not to be redivided, and that free movement was to be allowed between all its parts and to all the holy places, which would be controlled by the religious establishments. Most important of all, each national group of the population of Jerusalem would be entitled to political autonomy in its own territory.

Carter had resolved that the Arabs, in return, had to give Israel a real peace, with all that implied. This was not in line with Sadat's views: he still saw real peace and normalized relations "only in the next generation."

Nor was this all that bothered Sadat: he was also concerned by the obvious efforts Washington was making toward rapprochement with Damascus. He believed Carter was making grave tactical errors. Since they were after a comprehensive settlement, the Americans were trying to reach the Syrians, moderate elements in the PLO, and even—to get the PLO to participate in the peace process —the Soviet Union, which would take an active part. Sadat was afraid of this. He didn't want to cooperate with his pro-Soviet adversaries, and was afraid of Soviet conspiracy against him.

American courtship of Syria was obvious. Washington accepted the Syrian invasion of Lebanon with understanding as a move which would bridle the extremists in the PLO and stop the civil war in Lebanon. Sadat knew that Washington was trying to calm Israel, urging it not to take military action. Carter went to meet Syria's President Assad in Switzerland; later, American spokesmen said that the path to overall peace passed through Damascus. In Cairo this was interpreted as an American attempt to shift the center of gravity from Egypt to Syria, or at least to develop a second center of gravity.

Sadat was convinced that the American path would lead not to agreements at Geneva, but to a disruption of the conference. Assad had good reasons for objecting to Cairo's line. He was afraid it would bring Egypt to quicker agreement with Israel. He infected Jordan's King Hussein with his fears. Assad also rejected Sadat's compromise proposal to set up a preparatory working committee for the Geneva conference.

Sadat's distress increased sevenfold at the beginning of October when a joint American-Soviet declaration was made public at United Nations headquarters, in which Washington gave Moscow equal status in the peacemaking process and called for the Geneva conference to be reconvened no later than December. Israel was not the only one to be concerned that the Carter administration had helped Moscow reinforce its position in the Middle East; Sadat was afraid of a Soviet return by the back door.

Sadat's embarrassment was increased by the publication of a working paper, a few days later, formulated in Washington after negotiations into the small hours of the morning between President Carter and Israeli Foreign Minister Dayan, in which Dayan agreed to the participation of anonymous Palestinian representatives in the united Arab delegation which would attend the opening of the conference; these representatives would also take part in the working committees when matters relevant to the Palestinians were discussed.

Once the idea of an interim agreement for evacuation of part of the Sinai in return for partial peace had been dropped, now that Kissinger and Rabin were out of the act, there was no way to avoid the difficult problems of a comprehensive settlement. Instead of tackling well-defined, limited goals, the parties had to face apparently unbridgeable differences on the Palestinian question, the scope of Israel's final withdrawal, the nature of the peace, the role of the Russians and their Arab allies, and other complications arising from competition between Egypt and Syria. There was a wide gap between Sadat's and Begin's positions, and there was no way to compromise between Egypt and Syria on the ground rules for a Geneva conference. Carter's public commitment to a comprehensive settlement was threatened with collapse, and Sadat was very worried. A collapse of the efforts directed at Geneva, coupled with retreat from step-by-step diplomacy, could bring his whole peace strategy back to square one. He could not make an accommodation with the Syrians or the Russians, nor could he accept a prolonged deadlock. The path to Geneva seemed full of obstacles; Sadat felt that the conference had reached an impasse before it convened, an impasse that could lead to a war in which all Egypt's gains from the 1973 war might be lost. The impasse helped give birth to the idea of Sadat's new initiative and visit to Israel.

4 A REVOLVER UNDER THE PILLOW

Sadat's habit of playing his cards close to his chest, without consultations or partners, annoyed those close to him. When he is faced with an important decision he retires to one of the presidential residences to be alone for a few days. Later, when his decision has been made, he invites his aides to hear it. Veteran members of the government soon realized the difference between Sadat and his predecessor, Gamal Abdel Nasser, who—despite his proud and confident image—never made decisions on his own. Nasser considered matters together with his associates, hesitating before the final decision. The people around Nasser could influence him and attain independent positions of power, which led to a circle of strong, clever men, and unceasing competition in his court. The pyramid of Sadat's power had only one man on top, a man who did not like reading recommendations and reports and liked to surprise his aides—the expulsion of the Soviet advisers in 1972 and the war in 1973 are two examples. Sadat's advisers referred to the president, privately, as a latter-day pharaoh, despite their affection and respect for him.

Having dropped his bombshell in the speech before the

People's Assembly, Sadat withdrew into himself and left for home. His aides had to contend with the enigma on their own.

In his room in the gray office block on the "Black Square" in the heart of Cairo, Foreign Minister Ismail Fahmi hastily briefed his men. It was late; he told his aides to phone the newspapers and instruct the editors not to emphasize what Sadat had said about addressing the Knesset. "If possible," he said, "it would be best to omit the sentence altogether."

In his penthouse on Ben-Zion Boulevard in Tel Aviv, Yehiel Kadishai also thought that it "was not serious," that it was just "one of Sadat's tricks." Menachem Begin's loyal and energetic bureau chief had heard the pronouncement in a radio newscast. For a moment he wondered whether he should phone Begin's home in Jerusalem and draw his attention to Sadat's statement, but he decided that the declaration was not important, that it was only a phrase.

The phone rang in Begin's home at 7:00 a.m. on the day after Sadat's speech. The sixth prime minister of Israel had awakened at 5:00 a.m., as had been his custom for thirty-five years, dating back to his days as an underground leader, to listen to the BBC newscast and then to read the morning papers. The call was from Shlomo Nakdimon, a reporter who had been close to Begin for many years; he wanted the prime minister's reaction to Sadat's offer to come to Jerusalem.

Begin sighed. "I don't have the complete text of Sadat's speech and can't give you my reaction . . . I suggest that we wait until we have the full transcript."

Nakdimon felt his scoop ebbing away. "I've got the full version of what he said," he replied, and then got Begin's first reaction: "Regarding Sadat's readiness to meet us, even in Jerusalem, in the Knesset, if this is no mere phrase, I welcome his willingness and repeat the statement I made on taking office as prime minister, that I am prepared to meet President Sadat anywhere, including Cairo, in order to negotiate a true peace in the Middle East."

Obviously, the suggestion of addressing the Knesset seemed unbelievable to him. Like the heads of government in the United States, like the other Israeli ministers, the prime minister still saw a ray of hope in the Geneva conference. "Sadat can come to Geneva," Begin added when interviewed for an Israeli afternoon paper. "He can present his stand just as we will present ours. Neither side must turn its position into a prior condition." Begin rejected Sadat's demands for a withdrawal to the borders of June 4, 1967, and the establishment of a Palestinian state.

At 8:00 a.m. Begin's staff was waiting for him as he entered the anteroom leading to his office. They had just heard his reaction on the radio. "Was I all right?" Begin asked. They assured him that he had been. Pleased, Begin settled down to his usual work routine.

Begin had mixed feelings about Sadat: he both feared and despised him. He had joked with his aides many times at Sadat's expense and in closed meetings had given him various uncomplimentary nicknames. *Czodak*, Russian for "rascal," was the one most often used.

The *"czodak"* was, at that early hour, fast asleep. He had returned to his home in the Giza quarter, near the busy center of the city, late the evening before. His wife Jihan had been waiting for him. She had had twenty-four hours' warning of her husband's bombshell, and had encouraged and supported his decision. Despite his calm, she noticed that from that night on, her husband slept with a revolver under his pillow. She was not surprised. Years before, another Arab leader, King Abdullah of Jordan, had been assassinated after initiating peace negotiations with Israel.

That day, Sadat slept as usual until 11:00 a.m. Later he took his customary four-kilometer walk. His two heart attacks have left their mark, and Sadat looks after his health. Besides feeling a sense of historical mission, Sadat feels that time is short. When he was 57 he decided to devote himself to major objectives, leaving the minor issues to others. He developed a loathing for the daily routines of government; his short working day, from 11:00 a.m. to 4:00 p.m., is devoted to important matters only.

That morning, the surprising news caught up with Muhammad Hassan al-Tuhami in Al-Madinah, Saudi Arabia. The deputy prime minister of Egypt was on a hajj, a pilgrimage to the holy places of Islam. As someone close to the Egyptian president, Tuhami knew of Sadat's intention to say something about "being ready to go to the ends of the earth," but the meager information in the local papers indicated that Sadat had departed from the speech Tuhami had imagined he would make.

Tuhami was in a hurry. In a few minutes he was to take part in a ceremony on Mount Arafat, an important element in the pilgrimage to the holy places of Islam, during which seven stones are thrown at Satan. Tuhami was surrounded by a large number of pilgrims, all wearing seamless white sheets, who wanted to hear at first hand about Sadat's intentions.

"Don't you remember what the holy Koran says so clearly?" Tuhami asked the pilgrims, who did not know how to react to what had been said in Cairo. They listened attentively. "In Surat al-Asra, the chapter about the prophet Muhammad's night visit to the Al-Aksa Mosque, riding a legendary horse which could fly, it says that Allah would one day bring the Jewish people back to their land, one group at a time, and there he would put them to the final test . . ."

Tuhami fell silent for a moment and gazed at the faces around him. No one said a word. "Israel's victory in the 1967 war was the fulfillment of the Koran's prophecy about the success of the Jews," he said. "And now it is time for the test. Sadat is the foreign emissary whose task it is to warn the Jews, so that they will have no reason to complain that they were not informed before being put to the test . . ."

They hung on his every word. "And the test," Tuhami continued, "is whether Israel is prepared to give up the holy places to Islam . . ."

In the Egyptian newspapers, although headlines were devoted to Sadat's speech, the short sentence about his willingness to appear before the Knesset was lost in the sea of words or did not appear at all. Coverage was the same in Syria, Lebanon, and Jordan.

In an editorial in one of Tel Aviv's afternoon papers, the editor in chief poked fun at what the Egyptian president had said. "Sadat's speeches are all stratagem," he wrote. "The Egyptian president has come up with a new plum: for the sake of peace he is prepared to go even to Jerusalem . . . That fox knows that will impress the innocents in America—and that's where we will call his bluff:

for how can the man who refused to meet us in Washington come to us in Jerusalem?"

Sadat visiting Jerusalem sounded like a dream: both Arabs and Jews refused to believe it. Only two years before, the editor of the Kuwait paper *Al-Siyasa* had wanted to tour Israel for a series of articles but had been forced to drop the idea after being accused of treason and threatened with murder. The last time a citizen of an Arab state had visited Israel openly was in 1955, when the Egyptian journalist Ibrahim I'zat went for a few days. The Israelis had grown accustomed to regarding Arab pronouncements on peace as nothing but empty words.

At the State Department in Washington Sadat's pronouncement received an indifferent reaction. Coming as a surprise, it was given a cool, uncomprehending reception.

In Israel, as the day went on, momentum developed. In the afternoon Begin met with some visitors from the U.S. House Armed Services Committee. They asked him what he thought about Sadat's statement. "If the president of Egypt decides to come to Jerusalem he will be received with all the honor befitting for a president," Begin replied. "I will be happy to visit Cairo and see the pyramids . . ." he added.

Then Begin decided to appear on television the following day and speak directly to Egypt's 38 million inhabitants. The more he thought about it, the more he liked the idea. The idea of such a television speech had been broached earlier, and a date—October 10—had been set, but a heart attack had forced Begin to pass up the idea. Now he returned to it.

Friday afternoon, wearing his best gray suit, Begin faced the lights and cameras and reporters' pencils. Speaking in English, he declared: "Citizens of Egypt! This is the first time I speak to you directly, although it is not the first time I am thinking of you or talking about you. You are our neighbors, and always will be. For twenty-nine years there has been a tragic, completely unnecessary conflict between our country and yours . . ."

He went over the blood-soaked history of the relations between Egypt and Israel.

"We Israelis extend our hands to you. Our hand is not weak, as you know. If we are attacked we will always defend ourselves, as our forefathers, the Maccabees did, and be victorious. We do not seek a clash with you. Let us say to each other, and let this be a silent vow between our two nations: no more wars, no more bloodshed, no more threats . . ."

This last sentence was to become the catchphrase of the peace initiative, but Sadat was to be remembered as the man who gave it potency.

"In the holy Koran, in sura 5, our right to this land has been determined and sanctified," Begin continued, wanting to conclude his speech with some verses from the Muslim holy book. "Remember Moses' words to his people: 'Woe is my people. Remember Allah's goodness to you, when he appointed prophets from within your midst . . . Woe is my people, enter the holy land which Allah gives to you.' "

Begin's address made the headlines in the world press. Cairo radio and television interrupted their programs to react: "The address itself is welcomed by Egypt," but the official spokesman in Cairo criticized the fact that Begin had directed it only to Egypt and not to all the Arab countries. He added bitingly: "Begin quoted verses from the Koran to substantiate his claim, but he ignored others which contradict it." Indeed, there are many verses in the Koran which condemn the Jews to suffer degradation and poverty, having incurred the wrath of Allah.

Egyptian newsmen had not yet been briefed on Sadat's speech and the content of their articles reflected it: they did not know quite how to react.

Sadat continued to build up the tension. He reiterated his readiness to go to Israel "for a few days," in order to speak to the members of the Knesset about establishing a true peace between Israel and the Arab countries, during a conversation with the U.S. congressmen who had visited Israel the day before. The Americans swelled with pride. The first act of a historical drama was unfolding before their eyes.

Like a talented stage manager, Sadat prepared the background for the climax. Step by step he revealed the seriousness of his intentions. In each declaration he eliminated some of the queries, always leaving himself a path of retreat. In this way he captured tremendous interest, directing the spotlights at himself in anticipation of the event. To his aides he said: "We'll let the Jews grope in the darkness . . . we'll hold the reins of the game in our hands, and we won't let go." Sadat took care to leave his plans unpublished in full until the last possible moment. He realized, however, that in order to obtain a maximal response he would have to issue fresh signals every day.

Not every response was favorable. The Palestinians were the first to recover; they reacted to the pronouncement with predictable hostility. "Sadat is a bootlicking idiot," declared the spokesman of the Popular Front for the Liberation of Palestine.

On Saturday night when Begin arrived at a party at the Tel Aviv Hilton in honor of a French delegation, dozens of reporters and cameras were waiting for him. He was delighted to see the forest of microphones: "In the name of the government of Israel I officially invite the president of Egypt to come to Jerusalem . . ."

The hall resounded with applause.

"This is the invitation," Begin enthused. The hall echoed even more. The microphones caught the thunderous acclaim. The cameras did not miss the moment of excitement.

"Ahlan W'Sahlan," Begin concluded with an Arabic phrase meaning "Welcome."

5 "I HAVE THE HONOR . . ."

Reporter Israel Harel, at his home in one of the new settlements in Samaria, was not surprised to hear Chief of Staff Mordechai Gur's voice on the phone. Harel was a veteran paratrooper who had participated in the battle for Jerusalem in the Six-Day War and in the crossing of the Suez Canal in the Yom Kippur War. He is a personal friend of Gur and has helped write some of his books.

"Motta" Gur, the tenth chief of staff of the Israeli army, asked Harel to come to his home quickly. To save time, Gur had dispatched one of the cars at his disposal to collect him. Harel did not ask any questions, but set off.

A handsome, well-built man, Gur had a sharp tongue and unlimited self-confidence and was accustomed to expressing his opinions about political matters too.

He spoke to his friend freely and firmly. Early on Sunday evening the chief of staff did not yet know if Sadat would come to Israel. From the first Gur had not liked the idea of inviting Sadat to visit. He had said privately that before issuing the invitation Israel should find out from the Americans what the basis for continuing the dialogue between Israel and Egypt would be once Sadat returned home. It was not his job to concern himself with these questions, but Gur often said to his office associates that a visit to Jerusalem would give Sadat international renown as a man of peace while Israel would be represented throughout the world as the side responsible for every failure.

"We must not go forward too quickly," Gur said.

To his friend Harel he proposed a newspaper interview. Every such interview has to be authorized beforehand by the minister of defense. This time Motta Gur did not ask for an authorization, and certainly not from Ezer Weizman.

"It must be clear to President Sadat that he cannot deceive us again, as he did in the Yom Kippur War. We know that the Egyptian army is preparing for war against Israel in 1978, despite Sadat's declaration of willingness to come to Jerusalem," Gur dictated.

The reporter was surprised by Gur's bluntness. "Why are you taking that tone?" he asked. "What is the basis for your suspicions?"

"If one wants peace one doesn't hold aggressive maneuvers," Gur answered. He described in detail to the reporter what he knew about the Egyptian army's recent movements and habits. Harel had known nothing about them: not a word had appeared in the media.

A few weeks before information had come that Sadat was planning a war for February or March 1978. This had been discussed seriously by the cabinet.

"If we have to go to war, it's better to do it now," Weizman had remarked at that meeting.

Begin had ended the discussion by instructing the Israeli army to take steps to avoid surprise. The Israelis had noticed the maneuvers of Egyptian units along the Suez Canal front and had quietly drawn up their army facing them. Air reconnaissance flights had been increased and additional armored and paratroop units were sent to Sinai. President Sadat was informed of the Israeli reinforcements and he instructed General Gamassi to be on his guard. The Egyptians were afraid that Begin would embark on a preventive war. It was a quiet war of nerves, with maneuvers and countermaneuvers on a limited scale.

"I will be happy if Sadat comes to Jerusalem with the genuine intention of making peace," Gur dictated, "but the reliable information that has reached us indicates otherwise . . ."

Israel Harel put his notebook down. The interview had ended. He was still stunned by what General Gur had said so bluntly. "If I were prime minister," he said to the chief of staff, "I would dismiss you for a declaration like that!"

"If I have to choose between my responsibility as chief of staff, particularly after the Yom Kippur War, and the fear of being dismissed or reprimanded, my preference is undoubtedly for the responsibility I bear," said the man who headed Israel's armed forces. His predecessor had been dismissed after being charged with being taken by surprise in the 1973 war.

On Sunday morning there was still much confusion in Jerusalem. Though the radio was continually broadcasting guesses and news items about President Sadat's forthcoming visit to Israel, the members of the cabinet did not know what Sadat wanted. Would he come? When? Why? What was he up to? Their fears were tremendous.

The communications media in the U.S. and Europe praised Sadat's "historic step," describing it as "sensational" and "astounding." The exchange between Cairo and Jerusalem captured all the headlines. Sadat was particularly pleased that the information about his forthcoming trip to Jerusalem had been a complete surprise. "When I made that announcement," he said to the journalists he met that day, "my aides were horrified, but I am at peace with myself . . ."

Sadat never tired of explaining that his journey to Jerusalem was not tantamount to going to Canossa. He had no intention of abandoning to Israel a single inch of the territory conquered in 1967, but was going there in order to "beard the lion in his den."

In Cairo, General Ensio Siilasvuo of Finland, coordinator of UN forces in the Middle East, was summoned hastily by Egyptian War Minister Abd-el-Ghani Gamassi. Siilasvuo noticed the changed atmosphere. People talked to him about peace being just around the corner.

Gamassi received Siilasvuo in his office in the War Office, in the Heliopolis quarter. He wanted Siilasvuo to inform the Israelis that the bodies of three more Israeli soldiers had been found. The Egyptians were dismantling some of the former Israeli army strongholds along the

Suez Canal, in preparation for widening it. Beneath the ruins of what had once been the Bar-Lev Line they had found the bodies. Gamassi wanted the Israelis to be told that the bodies would be transferred to them as soon as possible. Siilasvuo recalled that on previous occasions the Egyptians had not handed over the bodies of Israeli soldiers without asking for something in return, usually the release of fedayeen or spies. This time the Egyptians did not ask for anything.

During the evening of November 13 or 14, at a conference at the Tel Aviv Hilton, Begin exchanged notes with his security men, who came and went several times. In one of the notes Begin agreed to participate in a joint television interview with Sadat. It was midnight in Israel when, tired and tense, Begin entered the room occupied by the manager of the Tel Aviv Hilton. The cameras were already whirring; the spotlights gave out immense heat. In New York the CBS newscaster Walter Cronkite talked by satellite to the two leaders in the Middle East. It was almost as if they were talking directly to each other. The television interviews took events a step further.

Cronkite asked Sadat: "Mr. President, when do you intend to make your visit?"

"As soon as possible," Sadat replied.

"Let's say within a week?" Cronkite asked.

Sadat replied: "You could say that. Yes!"

In the Hilton manager's office Begin listened through earphones.

Tuesday morning, November 15, 1977, began with an outburst of anger: Minister of Defense Ezer Weizman pounded his desk furiously. Prime Minister Begin contacted him several times. Weizman's office was inundated with phone calls from ministers, members of the Knesset, and friends. He rampaged through his office, seething and confused.

That morning *Yediot Aharonot* had published the interview with General Gur, printing his warning, "Sadat should know that if he is planning to deceive us, we will be ready for him," in large type. It was less than twelve hours since Sadat had declared his readiness to come to Israel "within a week." It seemed that Gur's timing was execrable. He had obviously not imagined that the interview would appear after it had become clear that Sadat was really prepared to come to the Knesset soon. At first it seemed the Gur interview would torpedo the chances of the Sadat visit and stain Israel's character.

Cairo responded immediately. "He's a naive man," an official spokesman said of Gur. "He has no political understanding."

"I'll fire him!" Weizman roared.

At that moment Gur was thousands of miles away. Weizman ordered him to return to Israel immediately. He had decided that if Gur did not have a convincing explanation he would instruct him to end his term as chief of staff at the end of December 1977, instead of April 1978 (which would be four full years after his appointment).

The morning of the fifteenth Begin dictated two letters. One was addressed to Sadat, and was an official invitation to visit Israel. The other was a personal letter to Carter. The letter to Sadat would be conveyed by the Americans. Then Begin went to the Knesset for formal approval of the invitation.

Begin was ceremonial and excited as he spoke. "The president of Egypt and I will speak peace to each other, and I am glad that neither side has presented any conditions for his visit."

The cabinet ministers were wearing formal suits, which they did not usually do. They knew that that session would be televised throughout the world. The members of the Knesset tried to catch the cameras from time to time, but the cameras were all focused on the prime minister's face. "The invitation to Sadat does not constitute an attempt to sow discord among the Arab nations," he said. "I am ready to conduct negotiations for peace and a peace treaty with all our neighbors . . . we believe that there is no reason for the quarrel between Egypt and us. It has been a long, tragic, unnecessary conflict. I invite Sadat to come here and start peace negotiations . . ."

There was silence in the chamber.

"I also invite the president of Syria, King Hussein, and the president of Lebanon . . ."

There was an interruption: "And will you invite Yasir Arafat, the chairman of the PLO?" asked Meir Wilner, representative of the Communist party, which supports the establishment of a Palestinian state.

Begin replied with a smile: "Wilner, there's no need to push. I hope that when Sadat comes here you won't heckle him . . ."

The Knesset chamber shook with laughter. Begin refused to read the contents of the invitation aloud. "It is not proper to make it public until the president of Egypt has read it," he said.

The members of the Knesset went to the rostrum to discuss the invitation. Finally, eighty-eight hands were raised to support Begin's motion to invite Sadat to address the members of the Knesset in Jerusalem. The three members of the Communist party raised their hands in opposition.

Later, again for the television cameras, Begin handed the written invitation to Samuel Lewis, the American ambassador. "Mr. Ambassador, I hereby give you a personal letter from me to Sadat, inviting him to come and visit our country . . ."

Not long after, in the American consulate in Jerusalem, the teleprinter clattered as it rapidly transmitted the invitation to Cairo. "My dear Mr. President, in the name of the government of Israel I have the honor of submitting you this heartfelt invitation to come to Jerusalem and visit our country. . . . Allow me to assure you, Mr. President, that the parliament, the cabinet, and the people of Israel will welcome you with warm enthusiasm . . ."

6 OPERATION SHA'AR

Begin still felt a fear of the unknown and the unexpected. He did not know precisely when, if at all, President Sadat would come to Israel. His dialogue with Sadat was still being conducted solely through the media. He wondered about Sadat's insistence on receiving a personal, written invitation, his not being satisfied with Begin's public speeches of invitation. Begin assumed that Sadat was afraid of anything that even hinted at a slight to his honor. A written invitation would commit the Israeli government to accord him a reception which would not be demeaning. Begin decided that if Sadat came to Israel he would be accorded all the honor due a head of state, as if there were no hostility between the two countries.

The first phone call on Wednesday to Begin's home in Jerusalem came at 6:00 a.m. from Samuel Lewis, the American ambassador, who said, "I guess that by Friday we will receive precise information about when President Sadat is coming to Israel."

"I am going to Israel without fear," Sadat said in an interview with BBC television. "Begin's hawkish government does not deter me. I am not afraid of strong governments, just as I am not afraid of the great powers."

Begin had scheduled a meeting with Weizman for that afternoon: Weizman had asked to meet him urgently. Begin assumed it was about the Gur interview warning Israel's people about the Sadat visit. The newspaper story had embarrassed Begin too, but he was not as angry as Weizman.

In Weizman's Tel Aviv office the atmosphere was cool, tense, and quiet. Weizman controlled his rage with difficulty. Chief of Staff Gur had arrived an hour before. On his way from Ben-Gurion Airport to the meeting with the defense minister he had already heard from his bureau chief and read in one of the afternoon papers that Weizman intended to conclude Gur's term as chief of staff early, reversing the decision of one week before.

Weizman's relations with Gur had alternated between the tense and the relaxed. Gur was an old hand at his job; Weizman was a new boy. Gur had unbounded self-confidence; Weizman was rather hesitant.

"Why did you do it?" Ezer Weizman asked.

Motta Gur explained that he had decided to make his views public out of a sense of national responsibility as chief of staff. He had not requested Weizman's authorization for the interview so as not to involve political strata in his opinions. Weizman refused to accept this explanation. He decided to reprimand him and end his service at the end of December 1977.

Gur was angry. He told Weizman that he would resign forthwith. Weizman said he would consult Begin before making a final decision.

Gur went to his home in a north Tel Aviv garden suburb to change from his civilian clothes into uniform and get back to his job as chief of staff. Weizman drove to Jerusalem to consult the prime minister.

On the Jerusalem road, near the large refuse dump outside Tel Aviv, a pedestrian was trying to cross the road. The driver, Yitzhak Azulai, turned the wheel of the car to the right. The car went off the road and overturned, injuring both the defense minister and his driver. A passing car took them to the nearest hospital, and Weizman was taken straight to the X-ray department. It was feared he was seriously hurt.

Gur had just put on his uniform when his bureau chief

phoned to inform him of Weizman's accident. Gur set off immediately for the hospital.

Begin phoned from his office in Jerusalem to the hospital's X-ray department, wanting to know how the defense minister was.

In the hospital, outside the X-ray department, Gur bumped into Reuma Weizman, the defense minister's wife. "This is his punishment," he said, wagging his finger at her. She was astonished.

In the evening a colonel arrived at Begin's office with a report from the army intelligence assessing the situation. Brigadier Shlomo Gazit, head of intelligence, posed this question: Has there been a change in Egypt's attitude to peace? He concluded that there had been no such change. In his report to the prime minister he wrote: "Sadat has changed his approach, not his attitude or his demands."

Like Begin, Sadat was tense. He flew to pay a short visit to his colleague the president of Syria, Hafez al-Assad.

"Do you mean what you said in your speech?" Assad asked. "Will you really go to Jerusalem?"

"Of course I'll go," Sadat replied. "I never say anything I don't mean."

"But how? How can you do it?"

Their meeting lasted four hours. At the end, the president of Egypt shook the Syrian president's hand. Assad was nervous and angry. "Listen," Sadat said. "Even if this is the last thing I do as president, I'll do it just the same! And if I fail, I'll admit that I was wrong and you were right and I'll hand in my resignation to the People's Assembly . . . Personally, I'm absolutely convinced that this initiative is necessary."

At a press conference in Damascus without Assad, Sadat was asked: "What do you expect from the visit?"

"Wait and see!" Sadat replied. "I haven't prepared anything except a speech. I have not asked to meet the cabinet."

"Will you really go to Jerusalem?"

"May Allah preserve me," Sadat ejaculated. "That's the thousandth time I've been asked that. The answer is yes! I only say what I mean."

He tried to be placatory. "President Assad and I agree on strategy," he said, "our differences are only about what is the right tactical approach."

Later, Assad said: "It grieves me greatly that I have not managed to convince him." He saw the Egyptian step as a betrayal of the Arab cause.

At the military air base at Abu Sweir, near the Suez Canal, the American ambassador to Egypt, Hermann Eilts, met Sadat when his plane landed, and handed him Begin's official invitation.

"Assad cannot force his opinions on me," Sadat said to the representatives of the media who surrounded him on all sides, "and I cannot force my opinions on him." The rift with Syria had opened. Sadat was to be abused and vilified.

There was a long history of misunderstandings between Sadat and Assad, beginning when Assad was a young pilot, a member of the Military Commission of the Ba'ath party, in comfortable exile in Alexandria during the short-lived Egyptian-Syrian union (1958–61). Assad, who came from a mountain village and was a member of the Alawi minority group, matured as a silent and thoughtful politician. He had never thought highly of Sadat's personality, regarding him as a bold, unprincipled adventurer whose true intent was to reach a settlement which suited Egypt, even at the expense of the other Arab states. Syria's maneuvers during the last few years had been intended to keep Sadat from doing this. The alliance between the two during the Yom Kippur War had not dispelled the suspicions; on the contrary, from the outset of the war each president was convinced that the other was working behind his back. Sadat was angry that Assad had agreed to a cease-fire before the Egyptian troops had completed their crossing of the Suez Canal. Assad believed that Sadat had used the Israeli counterattack beyond the Golan Heights to establish himself in the Sinai. He roundly condemned the Sinai disengagement agreements. Sadat had criticized the Syrian intervention in the Lebanese civil war. The two had competed openly for the right to set the tone among the Arab countries. The Syrians aspired to establish a new axis under their leadership, the so-called Arch axis from Beirut to the Mediterranean coast and Jordanian Aqaba on the Red Sea gulf. Egypt had tried unsuccessfully to draw Jordan and the PLO to its side. The ancient competition between the Nile valley and the Fertile Crescent around the Euphrates had been revived. Saudi Arabia's mediation at the Riyadh conference in October 1976 simply papered over the cracks of a deep-rooted rivalry.

Assad believed there was no logic in running madly after a settlement with Israel. The Syrians wished to gain time to strengthen their grip in Lebanon, where three divisions of their army faced the Christian militia and PLO fighters. Sadat was making a mistake by trying to obtain a settlement under American auspices, and the exclusion of the USSR from the negotiations seemed to the Syrians to sacrifice an important supporter. Assad remained faithful to the Ba'ath party's unbending doctrine: he was prepared to make "peace" with Israel only if Israel completely withdrew from occupied territory without any Arab commitment to recognition or normalization. Such a peace, of course, would only be a temporary cease-fire before continuation of the struggle to destroy the state of Israel in the name of the right of Palestinians.

Back in Cairo, Sadat summoned State Minister for Foreign Affairs Muhammad Riad, to offer him the post of foreign minister.

During a foreign ministers' conference in Tunis, Foreign Minister Ismail Fahmi, who still believed that Sadat did not really intend to go to Jerusalem, had told everybody so. Immediately before Sadat's trip to Syria, however, Fahmi realized that Sadat was going to do as he had said. He felt cheated. That very morning in an interview Fahmi had expressed support for convening the Geneva conference.

The next evening, after Sadat had returned from Syria, Fahmi submitted his resignation. "At this difficult stage through which our homeland and the Arab nation is passing," he wrote, "and because of the situation of emergency which has arisen, I feel that I cannot continue in my post and share in bearing responsibility . . ."

Fahmi was a professional diplomat with independent views. Generally considered one of the architects of Egypt's anti-Soviet line, he advocated "neutralizing" the U.S. in order to deprive Israel of its active help, while at the same time not putting all the Egyptian eggs in the U.S. basket, as Sadat had done. It was better, Fahmi claimed, to get the Americans out of the region than to allow them to get too much involved.

Two points especially affected Fahmi: immigration to

Israel, and the atomic issue. When Sadat talked about full peace in 1977, Fahmi made sure to add the unacceptable condition that Israel stop all immigration for several decades. This aroused angry reactions in Israel and slowed down the complex process of building trust. Fahmi did the same over the atomic question. Sadat had pushed aside the question of Israel's development of atomic weapons: he believed that the time had not come for demanding a decision. Fahmi ignored Sadat's directive, and together with Heikal made a series of demands about Israel's alleged possession of atomic bombs. But Sadat, when asked about it, dismissed the subject disdainfully, hinting in public that he did not think Fahmi was right.

Heikal encouraged Fahmi to resign while Sadat was still in Damascus. Osama al-Baz, director of the Foreign Ministry, tried to persuade Fahmi to postpone it, but was unsuccessful. Fahmi's resignation may not have surprised Sadat, but it disconcerted him. Then came another blow. Muhammad Riad not only refused to accept Fahmi's post but resigned immediately as second in command at the Foreign Ministry, in a demonstration of loyalty to his superior.

Other protests against Sadat's initiative mounted. In Iraq, Baghdad newspapers appeared with black borders. The forthcoming visit was described as a "national holocaust." Thousands of demonstrators shouted: "Sadat is a traitor!"

Syria declared a day of national mourning. Damascus radio broadcast "funeral" eulogies in memory of Sadat all day.

In Cairo, the PLO radio station attacked Sadat. Leaflets condemned his initiative. Students held spontaneous assemblies against him.

But hundreds of messages flowed into Sadat's office supporting him. And Mustafa Khalil, first secretary of the ruling Arab Socialist Unity party, phoned to say he had heard that Fahmi and Riad had resigned. He was aware of the dangers which threatened Sadat. "I want you to include me in the group going to Jerusalem," Khalil said. "Thank you," Sadat replied, "you're a true friend."

On November 17 President Carter phoned Sadat and Begin. To Sadat he said: "I congratulate you on your courageous decision to go and meet Begin in Israel. The eyes of the whole world are focused on you."

That afternoon the American ambassador to Israel visited Begin once more and told him that the invitation had been handed to Sadat and that the Egyptian president would indeed come to Israel. Now Begin was the only Israeli who knew exactly when Sadat would come to Jerusalem. In a previous conversation Lewis had asked him when the Jewish sabbath ended. Vice-President Hosni Mubarak of Egypt wanted to know if Sadat could arrive as early as 6:30 p.m. Saturday without violating the sabbath. Begin checked and determined that Sadat should arrive at Ben-Gurion Airport, at Lod, at 7:30 p.m., after the sabbath had ended, so that adequate preparations could be made. Another cable was sent from Cairo to Jerusalem: "The best time for us is 8:00 p.m."

"What kind of reception should I organize for President Sadat, low-keyed or high?" asked Dr. Eliahu Ben-Elissar, the bearded, forty-five-year-old director general of the prime minister's office.

"High-keyed," Begin said.

"What kind of ceremony shall we hold when the president comes?" asked Colonel Efraim Poran, Begin's military adviser, who had been appointed chairman of the restricted campaign headquarters.

"As if he were a friendly president," Begin said.

7 SAND SCREEN

Begin was not unmindful of Sadat's courage in proposing the visit to Jerusalem, but also he regarded Sadat's move as an act of weakness, even desperation. The Egyptian president would not have taken this risk, Begin thought, if he had had any choice. Furthermore, Begin had grave doubts about the seriousness of Sadat's intentions; some of Begin's advisers warned him that all Sadat wanted was an impressive show on television, designed as a trap for Israel.

Sadat was aware of the Israelis' confusions and suspicions, but he hoped his visit would shock public opinion in Israel and that Begin would prove himself the "de Gaulle of Israel," finding the strength to take decisions on withdrawal and concessions, as de Gaulle had in Algeria.

Each leader tried to read the other's thoughts from afar.

"I have studied Begin as a boxer studies his opponent before a fight," Sadat said. He reread Begin's *The Revolt*, while Begin reread Sadat's *Revolt on the Nile*. They studied psychological portraits, intelligence assessments, and expert recommendations.

Walls of blood, hatred, and stubborn belief of each in his own rightness separated the two men. Each had a deep sense of historical mission and an attachment to a religious heritage. Each bore not only the most ancient memories of a nation but a vision of redemption. In every speech Sadat mentions the seven thousand years of Egyptian civilization. Begin never misses an opportunity to refer to the legacy of Israel's prophets. Sadat quotes from the Koran, Begin from the Bible. For both, the past is not merely the justification for future hopes, but a powerful source of inspiration. Neither is orthodox in the usual sense, but both can be considered believers. Despite their sometimes mystical views, both have a close acquaintance with the dirty work of politics. They are mature politicians, without any illusions. Each has borne the burden of a negative image at home and a rich harvest of abuse accumulated along the way. Begin was once described as a "demagogue" and a "fascist" because of his extremist views. Ben-Gurion never addressed him by his name but said: "The man sitting next to Member of Knesset Bader." Sadat was considered an "adventurer" whom Nasser had called "Colonel Yes-Yes."

Neither Begin nor Sadat knew very much about the background of the other. Begin had never been to Egypt, had hardly ever talked to an Arab. Sadat had never visited Israel and knew virtually nothing about East European Jewry, from which Begin, like most other Zionist leaders, had sprung.

In the first decade of the century Brest Litovsk, also known as Brisk, was the regional town of the Polesie district. It was here that Menachem Begin was born in August 1913. Its mixed population had lived through many partitions and border changes among Russia, Poland, and Germany. It is remembered primarily because it was there, about a year before the end of the First World War, while the trench war was stalemated on the western front, that representatives of Germany and the new Bolshevik regime of Russia met and signed an agreement ending the war on the eastern front.

Muhammad Anwar al-Sadat was born in December 1918, in Mit abu al-Kum, a village in the Manufia region on the banks of the Nile. The villagers were extremely poor and could barely scratch a living from the soil along the great river.

Like the four thousand other villages in Egypt, Mit abu

al-Kum, saturated with Islamic orthodoxy, was far removed from the effervescent trends of the twentieth century. The village children were brought up on the ancient tales of the deeds of the legendary hero Abu Zaid al-Hilali, and on flowery verses that had been recited in the courts of the caliphs.

There was a large Jewish community in Brest Litovsk, and the Jewish youngsters learned in the youth and cultural clubs about the Zionist ideal, the attempt to find a national solution to the Jewish problem in Palestine, the land to which they turned each day in their morning prayers, the land whose name they never ceased to mention from the moment they learned to read Hebrew letters. The youngsters knew very little about that faraway land, the land of their dreams. They imagined it from Bible stories, from parts of prayers, from stories handed down from father to son, and from passages in Hebrew newspapers which had somehow reached them from Palestine.

Young Begin was distinguished by his voracious appetite for learning. Young Sadat was, to use his own description, "an unsatisfactory pupil."

Begin joined Ze'ev Jabotinsky's youth movement and wore its uniform, in preparation for emigrating to Palestine. His ability as a speaker who could move crowds was evident at an early age. Sadat's lean figure appeared at the first student demonstrations against the British.

Toward the end of the 1930s Begin and Sadat began their careers. Begin was appointed leader of Beitar, the youth movement of the Zionist Ze'ev Jabotinsky in Poland, which was said to number hundreds of thousands. In 1936 Sadat was one of the first lower-class boys to be accepted as a cadet at the aristocratic Egyptian Military Academy. He was an outstanding student there.

Begin fled from the German war machine that was mowing down Polish Jewry. His parents and brothers perished in the Holocaust. He fled to Vilnius, where he tried to gather around him the remnants of his colleagues from the youth movement. The Russian authorities did not approve of his political activities and, as he was playing chess one day, detectives knocked at the door of his house. He was arrested and sent to a labor camp in the snowy steppes of the USSR.

When the Second World War broke out Anwar Sadat

was serving as a junior officer in the Signal Corps at the Mankbad Camp in Sudan. Around the campfires he and his friends discussed their ideas about a revolution in British-controlled Egypt. On his return to Cairo he was attached to an intelligence ring operated by Eppler, a Nazi agent, from a houseboat on the Nile. Sadat kept track of Rommel's forces, which were approaching the Egyptian border. He was guided by the Arabic proverb "My enemy's enemy is my friend." Sadat participated in several operations designed to establish contact with Rommel's men. He openly admired Hitler and had a highly developed sense of underground activities. In 1942 the British uncovered him. He was arrested and his first wife and three daughters were left without financial support.

At the end of 1942 Begin was released from the Russian labor camp and reached Palestine, where he found his wife and many friends. Soon he was chosen to command the underground Irgun Zvai Leumi ("Etzel") whose aim was to banish the British rulers and establish a Jewish state. The Irgun used terrorist tactics against the British troops in Palestine. Begin, as its commander, was hunted by thousands of soldiers and policemen. He went disguised under several aliases as a lawyer, a rabbi, and a consumptive, and was never caught.

Sadat headed a small group that engaged in terrorism against the British in Egypt. He was arrested and sent to Cairo's central jail.

In the 1948 Arab-Israeli war, Egypt joined at the last minute, less from a sense of responsibility toward the Palestinian Arabs than from the fear that if it did not take part the Jerusalem king, Abdullah, would reap the harvest of victory alone. Many members of Egypt's ruling class objected to entering the war.

The humiliation of the Arab military defeat fed the atmosphere of unrest among the officers of the Egyptian armies, as it did among the other Arab armies.

At the end of the 1948 war Sadat was put on trial; after thirty-one months in prison he was acquitted. As an officer in the Egyptian Signal Corps he was stationed in Al-'Arish. From then on Israel was for him, as for many other Arabs, a fixed target. Erasing the shame of the defeat of 1948 was one of the major motivating forces of the time. Sadat listened to stories of the corruption and pollution which had gripped the troops. He followed the military trials of officers charged with buying rusty arms for bribes. He was astonished to discover how many errors had been made in the conduct of the war. Together with his friends he began planning the revolution.

In the young state of Israel Begin revealed himself to be an inspiring speaker. His party had won only 14 seats of 120 in the Knesset, but he spoke vehemently of how little had been achieved in the war. His opponents condemned him as a hothead; the protest demonstrations of tens of thousands which he organized in Tel Aviv and Jerusalem pushed him to the far end of the political spectrum. Many of his compatriots considered him an irresponsible politician. The Arabs linked his name with the slaughter of their coreligionists in Dir-Yassin, a village captured by Irgun soldiers at the beginning of the 1948 war. Begin was condemned to the frustration of being in opposition. He wanted Israel to occupy both banks of the Jordan River.

On July 22, 1952, Sadat was in Cairo when the revolution came. He was an active member of the Free Officers group, which sought to remove King Farouk from power. Sadat participated in the revolution, and it was he who read the first announcement over Cairo radio. The revolution was successfully completed the next day.

Here and there voices in Cairo asked that a way be found to make peace with Israel. "Make peace with Israel and reduce the budget," wrote Egyptian author Salameh Mussa. "Lead the nation instead of being the victims of its slogans!" But Mussa's voice was drowned by the shouts of the masses. Egypt was caught up in a spiral of hatred. Seeking legitimization for their absolute rule over Egypt, the Free Officers found new channels for their militant policy by bringing the Palestinian question onto center stage. The Palestinian question was no longer one of many problems of Egyptian foreign policy, but the center of the national struggle. All the channels of propaganda, the institutions of education, and the social organizations were mobilized to give this struggle ideological depth, to make the Egyptian public aware of its importance. In Israel the moderate line advocated by Sharet was defeated. The hawks had the upper hand.

Those years molded Israel's character as a country under siege. David Ben-Gurion's basic motive was to foil the

Arabs' plan of destroying Israel and, rather, to make Israel militarily the strongest state in the Middle East. To achieve this he used every means. His party, which had educated its youngsters in the social democratic values of Europe, suddenly found itself educating them toward militarism. The Israeli government's policy took the sting out of what Menachem Begin was preaching. The government, quietly and without acknowledgment, did almost everything that Begin had advocated earlier. Chief of Staff Moshe Dayan believed a clash between Israel and Egypt was inevitable. He worked toward it and Begin supported him from his seat in the Knesset. At this time Sadat was a leading proponents of pan-Arabism in Egyptian policy, which meant direct Egyptian involvement in the conflict with Israel as the touchstone of national integrity. Both Begin and Sadat desired the conflict.

In the autumn of 1956 another war broke out between Israel and Egypt. Israel attacked in the Sinai peninsula, in coordination with the Anglo-French campaign to gain control of the Suez Canal (which had been nationalized shortly before). On the eve of the war Ben-Gurion summoned Begin to his house. Ben-Gurion had a raging fever and when he had finished telling his old rival of the military plans Begin got up and went over to his bed. He shook his hand. "I congratulate you on your brave decision," he said. "You are guaranteed our support."

The war caused encounters of those who were to meet again during the peace initiative more than twenty years later. The architect of the war was Moshe Dayan. Sadat was at Nasser's side throughout his difficult hours. Tuhami was a cool and efficient messenger, who brought all the bad news from the front to Egypt's leaders as Nasser's bureau chief. Ezer Weizman, commander of an air force base, took part in two air attacks, one of them against an Egyptian destroyer which was shelling Haifa port and was captured immediately afterward by the Israeli navy. Ali and Gamassi commanded armored brigades in the Suez Canal region.

The Sinai campaign of 1956 cost only 180 lives to the Israeli side. The Egyptian price was much higher: thousands of soldiers were killed and 5500 were humiliatingly captured by the Israelis. In 1957 Ben-Gurion was forced to declare that Israel would withdraw from the Sinai peninsula. As a realistic politician he realized that he could not oppose a joint Soviet-American directive. The idyll between Ben-Gurion and Begin did not last long: Begin was angry at Ben-Gurion's "defeatism" and accused him of handing over the fruits of military victory. Thousands of Begin's supporters demonstrated in the streets near the ministries.

The 1956 war again made it clear to Israel's leaders that they would not be allowed to defeat a single Arab country in battle. After the war Israel received guarantees from the U.S. of free passage in the Gulf of Elath, the Red Sea, and Sharm al-Sheikh. The gateway to Africa and the Persian Gulf was opened. Egypt had to agree to demilitarize the Sinai peninsula and to allow posting of UN forces along the border on the Egyptian side.

Israel's 1956 victory put an end to the chances of a compromise—if there still were any—for many years. The link between the Israeli-Arab conflict and Egypt was strengthened after a war in which Israel was the partner of France and Britain, which had opposed Egypt's struggle for national liberation. When the Israeli army pulled out of Sinai in 1957, the Egyptians decided to observe the cease-fire, even though this meant loss of face. Nasser justified his policy as waiting for the best moment to strike; he compared the Zionists to the Crusaders. "Only eighty years after the conquest of Jerusalem the Arab nation succeeded in liberating Palestine," the Egyptian ruler used to say to the masses. Nevertheless, the Egyptians concluded that Israel was a continual threat to them as well as an active partner, always ready to fight, of the "sinking imperialist powers." Egypt drew even closer to Russia.

The border with Israel was quiet, but the Egyptian people were in a perpetual state of unrest. Messianic pan-Arabism swelled, fed by the undercurrents of traditional Islam. The Nasserist movement became a magic cure-all for the younger generation; it based itself on all the elements which regarded Israel as the major enemy of Islam, of the Arab countries, and of Egypt. Nasser fired the imaginations of millions of Arabs with the myth of Arab nationalism and a vision of greatness together with a recipe for social change. All the Arabs' strength was mobilized for the war against Israel. A popular slogan went: "We will throw the Jews into the sea."

Anwar Sadat, as chairman of the Egyptian People's Assembly, an important position, was involved at the highest level in the verbal war against Israel. Overshadowed by Nasser, it was difficult for Sadat to make an impression; his public speeches were not widely reported. He evidenced little affection for the Jewish nation, which he described as "a stiff-necked and brazen people, even toward its own god." His books, newspaper articles, and public speeches showed hostility toward Israel. "Israel was not created by chance," he wrote in his book *The Full Story of the Unity* (1957), "but in order to threaten the existence of the Arab nation, to prepare the way for its division, to exile its members, to rob them of their income, and to infiltrate Western influence . . . Israel is the point of the javelin directed at the heart of the Arab nation."

Twenty years before Sadat shook Begin's hand, the chairman of the Egyptian parliament had taken notice of the leader of the opposition in Israel. For Sadat Begin represented "Zionism unmasked." In one of his books Sadat accused Begin of aspiring to expand the state of Israel to the Nile and the Euphrates; Begin represented "the position that Israel wishes to hunt the Arabs like rabbits, one by one." Sadat's assertions were unequivocal: "Israel is a clear danger to the home of every Arab, to his income, his lands, and the skies above him."

Despite a wealth of published material it has always been difficult to ascertain Begin's attitude to the Arabs. As a Westerner, Begin, like most Israelis, tends to dismiss the culture of the East, but he has never said this in public. His party, Herut, pays lip service to the idea of peaceful coexistence with the Arab world. As a declared liberal, Begin still claims that the Arab citizens of Israel have equal rights. However, he has completely rejected the idea of establishing a Palestinian state alongside the state of Israel. In their heart of hearts the members of his party would like the state of Israel to consist only of Jews. A few extremists say it openly. Begin has hardly ever visited an Arab village; he tends to avoid giving special attention to the Arabs.

The revolution in Egypt raised a wave of expectations in Israel, too. It seemed that in a short while a new leaf would be turned in the relations between Israel and Egypt. David Ben-Gurion suggested a dialogue with the leader of the revolution, Gamal Abdel Nasser, an officer in the Egyptian army. Soon afterward Ben-Gurion resigned the premiership, but Nasser stated that he had "high hopes" of the personality of Moshe Sharet, Ben-Gurion's successor. Sadat was left on the sidelines.

Sadat, who sometimes accompanied Nasser on his tours of Egypt, noticed (as did Nasser himself) that the audiences followed Nasser's speeches attentively but expressed enthusiasm only when the Egyptian ruler spoke of Israel. Even in distant Bizerte, in Tunisia, Nasser's long speech was stopped by clamorous cries: "Palestine, Nasser, don't forget it!"

In 1970, after Egypt's defeat in the Six-Day War and Nasser's death, Sadat inherited an Egypt that was humiliated, approaching economic bankruptcy, and devoid of assets. The Israelis treated Egypt with undisguised contempt. One of Israel's most distinguished professors of Middle East studies described Egypt in a secret document as "addicted to hashish and subject to delusions." The assessment was that Sadat's regime was shaky and would not last long.

However, within a few years Sadat succeeded in establishing himself as a powerful ruler; it was his close aides who were not sure of their positions. The 1973 war granted him tremendous prestige and the aura of victory. Backed by his new status, Sadat began to change the course of the revolution. Egypt underwent a process of change in almost every sphere. Sadat claimed that he was merely adjusting misunderstandings, but his activities amounted to full de-Nasserization. Sadat felt secure at home on the eve of his trip to Jerusalem. There was no immediate threat to his regime; his main cause for concern was the continual erosion of Egypt's position of leadership in the Arab world. He was convinced that "without Egypt the Arabs can have neither peace nor war," but the other Arab leaders refused to accept his policy. From one speech to the next his disappointment with the other Arab countries, which demanded that Egypt pay the price of the conflict with Israel alone and unaided, became apparent. It was painfully clear to him that his country was heading toward a severe economic crisis which would only heighten its poverty. The decision to go to Jerusalem was, for him, a demonstration of his dissatisfaction with the

Arab countries, among other things. Sooner or later the others would have to follow in his footsteps. They would have to admit that they could do nothing without Egypt.

Sadat and Begin prepared for their meeting as a test of intentions. Sadat wanted to find out whether the price Israel was willing to pay to fulfill its dream of peace with its neighbors was compatible with Egypt's minimum demands. "Israel cannot have its cake and eat it too," he said. "It must choose between peace and territories." Begin wanted to find out if he could get peace without relinquishing the West Bank.

Sadat wanted peace for Egypt without abandoning the Palestinians. Begin wanted the opposite.

These conflicting approaches were to characterize the entire peace initiative. But now, two days before the journey, the sweet smell of optimism and hope was in the air.

8 "REQUESTING CLEARANCE TO LAND . . ."

On Friday morning, November 18, thirty-six hours before Sadat was scheduled to leave Egypt, many in Israel still did not believe that the Egyptian president would actually get to Israel. The dangers inherent in the visit, particularly if it were not successful, were being pointed out.

General Gazit, head of intelligence, led the questioners and tried to visualize what would happen should the two sides remain enemies after the visit and should there be no peace treaty. He and others spoke of the dangers that would then threaten the state of Israel. Sadat's visit would plant the seed of dissension among the people of Israel, they maintained, and for the first time, perhaps, the nation would be divided over the rectitude and justice of Israel's stand in the confrontation with the Arabs.

The accepted Israeli outlook assumed that the Arabs' avoiding direct negotiations with Israel was the best proof that they did not really want peace, just an Israeli pullback followed by some arrangement that would fall short of peace. Sadat's announcement of his visit to Jerusalem shook this conception. Further, Sadat's move implied normalization even before the start of negotiations. Thus in a most surprising way the long expressed Israeli demand for direct Israel-Arab negotiations without mediators was accepted. About 9:00 a.m. an Egyptian Boeing 737 landed at Ben-Gurion Airport at Lod. The Israeli population awakened to a normal workday, but before starting to their jobs they turned on their TVs to watch the miracle with their own eyes: the first Egyptian plane to land with official permission at an Israeli airport. Israel Television usually does not broadcast in the morning, but the historic importance of the event called for an exception. Millions in Israel and throughout the world watched as the plane carrying the Egyptian advance party landed.

Spectators applauded enthusiastically as the white plane with the parallel orange-and-yellow stripes rolled to a stop. Airport workers paused to stare at the Egyptian flag waving from the Boeing's tail. All eyes concentrated on the door of the plane; then the Egyptian flight steward peered out for a moment, the ramp was lowered to the ground, and the first person came through the door: Hassan Ahmed Kamel, head of the Egyptian president's office. He squinted into the bright light and forced a smile that barely hid his agitation. For a moment at the bottom of the steps he was confused, not knowing whose hand to shake fist. Two people approached him: Dr. Eliahu Ben-Elissar, director general of the prime minister's office, and Ephraim Evron, director general of the Foreign Ministry. Ben-Elissar solved the problem by extending his hand.

Confusion was general and had been for the last forty-eight hours, since word had come of the time of the visit. Nothing was ready; preparations had to start from scratch. At a hasty meeting in Begin's office someone remembered that the most splendid reception ceremony ever accorded in Israel had been for Richard M. Nixon in the early 1970s. It was decided to shake the dust from the old file.

The most difficult problem was security. Too many people would like to kill Sadat. Some of the million Arabs living in the territories occupied by Israel considered the Egyptian president's visit a betrayal. It was decided to surround Sadat and his entourage with a security ring exceeding any ever set up in Israel. Tanks were distributed among the thousands of soldiers, police, and men of other security services. Large numbers of men were stationed on the road from the airport to Jerusalem and in the city. A supreme effort was made to eliminate all possible options to strike. Before Sadat had even left Egypt, helicopters were flying low over the Judean desert in the Jerusalem area to forestall any attempt to set up Katyusha rocket launching stands. At night, police and other security forces knocked on certain doors in the occupied territories and took known leading Arab instigators into custody to prevent the organization of demonstrations, riots, or sabotage. The detainees were told that as soon as Sadat left Israel they would be freed.

Those in charge of the Zahal (Israeli defense forces) orchestra were telephoning to Paris, London, Nicosia, and Athens, trying to get the score of the Egyptian national anthem. Finally someone recorded it from the radio; the first rehearsals had to rely on the tape. Flags were snatched from the sewing machine in a Jerusalem workshop and carted straight to flagpoles on the city's streets.

The horde of security men, who had come with the Egyptian plane, were very tense. Having been forbidden to talk with correspondents, they were not partners to the general excitement. Applause accompanied them to the airport restaurant, but even this did not bring a smile to their faces.

"What are we feeling?" one of them nevertheless responded. "Exactly what you would be feeling were you to come to a land that is considered an enemy country." Then he added: "People have gotten to the moon, so what is the big problem about getting to Israel?"

Hassan Kamel was pleased to learn that President Sadat would stay at the King David Hotel in Jerusalem, where Nixon and Kissinger had stayed. Prime Minister Begin had decided that Sadat would be put up at the King David because of its aura and status, although the security men had wanted the Hilton, where security would have been easier to enforce.

The Egyptian head of protocol asked which sites in Israel Sadat was obliged to visit, in accordance with ceremonial etiquette governing visiting heads of state.

"Yad Va-Shem," answered Ben-Elissar at once.

"What is that?" asked the Egyptian official.

"It is the largest Israeli memorial to the victims of the Holocaust during the Second World War." This memorial, on a hilltop in the outskirts of Jerusalem, houses documents, photographs, and other memorabilia commemorating the story of the death of 6 million Jews at the hands of the Nazis, preserving the record for future generations. It is accepted practice for any foreign head of state visiting Israel to spend time at Yad Va-Shem. More than any previous prime minister, Begin imputes great importance to these visits.

The head of the Egyptian president's office immediately agreed, surprising Ben-Elissar by his alacrity. Ben-Elissar added that it was also customary for a visiting head of state to place a wreath at the eternal flame burning in the Knesset square in memory of the Unknown Jewish Soldiers. He suggested that Sadat place a wreath of his own. There was no problem.

Ben-Elissar wanted to find out how long Sadat intended to remain in Israel but had to approach the issue tactfully, to avoid offending his visitors. "You are welcome to be our guests as long as you like," he said, "but we would like to know the duration of the visit so that we can make all necessary arrangements."

Kamel said, "We shall remain in Israel until Monday afternoon, and are very anxious that arrangements be made in such a way that our plane lands in Cairo while there is still daylight . . ." The Egyptians wanted the landing to be before dark to facilitate the organization of a mass welcome for Sadat upon his return from Israel.

Late that afternoon the delegation returned to Egypt, leaving the security men in Israel. An armored limousine was borrowed from the American embassy. The Hadassah Hospital in Jerusalem was supplied with reserve blood matching the blood types of Sadat and his colleagues. Operating theaters were placed on an emergency footing.

The Egyptians had insisted that the entire visit be transmitted live to Egypt, leading the Israelis to realize that Sadat had devised his trip to Israel as an impressive television operation. Egyptian TV had already shown the landing of the first Egyptian plane in Israel and millions in Cairo and other Egyptian cities had watched the historic event. The Egyptians were surprised at their gracious, deferential reception.

For several days the Israelis and Egyptians had been careful to avoid any special espionage activities near their border. Routine photography flights were stopped. IDF headquarters and the Egyptian War Office issued instructions that nothing was to be done that might be interpreted by the other side as a hostile act.

But during the evening Yigael Yadin, deputy prime minister and acting minister of defense, burst into Begin's office in Jerusalem. He called Ephraim Poran and Arieh Naor, respectively Begin's secretary for military affairs and the secretary of the cabinet, into a private room.

"I have just come from a consultation with the chief of staff in Tel Aviv," said Yadin tensely. "The Egyptian army has been put on the alert."

There was silence in the room.

"The whole thing may be a bluff," Yadin went on. He had been a member of the committee of inquiry into errors and oversights in the IDF's conduct of the Yom Kippur War. Yadin, like many Israelis, still suffered from the trauma of that war.

Yadin suggested the immediate mobilization of large forces of the reserves. Poran and Naor told him this was not to be done without the knowledge of Begin and Defense Minister Ezer Weizman. Poran used the direct telephone line to speak to them. Begin refused to hear of mobilizing the reserves. He felt that any such call-up would immediately be leaked to the media, causing an uproar and possibly even leading to the cancellation of Sadat's visit. Weizman, bedridden as a result of an accident, was furious. "I'm going back to my job as defense minister," he roared over the phone to Poran. "That bald ass is mobilizing the whole army for me already!"

The Egyptian army had in fact been put on the alert, but only because of the alert declared in the Israeli army for the duration of Sadat's visit, a step that had been taken by the IDF out of fear of surprises on the part of the Egyptians, other Arab states, or Palestinian organizations. Egyptian Minister of War Gamassi, on being informed of Israeli troop movements, had instructed his front-line forces to enter a state of preparedness. This mutual misunderstanding was an excellent illustration of the inflammatory foundations on which the Middle East lived.

In Ismailia on the banks of the Suez Canal, Sadat seemed to be at an impasse. Recent high-level resignations were a severe blow. He knew that he could not leave the posts open even for a few hours; he appointed Dr. Boutros Ghali as acting foreign minister. Ghali had to join the entourage leaving for the historic visit to Jerusalem on only a few hours' notice. He was ready. The man who added the ideological dimension to Sadat's initiative was a theoretician of rather ascetic appearance, a tall, slender man with slightly hunched shoulders and heavy-rimmed eyeglasses. He was an outstanding member of the Egyptian intellectual community, with no previous governmental experience. In spirit Ghali was a stranger to the pomp and circumstance of Sadat's immediate retinue, but he was to be responsible for adding polish and sheen to the president's gruff style, for giving historic depth and visionary uplift to a crucial moment in history.

Ghali had been the first—and almost the only—Egyptian to dare to consider the concept of peace and agreement with Israel not as a diplomatic slogan but as a practical possibility. As editor of an influential quarterly, he began a reassessment of the contents and targets of Egypt's peace strategy immediately after the Yom Kippur War. For a while he used the transparent cover-up of engaging in an exercise of predicting the future. Gradually, however, he developed the approach of confrontation in peace, with peaceful, armed coexistence. He suggested a settlement that would put an end to active military conflict, but not to the armaments race, by diverting the focus of the conflict to political, economic, and cultural planes. "The goal is not necessarily the liquidation of the state of Israel," he wrote, "but a struggle for the souls of its inhabitants, drawing the Jews away from Zionism and fusing them in the melting pot of Arab nationalism."

Ghali's life prepared him for his role in the conflict with Israel. He is the son of an aristocratic Coptic family that has been central in Egyptian political life for a century. In 1919 his grandfather, then prime minister, was murdered by fanatic Muslims because of his closeness to the British rulers. His grandfather also conducted negotiations with the founder of the concept of the Jewish state, Theodor Herzl, about granting a charter for Jewish settlement in Al-'Arish, on the border of Palestine and Egypt. The Copts were always suspected of coldness toward Arab nationalism and sympathy for the West; later, of pro-Israel bias. In today's Egypt it is not hard to find manifestations of hostility toward the Copts. Even Sadat has not blocked laws that discriminate against them.

For many years Ghali has been married to a Jew, which is unusual in Egypt. His wife, Leah Nadler, is the daughter of a candy manufacturer who fled from anti-Semitic persecution in Rumania and settled in Cairo. Her mother's family traces its origins to the Israeli town of Safed. Ghali met his wife while he was studying in Paris. As time passed, her whole family left Egypt, some of them becoming Zionists and going to Israel. Through his wife's family Ghali learned of the Jewish problem at first hand and sought a solution: a non-Zionist alternative for Israel's population.

On Saturday no television or radio station in the world ignored Sadat's forthcoming visit to Israel. Over a thousand journalists had gathered in Jerusalem. The most insignificant details were being photographed from every possible angle; the airwaves were filled with commentators describing events that were still to be. Preparations were almost completed.

At 10:00 a.m. a meeting was held in Begin's home to discuss who would be invited to the state dinner planned for Sunday evening.

The gathering at Begin's home was festive, with red wine and cake baked by Mrs. Begin. At the last moment Begin decided to change the route by which Sadat would travel from Lod to Jerusalem. For security reasons it had been planned to bring him via a new road which was not yet open to general traffic. "We'll drive on the main highway," Begin told Inspector General of Police Haim Tabori. This decision caused the transfer of thousands of soldiers and policemen over a good many kilometers to ensure the safety of the main road.

That evening at Abu Sweir Air Base there was a brief, not particularly impressive ceremony preceding the short flight to Lod. Sadat made a great effort to retain his composure.

In the control tower at Ben-Gurion Airport the flight superintendent adjusted his earphones to hear the Arabic-accented English of the pilot of Sadat's Boeing: "Egyptian airplane, Egypt 01 on special flight, requesting clearance for landing."

The plane was two minutes early and the pilot asked whether to circle the field or land at once. He was instructed to land at once. At 8:01 p.m. the wheels of Egypt 01 touched the asphalt strip. Three minutes later the plane taxied to a stop at the reception area. Twelve spotlights illuminated the white Boeing with the flag of Egypt painted on its tail.

The first passenger out was a plump woman who toddled down the ramp and broke into a run, making straight for the journalists' platform. She was from Egyptian television and was rushing to transmit the description of Sadat's arrival in a live broadcast. Dozens of photographers and reporters from Cairo followed her out of the plane and remained crowded around it, creating a barrier between it and the Israeli president, prime minister, and other illustrious guests. Pandemonium broke loose.

Millions of eyes were glued to the door of the Boeing—but no one came out. Tensions grew and then Sadat's military aide appeared in impeccable dress uniform.

After him a man in a gray suit, his features fixed and tense, appeared at the top of the ramp.

At that moment something indescribable tugged at the hearts of millions in Israel, Egypt, and the world as a fanfare of trumpets and enthusiastic applause greeted the visitor.

The president of Egypt, Muhammad Anwar al-Sadat, was on the soil of the state of Israel.

9 NO MORE WAR

Tears rolled freely in the first moments of Sadat's visit.

"The last time I cried was during the October War," said an American Jewish journalist, John Peters. "But this time the tears are of a different sort." Isam Maghribi, a twenty-four-year-old law student at Cairo University, said, "I found myself trembling and then I began to cry. I was overcome at seeing the honor an enemy bestowed on my president."

At 8:03 p.m., Rehabam Amir, chief of protocol for the Israeli Foreign Ministry, walked up the ramp to greet Sadat. "I'm at your service," Sadat said to him as the two descended to the waiting president and prime minister of Israel. In accordance with protocol, Sadat shook hands with President Ephraim Katzir first. Begin's excitement mounted. "I await you, sir," Begin said when his turn came, "and my ministers await you too."

For a second, Sadat and Begin locked eyes. Begin has never revealed what went on in his mind during those first tempestuous moments of encounter. Sadat has recalled thinking, "The people are absolutely stunned."

The strains of the Egyptian national anthem followed by the Israeli national anthem, a twenty-one-gun salute, a military honor guard—all were laid on to welcome the Egyptian president. The long red carpet was lined with VIPs. Sadat, who had asked to be introduced to Mrs. Golda Meir, shook hands with her warmly. "I've looked forward to meeting you for a long time," he told the former prime minister of Israel.

"But you didn't come . . ." she retorted.

"Well, now I am here." The two former adversaries smiled warmly at each other.

Sadat moved down the reception line. He recognized many of those present.

"I had planned to capture you over there," he told the minister of agriculture, General Ariel Sharon. Both knew he was referring to the west bank of the Suez Canal, which Sharon had taken in the October War.

"And I," Sharon replied at once, "am glad to welcome you here."

To Motta Gur he said: "I wasn't bluffing." Gur laughed, bringing a smile to Sadat's face.

When he faced Dayan, Sadat had little to say. He shook hands and said only, "Moshe." Deputy Prime Minister Tuhami, who walked just behind Sadat, paused in front of the man he had met in Morocco: "You said you were waiting for a phone call." Tuhami smiled broadly. "Here we are."

After the Six-Day War the press made much of Dayan's statement that he was waiting for a phone call from the Arabs in order to talk peace with them. This phrase was often quoted as an illustration of Israeli arrogance following the 1967 victory. Sadat and his entourage noticed that Arab leaders from the administered territories were not at the airport. It was a bitter pill.

Sadat and Katzir sat in the black limousine borrowed from the American embassy. There was a moment of embarrassment. Silence prevailed as the large black car sailed out of the airfield into the night on its way to Jerusalem.

It was Sadat who broke the ice. "Mr. President," he said, "how strange it is . . . This is the first time that I have ever shaken hands with people whom I have been fighting all my life, with all my strength and conviction. How is that—how could this come about?"

Katzir remained silent.

"Arik Sharon," asked Sadat, "what exactly does he do today?"

"He is minister of agriculture, and we respect him greatly for his courage and daring."

"Ah," Sadat mused, "if I had caught him then, when he crossed the canal in 1973 . . . I do not envy him now."

"In the 1973 war, he behaved as people behave in war," Katzir said.

Sadat looked straight at the Israeli president. "Courageous, daring, and aggressive military men . . . believe me, Mr. President, a serious statesman has got to be very wary of them . . . I personally am very cautious with regard to my own brave heroes."

Sadat went on to speak of himself, his peasant background, how he thinks of himself as neither a statesman nor a general, but a villager. He spoke of his wife, saying she was extremely gifted and that she loved him very deeply. "She is so keen to do well in her studies that she is hardly ever at home. But love, as we all know, makes up for everything."

Night had fallen as Jerusalem awaited Sadat's arrival. The sharp cold air of the capital had kept hundreds of thousands of its inhabitants at home, watching the great drama unfold on their television screens. From every apartment the voices of radio and TV commentators blared. Thousands lined the pavements to cheer the long convoy as it wound its way through the main streets of Israel's capital. Thousands of security and police personnel, and troops tense with anxiety, mingled with the crowd.

At that moment, an angry crowd was carrying a distorted image of the Egyptian president through the streets of Damascus. An effigy of Sadat was thrown into a bonfire. In Libya, the Egyptian legations were attacked by a mob that raised the flag of the three-nation federation, crying, "Sadat-Cohen is going to rebuild the Temple for the Jews." There was opposition at home. In a Cairo suburb, Palestinian students organized a demonstration at the head of which they pushed along a casket. "We shall dig your grave, O Sadat," they chanted. The stormy demonstration was broken up by young Egyptians. They attacked the demonstrators, but before they were driven away from the dark alleyways, the demonstrators cried out, "There is no God but Allah and Sadat is his enemy." Insults were hurled at Sadat by radio commentators in Damascus, Baghdad, and Tripoli. An entire dictionary of offensive insinuations and invectives were hurled at him.

Sadat feared that the Israel defense establishment had not exactly welcomed his extraordinary initiative. He had seen an interview with Chief of Staff Motta Gur in the newspapers and believed that the interview was only the first manifestation of certain undercurrents. When reports reached him of Weizman's accident, Sadat assumed that it was a fabrication and that Weizman, one of the more aggressive cabinet ministers, had sought an excuse to absent himself from the welcoming ceremony. It was of the utmost importance to Sadat to win the confidence of Israel's defense establishment. In the car en route to the capital, his anxieties were assuaged. President Katzir informed him that the Israeli defense minister had indeed been injured in a terrible accident.

Weizman had watched the welcoming ceremony on television, from his hospital bed. He was in pain and his doctors had given instructions for him to rest the following day as well. But that would be the day Sadat was to appear before the Knesset and Weizman was determined not to miss the historic occasion. He called his doctors to his bedside. "I'm going to the Knesset tomorrow," he told them. He asked them to prescribe a painkiller that could be administered by injection, and instructed his staff to arrange a helicopter for the journey.

At the King David Hotel in Jerusalem, Begin accompanied Sadat to his fifth-floor room. It was late and both he and Sadat were emotionally drained. The president and the prime minister were left on their own; on the other side of the door, Ben-Elissar instructed the security officer not to allow anyone to enter Sadat's room. Begin uncharacteristically kept no written record of his conversation with Sadat that evening. Nor did he ever speak about it at length to anyone, and only a sketchy account can be pieced together.

Sadat smiled. "I've been to Moscow three times," he said, "and every time Kosygin said, 'You are the guest, will you please set the ball rolling?' Well, now I am here."

The conversation was held in a relaxed atmosphere. Sadat told Begin that he would not be able to make a separate peace, that he had come to Jerusalem to discuss the Palestinian issue.

Begin hoped that he would soon be paying a visit to Cairo. He regarded such an invitation as a suitable reciprocal act, a matter of courtesy. But that would not suit Sadat. He did not think Begin would be accorded an enthusiastic welcome in Cairo and might even be endangering his life. "We like each other," Begin said, but to no avail. Sadat did not invite him to Cairo.

The subject of restoring Egyptian sovereignty to Sinai was apparently raised. Begin reportedly told Sadat he was ready to return all of Sinai to Egyptian sovereignty. Sadat, it seems, did not grasp the fine distinction between "returning all of Sinai" and Begin's phraseology, "returning sovereignty over it." For years Begin had objected to total withdrawal from the peninsula.

"I would like to set your mind at rest," he told Begin. "My striking force will not move east of the passes once you withdraw from Sinai."

Immediately after this conversation, Begin met with Yigael Yadin, who was in the next room. "Listen to this," he said to Yadin. "I explained our security problem in Sinai to Sadat. At first he said he was ready to have a demilitarized zone extending thirty to forty kilometers from the international boundary. When I explained to him again that such a distance would still be within gun range, he agreed with me and said, 'I've got to keep my army in the region up to the Sinai passes [which are 30 kilometers from the Suez Canal], but the rest of the area can be demilitarized.'"

Some believe that the promise to return the Sinai peninsula to Egyptian sovereignty was made earlier, during Dayan's meeting with Tuhami in Morocco. Tuhami reported later that Dayan had said of Sinai, "You can have it—it's all yours." Those who maintain this view argue that this was Sadat's precondition for his visit to Jerusalem. Whatever the case, quite a few misunderstandings sprang up later, mainly over the complex issue of Israel's intention to withdraw from the Rafa salient, and over an Egyptian military presence east of the passes in the peninsula.

The issue was never brought to the cabinet ministers for discussion; instead, they were presented with a fait accompli. As on many other occasions, a vital decision was taken by the prime minister alone, without ministerial consultation or approval. Begin was not spared criticism about this.

The conversation between Sadat and Begin ended on a note of cordiality. "Whatever happens," Sadat said, "we shall remain friends." Begin shook his hand, and as he turned to leave the room said, "I am a man who keeps his word. Believe me."

It was late at night. From his fifth-floor window at the King David Hotel, Sadat looked over the breathtaking view before him: the walls of the Old City, the golden dome of the Mosque of Omar, Mount Scopus and the Mount of Olives, the myriad lights from houses.

Begin returned home, where his family and friends were waiting to hear all the details of his first meeting with Sadat. "The discussions brought us together as friends, and we believed each other," he told them. "A real relationship developed between us. We told jokes. I told him about our revolt against the British, and he told me some of his memories. Everything was very personal."

Next morning Sadat awakened early and prayed. It was Sunday, November 20, 1977, the Day of the Sacrifice, Id-al Adha, a holiday sacred to millions of Muslims. It was the day that marked the end of the holy month of Ramadan. Sadat had intentionally chosen this day for the prayer services at the Al-Aksa Mosque. Sadat had been informed that only five hundred Arabs and members of the entourage would be permitted to attend the special service at the mosque, for security reasons, though the mosque and the square around it can hold as many as 20,000 people. Sadat feared that a small turnout would be interpreted as a victory for the PLO, which had called for a boycott of the prayer service. He asked that the gates be opened wide. Some 6000 Muslims joined the prayer service, all enthusiastically greeting the president.

From this sacred Muslim site, Sadat went to Yad Va-Shem, the memorial to the Jews killed in the Nazi Holocaust. Sadat arrived and was handed a skullcap.

"What's that?" he asked.

"It's a *kippah*, a head covering," Begin answered. "It is our custom to cover our heads during prayers or when entering a house of prayer."

Sadat listened and said very little. He only asked how a copy of the secret Soviet-German agreement on the division of Poland had reached Israel. Begin used the opportunity to teach Sadat a lesson for the future: "All this befell us because we had no state of our own and no country that was the state of our fathers, and consequently we had no protection."

Sadat nodded. In the visitors' book he wrote, "Let us put an end to all the suffering of the human race."

Sadat was visibly tired by the time he arrived for lunch with Israeli officials. At the luncheon, mutual suspicion separated the visitor and his hosts. From the first moment the Israelis perceived that Sadat did not trust them. The meal had been prepared by his personal chef and Sadat had even brought his own cup from Cairo. At one point Begin and Sadat spoke of their heart conditions.

"You look very good for a man with your illness," Sadat said.

"You too look very well in spite of your illness," Begin responded.

"Do not eat the watermelon," Sadat warned his host. "The cellulose is harmful to the stomach."

After lunch Sadat went to his room to polish the speech he was shortly to deliver to the Knesset.

Tension was high among the Israeli cabinet members. Though they shared in the general euphoria, some were worried. It was evident to almost all the ministers that it would not be possible to send Sadat home empty-handed. Sharon had suggested, at a cabinet session during the week, that as a goodwill gesture Sadat, upon his arrival, be offered Egyptian civilian administration of Al-'Arish and the right of passage on the roads leading to the desert city. The idea appealed to Begin, but Dayan rejected it: "Sadat is not coming to get crumbs," he said. The matter was dropped. Begin wanted to know in advance what Sadat planned to say to the Knesset so he could prepare a reply, but the Egyptians said no.

The atmosphere at the Knesset was both festive and tense. For the first time in its history the audience would be permitted to applaud a guest. Special rules of protocol were devised, and no effort was spared to demonstrate the respect Israel had for the president of Egypt. The entrance of the Egyptian and Israeli presidents was a breathtaking moment. The guest from Egypt was greeted with a bugle call and loud, continuous applause. Hardly anyone noticed that several Knesset members remained seated and refrained from clapping.

Among those at the cabinet table was Ezer Weizman. He smiled at everyone but was unable to hide his pain. He was brought to the entrance of the hall in a wheelchair, but made his way to his seat with the aid of a cane.

Sadat walked up to the rostrum. Unknown to him a voice stress analyzer was attached to the microphone. Later it would be found that the needle jumped slightly when Sadat spoke about reconciliation. He spoke in Arabic, and the eight hundred members and guests in the Knesset followed the translation with earphones.

Sadat emphasized the human aspects of his daring mission: the concern for life, for loss of life, for mourning. "We, all of us, are still suffering the consequences of four fierce wars waged within thirty years. All this, at a time when the families of the 1973 October War—these families are still moaning under the cruel pains of widowhood and bereavement of sons, fathers, and brothers . . . Any life lost in war is a human life, whether of an Arab or Israeli. A wife who becomes a widow is a human life who is entitled to live a happy family life, whether she is Arab or Israedi. Innocent children who are deprived of the care and compassion of their parents are ours."

He went on: "Many long months during which peace could have been brought about have been wasted over differences, fruitless disputes and discussions of the procedure for the convening of the Geneva conference, all showing thoroughgoing suspicion and absolute lack of confidence."

The audience was deeply moved by the personal, warm words on mourning and wars. But then Sadat adopted a sharper, more outspoken tone. "Frankness makes it incumbent upon me to tell you the following," he said. "First, I have not come here for a separate agreement between Egypt and Israel. This is not part of the policy of Egypt. The problem is not that of Egypt and Israel. Any separate peace between Egypt and Israel, or between any Arab confrontation state and Israel, will not bring permanent peace based on justice in the entire region. Rather, even if peace between all the confrontation states and Israel were achieved, in the absence of a just solution to the Palestinian problem there will never be the durable and just peace upon which the entire world insists today.

"Second, I have not come to you to seek a partial peace—to terminate the state of belligerency at this stage and put off the entire problem to a subsequent stage. This is not the radical solution that will steer us to permanent peace. Equally, I have not come to you for a third disengagement agreement in Sinai or in the Golan or in the West Bank, for this would mean that we are merely delaying the ignition of the fuse, and also that we lack the courage to face peace, that we are too weak to shoulder the burdens and responsibilities of a durable peace based on justice."

Sadat sipped from a glass of water and continued: "You must give up forever your dreams of invasion and the belief that strength is the best way to deal with the Arabs. . . . I have come to Jerusalem the City of Peace, which will always remain a living embodiment of coexistence among believers of the three religions. It is inadmissible that anyone should conceive of the special status of the city of Jerusalem within the framework of annexation or expansionism: it should be a free and open city to all believers. Above all, this city should not be severed from those who have made it their abode for centuries . . . let us make no mistake about the importance and reverence that Christians and Muslims attach to Jerusalem."

Tension rose in the Knesset. It was clear that Sadat was not mincing his words. The ministers and Knesset members had deluded themselves, thinking that Sadat would choose fine words and make only noncommittal remarks.

"Let me tell you without the slightest hesitation that I have not come to you under this dome to make a request that your troops evacuate the occupied territories. Complete withdrawal from the Arab territories occupied after 1967 is a logical and undisputed necessity. Nobody should plead for that."

Sadat did not balk at harsh words to get to the core of his speech: the Palestinian problem. Dayan listened with concentration, eager to see if Sadat would take his suggestion and refrain from mentioning the Palestine Liberation Organization. Much of the success of the speech, and perhaps of the entire visit, depended on whether the PLO would be mentioned. It was not.

"As for the Palestine cause," Sadat continued, "nobody can deny that it is the crux of the matter. Nobody in the world can accept today slogans propagated here in Israel, ignoring the existence of the Palestinian people . . . even the U.S. has opted to face up to reality and facts, and admit that the Palestine problem is the core of the conflict, and that so long as it continues to be unresolved, the conflict will continue to get worse, reaching new dimensions. It is unthinkable that peace be attained without the Palestinians . . . The solution lies in recognizing a state for the Palestinian people . . ."

Sadat went on to present his conditions for peace: an end to the Israeli occupation of Arab lands conquered in 1967 and the recognition of the fundamental rights of the Palestinian people and its right to an independent entity. There was nothing new in these conditions. In Israel there was a broad consensus never to revert to the 1967 borders or to allow the Palestinians to set up their own state.

Weizman leaned over toward Dayan and passed him a note: "We've got to prepare for war." Begin's face became even grimmer. "That's an ultimatum," he said in an audible whisper.

"Tell [your sons]," Sadat went on, "that the past war was the last of wars and the end of sorrows. Tell them that we are in for a new beginning to a new life. A life of love, prosperity, freedom, and peace. You bewailing mother, you widowed wives, you the son who lost a brother or a father, all you victims of war, fill the earth and space with recitals of peace."

The audience in the Knesset, taken aback by Sadat's outspokenness, responded with weak applause. Begin, Sharon, and Gur did not join in.

Begin is one of the most forceful speakers in Israel; his bitterest foes praise his eloquence. He almost never reads from a written text, but writes only a few key words on slips of paper. Since he had not been able to study Sadat's speech in advance, he had no choice but to improvise. Sadat had attempted to appeal to the people of Israel over the heads of their leaders to make concessions and compromises; he had presented uncompromising attitudes.

Since Sadat's speech was replete with religious comments, Begin, too, chose to open with Bible stories. He recalled the sacrifice of Isaac, in the course of which Abraham, "our common father," was submitted to a terrible ordeal. Begin apparently chose this vein to highlight what was shared between the two leaders, to restore Israel and Egypt to their common glorious past while at the same time referring to the present: "The flying time from Cairo to Jerusalem is short, but the distance between us, until yesterday, was infinite. President Sadat, with great courage, has crossed that distance."

Begin presented his conditions for peace: "What we want is a full, true peace, and absolute reconciliation between the Arab people and the Jewish people . . . peace treaties, in which we shall end the state of war. There is no need to separate the peace treaty from ending the state of war . . . The first article of the peace treaty will be the termination of the state of war, and forever. We wish to establish normal relations between us . . . and that you, Mr. President, should have a loyal ambassador in Jerusalem and that we should have an ambassador in Cairo . . . We propose economic cooperation for the development of our two countries. The combination of the Arab and Jewish genius could turn this region into a paradise on earth. Come to visit us and we shall go to visit you.

"I propose that everything be negotiable . . ." But on Jerusalem, Begin left no room for doubt. As this issue had been so emphatically presented by Sadat in his speech, Begin made it unequivocally clear that the city "which was reunited" would never be divided again.

Begin's speech made a most unpromising impression on the Egyptian delegation, including Sadat. The translation from Hebrew to Arabic made the nuances even sharper than the original. The Egyptian delegation had expected cordial, hopeful words from the prime minister of Israel, even the declaration of certain concessions. But Begin made it clear that this was not to be. He presented the adamant Israeli position; this was, he felt, only the beginning of a long process in the course of which he would be forced to "bring the price down."

The last speaker was opposition leader Shimon Peres, who, unlike Begin, chose to overlook Sadat's remarks on the Palestinians and stressed only the historic link between the Jewish people and Palestine. ". . . a way must be found to give expression to the Palestinian identity without endangering Israel's security."

The reaction of the Minister of the Interior Joseph Burg was perhaps most to the point: "Sadat's speech was frank and presented his position clearly; Begin's was too. The job now is to build a bridge between the two speeches."

Sadat was escorted from the Knesset to Begin's office, where the prime minister introduced him to Ezer Weizman. Weizman, leaning on his cane, limped toward Sadat. Weizman, a man of great charm and appeal, at once established a warm rapport with the Egyptian president. Sadat, for his part, made and would continue to make a special effort to win Weizman's favor. Sadat was eager to get to know the defense minister, who was known as a hawk and had been mentioned as Begin's possible successor. Sadat hoped that through Weizman he could learn the defense establishment's evaluation of his peace initiative. "Weizman is agreeable company and has a penchant for merriment," Sadat once said, "but behind that outward lightheartedness there is deep unrest in his face due to the political life, for he much prefers the military life. His gaiety is a cover for a true tragedy: he has a son who fought and was severely wounded on the Bar Lev line in the October War . . . How can such a man not long for peace?"

Sadat and Weizman met again that evening at a banquet at the King David Hotel. Cordial greetings on the birth of Sadat's granddaughter were not of much help; the outspoken speeches in the Knesset only a few hours earlier had created a tense atmosphere. The guests did not know what to say, and the mood was oppressive.

Weizman tried to break the tension by telling a joke about his service in the Royal Air Force in Egypt during World War II. Then he went on to talk of the local Egyptian girls. This, however, only caused greater embarrassment.

Sadat's relative Osman Ahmed Osman spoke of the reconstruction of the Suez Canal, and spoke at length on the rebuilding of houses in the towns destroyed during the war of attrition. "I know the place," Weizman said. "An Egyptian sniper caught my son there—with a bullet that hit him between the eyes."

71

"War is war," said Sadat. "But we are on the way to making peace. I wish him a speedy recovery."

"The president's younger brother was killed too," Tuhami added. "He fell flying a fighter plane near Bir-Gafgafa in the Yom Kippur War."

Begin added, "There are two ministers at this table whose brothers were killed in the 1948 war—Dayan and Yadin."

Yigael Yadin turned to Tuhami and said: "Don't you think it would be worthwhile issuing a joint communiqué?"

"A wonderful idea," Tuhami answered.

"You are going back tomorrow. Let us try and formulate it now."

A waiter brought over a paper napkin. Handing it to Tuhami, Yadin said, "You write and then we shall know what you want." The Egyptian deputy premier suggested writing "divine visit" but Yadin demurred. "OK, then I suggest 'providential visit' instead." Before passing the napkin to Begin, Yadin asked Tuhami whether he could say that the wording was also approved by the president of Egypt. "Well," Tuhami responded, "the president has not seen it, but insofar as I can read his thoughts, this is what he would have done if you had asked him."

"Why did you wish to use the word 'divine' or 'providential'?" Yadin asked.

"You must realize," Tuhami responded, "that that is the key to understanding this entire visit here. We regard the visit as a sacred, religious mission."

Yadin handed the napkin to Dayan, adding a note: "What do you think?" Dayan read it and replied: "I have no comment."

Only then was the napkin handed to Begin, who immediately replied with a note of his own. "I don't care for 'providential.'" He showed the statement to Sadat, who crossed out "providential" and wrote "courageous." Begin immediately called over his adviser, Yehuda Avner.

"Shakespeare this formula for me, will you?" he asked. "Shakespeare" was his own turn of phrase, when he wanted something drafted in fine English. Avner, who was expert at it, went out to polish and type the text of the joint statement, which emphasized Sadat's initiative and stressed that talks were to continue.

"You see," Tuhami said, "in spite of everything we've managed to get something done."

The dinner was over, and Begin suggested to Sadat that they hold a meeting right away to continue the talks.

Yadin was getting ready to drive home when Boutros Ghali approached him: "Our bosses have gone to talk to each other, and Mustafa Khalil would like to speak to you and Weizman." Mustafa Khalil, secretary of the Arab Socialist Union, the Egyptian ruling party, was a close friend of Sadat's.

The four talked into the small hours of the night.

The two Egyptians painted Egypt's problems in grim hues. "Did you know that every year one million babies are born in our country?" Ghali remarked. "And that today one million Egyptians—from professors to prostitutes—are working in other Arab countries?"

Khalil dwelt more on military issues. "We know that we wouldn't have a chance of winning a war and we also know that you have the atom bomb. Egypt doesn't have a military alternative and we have to seek a different solution. You've got to believe Sadat."

Weizman explained his Zionist approach to security matters. He concentrated mainly on the future of the West Bank. Khalil replied with arguments about the West Bank. "For Egypt this represents a difficulty of the first order," he said, "even if you are right." Before they bade each other good night, Khalil said Sadat had requested an immediate report of the conversation. He disappeared into the president's room.

The time available did not allow in-depth discussions on the nature of the peace, but by the second evening it was agreed that the talks should continue. A framework for further contacts was concluded, including meetings between ministers, exchange of notes, and telephone conversations.

The next morning one of Sadat's bodyguards was found dead in his bed at the King David Hotel. The Israelis were greatly worried, fearing they might be held responsible. An Israeli doctor found that the bodyguard had died in his sleep of a heart attack. The Egyptian delegation's physician examined the body and confirmed the diagnosis. Both sides were anxious; they realized that if the report got out, it would lead to endless rumors, suspicions, and recriminations. They decided to keep the incident quiet. Nothing would be leaked to the public. But how would the body be brought to the aircraft without arousing the suspicions of the press corps? The Egyptians placed the body of their colleague in a large crate, which was transported to the airport along with their luggage. It was placed on the cargo plane that accompanied Sadat's aircraft.

The death of his bodyguard only added to Sadat's depression. Begin's Knesset speech of the previous day now lay before him in accurate translation, but this did little to dispel his belief that Begin was intransigent. It was Begin's style, not his words, that had done the harm. The Egyptian journalists were briefed accordingly and soon the entire community of journalists learned of Sadat's disappointment, and reported it extensively.

Sadat's speech had presented the classic Arab position: peace in exchange for territories. It was a simple equation that could easily be understood by the world. The media, therefore, presented Sadat as the party willing to give. He had taken a risk and Israel had not yet made an appropriate response. The Israelis were portrayed as obdurate and uncompromising.

Sadat made a good impression on the Israeli public: relaxed, reasonable, courteous, and well dressed. Unlike Israeli leaders, he maintained a distance from his associates. They did not speak in his presence unless he literally nodded his consent. There was no doubt that he alone determined what was to be said, and to whom.

There was no rapport between Sadat and Begin, but Sadat's relationship with Weizman warmed quickly. On the morning of the second and final day of the visit to Jerusalem, Weizman was invited to the royal suite at the hotel, with Begin's knowledge.

Weizman limped on his cane. At the door of the room, he waved it like a rifle, in salute: "My compliments on the surprise you sprung in the Yom Kippur War," he said. Sadat was pleased. Weizman had touched on one of Sadat's sensitive points. Ever since October 1973, he had missed no opportunity to sing his own praises over the surprise he had inflicted on the Israelis.

Sadat looked up at the tall defense minister. "Thank you, but I suggest that we do not speak of war."

"Your speech yesterday in the Knesset was very tough," said Weizman. "I hope it's like in business—you start high and then scale down your demands."

Weizman led Sadat to the window. He pointed to the Old City of Jerusalem. "A great deal has changed in the region, and a great deal has been rebuilt," he said. "You cannot suddenly go back eleven years. Today there is a different reality."

The conversation touched on peace agreements, on abiding by political commitments. "After all, the controversy between us did not begin with the '67 war," Weizman said. "I, for example, began to fight when I was just over fourteen. Agreements are signed between nations and not only between leaders."

Weizman hinted to Sadat that even if Sadat were to sign a peace treaty with Begin, such an agreement would not necessarily last long. Did Sadat get the message?

"Ezra," Sadat said (he persisted in saying "Ezra," not "Ezer"), "you can believe me and put your trust in what I say. Whatever I say—I stand by it. That is my way."

"May you live to be a hundred and twenty," Weizman said. He was hinting that the Egyptian president was not immortal, and that the peace agreement might be worthless upon Sadat's death.

Sadat, pretending not to get the hint, said, "That's too long."

"Then may you live to be a hundred and look as though you were twenty."

Sadat spent the morning meeting factions of the Knesset. Nothing startling was said, but he came away deeply impressed by his meeting with Golda Meir, his adversary through so many years. "I am old already," said Meir, "and hope still to see the day of peace."

"You have many years yet to live with us," Sadat answered.

"Ah, but it was you who always called me 'old lady.' "

Sadat burst out laughing. Indeed, he had in his speeches attacked the obduracy of the "old lady in Israel." Golda now paid him back. As she finished her address, she handed Sadat a gift for his newly born granddaughter and a modest gift for himself—a silver cigarette case.

In the afternoon Sadat and Begin sat on the colorful

stage of the Jerusalem Theater, facing two thousand representatives of the media. It was a highly charged, emotional occasion.

The first question was expected, and was repeated several times in the course of the press conference. It was directed at Sadat: "When are you going to invite Begin to Cairo?"

From the start of the visit it was evident that Sadat had no intention of inviting Begin to Cairo, a step that appeared superfluous to him so long as Begin did not accept his terms for signing a peace treaty. Sadat guessed that Begin was eager to go to Cairo as soon as possible, and he knew that he did not have an adequate reply to the question of why he had not invited him.

"I hope we shall meet soon to continue the peace talks," Begin told him on one occasion, in an attempt to get an invitation to Cairo. "Certainly. We shall meet in Sinai and continue," the Egyptian president had responded.

"Why not in Cairo? Conditions in Sinai are not suited for such a meeting."

"We could hold the meeting at my home in Ismailia," Sadat compromised. "In your honor I shall bring the People's Assembly to Ismailia and you will be able to address its members there."

The televised press conference was viewed by millions. From Sadat's standpoint, the public coverage was successful beyond all expectations.

Among the gifts Sadat took away when his visit ended were a copy of *The Revolt* by Menachem Begin, three urns from the age of the patriarchs, and eight oil lamps from the Maccabean period.

Sadat returned home. Millions watched him as he passed through the streets of Cairo. He passed under honor arches and waved in all directions, in the joy of achievement and victory.

Israel tried to go back to everyday living. The Israeli economy had registered a loss in production of a half billion Israeli pounds. The Israelis felt as though the wheel of history had made a complete turn. A few days later, Ezer Weizman addressed the senior generals of the Israeli army. Asked to evaluate events, he said: "There are many dangers inherent in the situation. I am not one of the most

Veto Cites Procedure on St

Jan. 2 (AP) — Presi-
vetoed a bill to require
h effects of the defoli-
'' He said that the bill
nstitutional Congres-
nt on Presidential

ted to a provision giv-
Congress the power to
ation's design for the
resident said would be
thout the bill.

he strongly supported
y into the effects of
health. Dioxins are
orange,'' a defoliant
Vietnam War that is
isorders of the skin,
rvous system.

id that several studies

into dioxins were already being carried
out by various arms of the Administration and that a study like the one required
in the bill was planned by the Department
of Health, Education and Welfare.

Calls Provision Unconstitutional

Mr. Carter said he had vetoed the bill,
the first he has disapproved during the
current Congress, because of an ''uncon-
stitutional requirement'' that the director of the Office of Technology Assessment, an arm of Congress, approve the
study's design before the Adminstration
could go ahead with it.

Mr. Carter noted his longstanding objections to ''legislative veto'' provisions,
which give one or both houses of Congress
the ability to override certain administration actions. Mr. Carter takes the posi-

East Rive

Letters

Where the P.L.O. Stands i:

To the Editor:

It is hard to believe that anyone would dare maintain that the P.L.O. has "helped the hostages" in Iran, but Aziz Ghannam makes that claim in a Dec. 19 letter.

The P.L.O. made a brief and transparent public relations attempt to "mediate" with the Iranians. It clearly envisioned a repeat of last summer's Ankara farce, in which Turkey "rewarded" it for ending the seizure of the Egyptian Embassy by an allied terror group. However, the P.L.O. soon reverted to its complete support of the Iranian terrorists, forgetting its slogans about a "secular democratic state" to embrace the Ayatollah, who has been aptly described as the Führer of Islam.

The P.L.O.-Khomeini connection is a long and close one. P.L.O. presses in Beirut ran off propaganda for Khomeini while he was still in Paris. Hundreds of his warriors were trained in P.L.O. camps in southern Lebanon (even now Iranians are clamoring to join the P.L.O. in those very camps for its *jihad* against the Israelis). Ghotbzadeh and other Iranian leaders have close P.L.O. connections. P.L.O. and P.F.L.P. members have been reported both among the "students" inside the embassy and outside among the mobs. The only picture other than that of

Khomeini anywhere n is that of Arafat, on the

P.L.O. comments du should not be forgotte head of the P.L.O. "The P.L.O. is not an i tween Iran and Amer tory by the Iranian na fluence of American the region should be c tory for the P.L.O." Palestinian people ha eternal ally in Iran an Arab nation will supp people who are followi Ayatollah Khomeini against U.S. imperiali port Iran's stand a mediators" (Nov. 19).

Both at the Arab Le Tunis and at a gather P.L.O. proclaimed its with the Iranians. On rut newspaper As "P.L.O. chief Yasir Ar military assistance to the U.S. intervenes to hostages."

CBS News reporte "When Washington r of military interventi say an unknown numb guerrillas joined the the compound and called 'technical

Pakistan Falsely Blamed

the Iranian Crisis

the embassy ont gate.

g this ordeal Hani Hassan, heran office: rmediary be-

... Any vic-n over the in-peralism in sidered a vic-v. 13). "The e found their firm that the t the Iranian in the steps of his struggle ... We sup-we are not

e meeting in in Paris, the tal solidarity v. 17 the Bei-ir reported: at has offered in in the event ease the U.S.

on Dec. 12: ed the threat U.S. experts of Palestinian anians inside vided what's assistance'

.... [They] mined the embassy grounds and walls." Arafat on Dec. 7: "Tell Imam Khomeini to give the order, and we will obey and move to strike U.S. imperialism and U.S. imperialist interests at any time and in any place."

This is a fraction of the evidence linking the P.L.O. to Khomeini's terrorism. There is a larger connection. Neither the embassy seizure in Tehran nor much of the terrorism now plaguing the world would be thinkable without the success of the P.L.O., which has seized embassies, killed U.S. diplomats Cleo Noel and Francis Meloy, blown up commercial planes in flight, bombed buses and markets and murdered schoolchildren.

Despite all this, it has had success in promoting the cause of the recently fabricated "Palestinian people" (will the "ethnic Arabs of Iran" begin to demand "the legitimate rights of the Khuzistanian people"?) Before the Teheran outrage, the Carter Administration and others were intent on legitimizing and appeasing the P.L.O.

It will be fascinating to see if, once the Teheran crisis has passed, the Administration will relapse into appeasement of the P.L.O., and thus again encourage terrorists everywhere, including the U.S.   HUGH FITZGERALD
Cambridge, Mass., Dec. 27 1979

When Regular Bus Runs

CARTER TO DISCLOSE FUND-SHARING PLAN

Aides Say a $6.9 Billion Proposal Retaining Money for States Is to Be Announced Today

By STEVEN R. WEISMAN
Special to The New York Times

WASHINGTON, Jan. 2 — President Carter plans to announce tomorrow a proposal to renew the $6.9 billion general revenue-sharing program for states and local governments, tied to a mechanism to encourage states to ease the financial burdens of cities and counties, Administration sources said tonight.

The announcement would be a triumph for the coalition of representatives of state and local governments who have been fighting to persuade Mr. Carter to drop his long-stated opposition to the concept of giving money to state governments with no strings attached.

Representatives of the various lobbying groups, including the United States Conference of Mayors, the National League of Cities and the National Governors Association, are scheduled to arrive at the White House tomorrow for the announcement.

Reversal of Earlier Position

The political pressure from these and other groups persuaded Mr. Carter to retain revenue sharing at full strength, Administration officials said. Mr. Carter's previously stated position had been to eliminate a $2.3 billion portion of revenue

Carter

WASHINGTO
dent Carter toda
a study of the he
ant "agent oran
contained an u
sional infringe
power.

Mr. Carter ob
ing an employee
veto the Admini
study, which the
carried out even

Mr. Carter sa
the proposed st
dioxins on hum
found in "agen
widely used in
now blamed fo
heart, lungs and

The President

optimistic, but I am not pessimistic either. If this move fails, war will break out . . ."

"Sadat is a very courageous man who has risked his life," the defense minister concluded. "If I were Lloyd's I would not issue him a life-insurance policy."

10 EARTHQUAKE

Sadat's visit to Israel hit the country like an earthquake. Euphoria reigned. Hundreds of thousands of hopeful words were written about the coming cooperation in agriculture, trade, industry, and tourism. A Tel Aviv travel agency published advertisements for forthcoming tours to the Pyramids and pleasure cruises down the Nile. Peace songs topped the charts. There were public debates on topics like: "What changes will peace bring?", "Israeli-Egyptian relations," and "Israel's integration in the area." The joy grew. "The mood in Israel is always swinging like a pendulum between catastrophe and festivity," Ezer Weizman was wont to say. "Yesterday was a catastrophe—today they're organizing festivals."

Immediate changes were instituted in Egypt's official propaganda line. The term "enemy," used by radio announcers when referring to Israel, was dropped; Israel was now referred to as the "adversary." At Radio Cairo's military section, the program "The Sounds of the Battlefront" gave way to a new program: "Flags of Peace." Radio broadcasts and newspaper articles no longer called the Palestine Liberation Organization the sole representative of the Palestinians.

The Egyptians had been afraid that the Israelis would insult their president, perhaps even make an attempt on his life. The cheering throngs in the streets of Jerusalem and the applause at the Knesset convinced them that the Israelis were not so bad after all. A flood of telegrams of support were sent to Sadat's office. Notable in their enthusiasm were writers and other intellectuals, who as far back as 1972 had called on Sadat to work toward a compromise instead of accepting a situation where "university degrees were thrown away on the sands of the battlefield."

The journalists accompanying Sadat took a quick peep at Israel and returned home with wide-ranging theories: "They don't have a military regime there as we had thought," wrote one. "Israel is green, while the territories are yellow," said another, who derisively told his readers how he had bought a can of "Holy Land air" in Jerusalem.

But other voices were being heard in Egypt: Ismail Fahmi, who had resigned as foreign minister to protest the initiative, said of Sadat: "He wants to open a psychiatric clinic to cure the Israelis. There's a difference between a well-thought-out initiative and a television performance." Leftists distributed anti-Sadat proclamations, one group criticizing the initiative without rejecting its basic aims, another opposing the entire move, including its underlying principle. The Egyptian ambassador to Belgrade resigned, rejecting Sadat's initiative.

In Washington, confusion continued. "The superpowers don't like surprises," said Fahmi. President Carter and his advisers were afraid that Sadat's visit to Jerusalem would ruin the American plan to reconvene the Geneva conference. The State Department and the White House had not given up the idea of reconvening the conference with the participation of the superpowers and the Arab confrontation states, as well as representatives of the Palestinians.

The Americans—though they didn't say it too loudly—were also afraid of being pushed out of the negotiating process. They wanted to be involved in every stage of the discussions. It was clear to officials that without reliable information about what was going on, they would be dragged along with events instead of being in control of them.

The Russians reviled Sadat. It was clear that they had

lost any chance of influencing the peace negotiations. Washington was afraid the Egyptian move would have a negative effect on detente.

Confusion also reigned among segments of the Israeli public, particularly among Begin's most enthusiastic supporters, who still believed in the need to govern the West Bank as an integral part of the historic land of Israel, and believed the coming peace negotiations would force Begin and the other members of his cabinet to relinquish their basic convictions. Shouts of protest were heard from the right, including some of Begin's closest friends. Anxiety prevailed in the Jewish settlements set up in the territories taken in the 1967 war; there was fear that Begin would be unable to withstand the pressure for retrenchment that would arise from the peace process and Sadat's daring initiative.

Sadat, hoping for support in the Arab world, looked for it in Saudi Arabia, whose political and economic power had soared in recent years. As soon as he returned to Cairo from Jerusalem he reported on his visit to Saudi Arabia's strong man, Prince Fahd, hoping to keep the Saudis informed and involve them in his peace initiative. But the Saudis reacted coolly, and did not take a clear stand for a long time. The Riyadh government issued a statement that it insisted on guaranteeing the legitimate rights of the Palestinians, withdrawal to the borders of 1967, and the return of East Jerusalem to Arab control. The Saudis did not move a finger to help or hurt Sadat, choosing to sit on the fence.

All the sides involved in the Middle East conflict knew that peace depended on finding a solution to the West Bank problem. This region, which had been held by the Israelis since the 1967 war, was inhabited by hundreds of thousands of Arabs; but many Israelis, particularly Begin's supporters, saw it as an integral part of the historic land of Israel promised to the Jews in the Bible. Israel also had good security reasons for holding on to this area: the West Bank was on Israel's old border and any military action originating there could sweep past the old border very quickly, endangering Israel's security and its very existence.

After his trip to Jerusalem, Sadat no longer had any hope of working together with the Palestine Liberation Organization, and Israel refused to have any contact with the terrorist organization.

Sadat therefore fell back on an old idea: handing back control of the West Bank to Jordanian King Hussein for an interim period. Sadat asked for an urgent meeting with Hussein, and they met in December 1977. Sadat tried to persuade the king of Jordan of the advantage to him if the West Bank were put under his control for an interim period. "It justifies the risks involved," he said.

Hussein hesitated. He was hurt by the fact that Sadat was always surprising him and that he hadn't been told anything about his plan to go to Jerusalem. Hussein showed no interest in opposing the entire Arab world, which at a conference in Rabat, Morocco, declared that Hussein had no right to rule the West Bank.

Hussein neither rejected nor accepted Sadat's proposals. He waited in Amman and hoped that Israel, under American and Egyptian pressure, would have to issue a "declaration of principles" which would enable the negotiations to progress and serve as a basis for Jordan's joining the peace talks. Hussein issued a statement praising Sadat's courage in going to Jerusalem but stressing the need for Arab solidarity. Hussein was afraid that Sadat's initiative would fail, and the king of Jordan had to take into consideration the threats of Syria and the PLO.

Secret meetings between Hussein and the Israelis started even before the 1967 war. The first to meet with Hussein after the 1967 war was Minister of Labor Yigal Allon, who drew up a plan for solving the problems of government and peace in the West Bank. At the meeting at the beginning of 1968, this Allon plan was presented to the king. With the aid of a wall map, Allon explained the plan's essential points to Hussein. The plan was aimed at ensuring Israeli control of the Jordan Valley and the passes to the West Bank, but not Israeli rule over the population or over all the territories.

In his talks with the Israelis Hussein was frank, continually repeating his main position: "In order to sign a peace agreement with Israel, I have to get everything back, down to the last square centimeter of occupied territory, including Jerusalem, and especially Jerusalem." If they're not willing to give back everything, the king said, the Israelis would have to swallow their pride and deal with Arafat.

Nearly all the Israeli leaders met with Hussein. The meetings were held, among other places, in the Negev and in Tel Aviv. Prime Minister Yitzhak Rabin met Hussein at least eight times. The king gave Allon a sword and Abba Eban a gold pen. Rabin gave the king a present, a Galil rifle made by the Israeli military industries.

From time to time the Israelis would again propose the Allon plan to the king, but they finally dropped it when Jordanian Prime Minister Zayid Rifai remarked: "Yigal, enough of this plan of yours! It's out of the question!" Hussein warned Rabin, "Sadat will betray you—just as he betrayed me." "Sadat is cunning," he used to say. While telling the Israelis not to trust Sadat, he often reported to Sadat on his secret contacts with the Israelis.

Hussein reached a secret agreement with Allon on an ambitious project, which has not yet been realized, for digging a canal from the Jordan River to the Mediterranean Sea, to run power stations, to carry light shipping, and to prevent the drying up of the Dead Sea, from which both states extract bromine and potassium compounds. Hussein accomplished many tangible arrangements with the Israelis connected with the territories: open bridges for the movement of Arabs and foreign tourists, normal trade arrangements, and the like. He was angry that the Israelis allowed PLO supporters to replace those loyal to Hussein in important positions in some places in the territories, and he felt cheated by not being allowed to take part in the 1974–75 interim agreements. He was interested in reaching an official interim agreement with Israel along the Jordan Valley, but Rabin's government was afraid that any withdrawal on this front would necessitate a referendum, the results of which could not be assured. The Israeli counterproposal that he take administrative responsibility for the territories—"the functional arrangement"—was angrily rejected. The king told the Israelis they needn't worry about his influence on the Palestinians weakening. His adviser and friend Zayid Rifai said at one of the meetings: "You'll see! The king just has to set foot on the West Bank and they'll line up in a long row from Jericho to Jerusalem to kiss his hand."

Hussein was the first to hold direct talks with the Israelis —he went about it continuously and methodically—but he was careful to preserve secrecy. Now, when Sadat called him to come into the limelight, he felt doubtful.

As opposition to Sadat in the Arab world raged, the Egyptian president was condemned as a traitor. He doubled his bodyguards; there were fewer advance announcements of his movements within Egypt. He grew bitter as his attempts to find support in the Arab world failed. "The Syrians always wanted us to do their dirty work for them," he said. "I'm a hundred years ahead of them."

The anger against Sadat culminated in a pan-Arab conference called to find ways of foiling the expected peace negotiations between Egypt and Israel. The conference took place in December in Tripoli, Libya, and from the first was torn by crises and disputes. The Iraqis assailed Syria's President Assad for not having rejected the very idea of a political settlement with Israel, and for criticizing the PLO. Clashes broke out in the Palestinian delegations. Dr. George Habache accused another Palestinian leader, Yasir Arafat, of "tacit cooperation" with Sadat. Habash would not forgive Arafat for having been present when Sadat announced his intention to go to Jerusalem. The Libyan ruler, Qaddafi, demanded that the participants in the conference not be content with breaking off relations with Egypt; he called—in vain—for a campaign to overthrow Sadat. (During the months before Sadat's initiative, Qaddafi had tried to stir up a rebellion in Egypt against Sadat, but to no avail.)

The conference ended in chaos: the Iraqis left in protest at the rejection of their proposals, and Arafat did not appear at the final session, sending one of his associates to sign the joint declaration. The declaration announced the setting up of a "rejection front" which included, on paper, a mutual defense treaty between all the countries with the exception of Iraq. It was agreed to freeze diplomatic relations with Egypt and to widen the Arab boycott, used against Israel, to include Egypt. The participants also agreed to demand the removal of the office of the Arab League from Cairo and to boycott its meeting in the meantime—and, of course, to sever all air and communications links with Egypt. However, the "rejection front" remained only a symbolic union and never engaged in any real coordinated actions.

Even before going to Jerusalem, Sadat had realized the

need to create momentum for the peace process. He made up his mind to call for a conference as soon as he returned from his trip to Jerusalem. He dropped hints about it during his talks with Begin, but neither side gave it much thought. The assumption in Israel and in the United States was that the next step would be the reconvening of the Geneva conference.

A few days after returning to Cairo, Sadat issued a call for a conference to lay the groundwork for Geneva. He tried to pull the rest of the Arab states to the negotiating table by inviting all the countries which had attended the original Geneva conference. He had no doubt of the results: "Whoever comes—comes!" he said. He wasn't naive enough to believe that his rivals in the Arab world and the Russians would really come to Cairo. He knew almost from the beginning that only Israel, and perhaps the United States, would agree to take part in the play which he was stage-managing.

Sadat acted forcefully, closing down the cultural centers of the eastern bloc countries which had reviled him, and breaking off diplomatic relations with the countries that took part in the Tripoli conference. At the same time, he opened Egypt's doors to Israeli reporters.

While the first Israeli journalists were wandering around Cairo, in December 1977, Foreign Minister Dayan was in Rabat, Morocco, again for a second secret meeting with Egyptian Deputy Prime Minister Tuhami. The atmosphere was much better than it had been the first time. The talks were straightforward and to the point. Dayan offered Egypt sovereignty over the entire Sinai peninsula, stressing that this was only a "suggestion," not a "proposal." The difference was clear: a suggestion is an offer for the sole purpose of negotiations and is retracted if rejected; a proposal binds the proposer even if the offer is rejected.

The Israeli foreign minister also suggested the demilitarization of the area east of the passes, some 30 kilometers from the Suez Canal, while allowing the Israeli settlements in the Sinai to remain under the flag of the UN.

"If you reject this suggestion," Dayan said, "we'll have to think of some other way."

Tuhami had come to the talks alone; he took no notes, but Dayan's aides made sure there was a detailed protocol. At one point Dayan turned aside and wrote down a list of suggestions. He asked Tuhami to transmit the hastily prepared document to Sadat. Tuhami refused. He suspected that Dayan wanted to set a precedent for communicating via messages instead of through the Americans. He looked at the points noted down by Dayan and said: "I don't have to transmit it to the president, I can give you an immediate answer." He then shot off his answers to each section.

Dayan had the impression that his suggestions could serve as a basis for negotiations. Later there was an argument between him and Tuhami about what was said there, especially on the question of an Arab presence in Jerusalem.

Dayan told his colleagues in the cabinet that Tuhami insisted on a complete withdrawal from Sinai. Dayan had been adamant on the question of the settlements. He had told Tuhami that there was no reason why Israeli citizens couldn't remain in Sinai and had made it clear to him that Israel's only interest in Sinai was one of security, to prevent a surprise attack on Israel. "Any arrangement that will ensure that will be acceptable to us," Dayan told him.

In Cairo, Sadat realized that challenging Israel's refusal to allow any representative of the PLO to participate in the peace negotiations might torpedo the entire initiative. He decided to give in to Israel by evading the problem. On the eve of the opening of the conference in Cairo, he sent a message to Arafat asking if he was willing to allow Palestinian representatives who were not members of the PLO to take part in the conference, as a basis for the start of negotiations. Israel had quietly agreed to this. "I suggest that you accept this proposal and begin this way," Sadat recommended to Arafat. "Later, things will go the way the Arabs want them to."

Arafat was not willing. In a private message to Sadat, he wrote: "You must remember that Syrian cannons are directed toward the window of my office. No political pressure used on me can possibly outweigh that kind of pressure."

For three days there was no official reaction to the invitation to the Cairo conference. Silence reigned in the White House and the State Department.

Begin received the invitation just as Dr. Eliahu Ben-Elissar walked into his office. The director general of the prime minister's office had brought some documents for Begin to read.

"Eli," Begin said, "you will head our delegation to Cairo."

Ben-Elissar was stunned, but in fact the bearded, well-dressed official, Begin's spokesman in the Likud movement, was a good choice, with his distinguished appearance, discretion, and background as the prime minister's personal representative.

Sadat was angry at the naming of Ben-Elissar. He had hoped for a more prominent representative and sensed that there was no hope of purposeful negotiations within this framework. He called in his ambassador to the U.S., Dr. Ismet Abd-el-Magid, a graduate of the Sorbonne who had filled ministerial posts twice. The inexperienced Ben-Elissar would have to face a polished, accomplished diplomat.

It wasn't clear to Israel what the Egyptians wanted to discuss in Cairo. The Egyptians weren't saying anything about it.

Before Ben-Eilssar left as Israel's first official envoy to Cairo, Dayan handed him a letter, from which Ben-Elissar understood that he would not have much to do. Dayan set strict limitations on his freedom to negotiate and forbade him to deal with three topics: the Palestinian problem, territorial compromise, and the reconvening of the Geneva conference. He was also asked not to go into details on questions that might involve the state of Israel in a dispute. Only one, very general, topic was left for possible discussions with the Egyptians: the text of a peace treaty.

Apprehension surrounded the preparations for the departure of the first Israeli delegation to Cairo. It was felt that the delegation might be exposed to the danger of personal attack by Palestinians, Libyans, or other Arabs who opposed Sadat's peace initiative, including some Egyptians. The Egyptians promised full cooperation about security.

The other members of the Israeli delegation were the Foreign Ministry's legal affairs adviser, Dr. Meir Rosenne, and the head of the IDF general staff's planning department, General Avraham Tamir, whose presence would suggest to the Egyptians that even at this stage, steps should be taken to prevent the start of an accidental war. Weizman was afraid of fighting breaking out as a result of a misunderstanding. He told Tamir to agree to install a hot line, to agree to the thinning out of forces in the areas of the front and to holding military exercises far from the front lines. Weizman had not forgotten that because of a misunderstanding, the deputy prime minister of Israel had wanted to mobilize a large segment of the reserves only twenty-four hours before Sadat's visit to Israel.

For a day or two the state of Israel relived the glorious hours of Sadat's visit. Three El Al pilots, who had been captured by the Egyptians while serving in the reserves as fighter pilots in the Israeli air force, were chosen to fly the first Israeli planes to Egypt. On the side of the plane the word "peace" was written in large letters, both in Hebrew and Arabic. Early on the morning of December 13, 1977, El Al's Boeing took off for Cairo airport.

In the space of one hundred minutes a thirty-year gulf was bridged.

11 THE HANDS OF TIME

Winter winds welcomed the first Israelis to land at Cairo International Airport. It was bitterly cold. The Israeli delegation was given a very modest reception; a handful of journalists and minor officials were the only witnesses to the historic occasion. A large number of soldiers and security personnel surrounded the El Al plane. Greetings were not exchanged, and had it not been for their general excitement the Israelis might have been inclined to take offense.

Cairo remained unruffled as a fleet of minibuses made their way through its dusty streets to the Mena House hotel, in the shadow of the pyramids. Only the nervous howling of the police and security cars hinted at the presence of the excited visitors, who were eagerly taking in their first sights. The tree-lined road near the pyramids which led to the hotel was bordered by hundreds of soldiers. A heavy guard had been placed at the gate of the English-style hotel.

Once Sadat had invited the Israelis to a conference in Cairo, individual Israeli journalists made haste to find a way of entering Egypt. They flew from Tel Aviv to Cairo via Athens (there were no direct commercial flights, of course). One of them, Ehud Yaari, Israeli television's expert on Arab affairs and coauthor of this book, had set out without the explicit permission of the directorate of the Broadcasting Authority. He was accompanied by a producer, Alex Giladi. When the American plane was about to land the two men sent a note to one of the stewardesses: "We are two Israeli journalists and do not expect there to be any problems. Just to be on the safe side, please tell the captain to make a note of it."

At the airport the two men placed their blue Israeli passports with the emblem of the state of Israel on the passport control counter. They were very excited. The officer took the passports indifferently and looked inside them. "*Ahlan, ahlan*" ("Welcome"), he said, smiling broadly.

The tension broke all at once. The passport officer waved the passports in his hand and shouted: "The Israelis have arrived!" There was silence in the hall, followed by an outburst of applause.

Officers of the Egyptian general security service accompanied the Israeli journalists in Cairo. The security men were simultaneously bodyguards, guides, and supervisors. Every hour they reported by phone to the headquarters of the general security service about the activities of the Israeli newsmen. They also had to write detailed reports. Well-trained professionals, polite and good-tempered, they helped the Israeli journalists to break through barriers of paperwork and confusion in the various ministerial offices, but in accordance with their instructions they also restricted the Israelis' movements. They were the nearest representatives of Egypt for the Israeli reporters. Through long conversations and courteous behavior they cultivated the Israelis' goodwill toward Egypt, doing their utmost to keep them away from negative subjects, such as opposition to Sadat or the ugly sights of the slum areas. They made sure that everyone who came into contact with the Israelis behaved suitably. Through them the Israelis learned that Egypt had remained a police state even after Sadat's liberalization. The security police card worked wonders wherever it was shown. Deference toward the security police was shown even by important journalists and senior government officials. No one wanted to get in trouble with them.

Television viewers in Israel did not participate in the

first experiences of the Israeli journalists in Cairo, since the government of Israel forbade the broadcast of the programs sent by Yaari and Giladi via satellite. Moshe Dayan was angry that they had made it to Cairo in such haste; he claimed that the journalists had disturbed the negotiations, and demanded their immediate return home to stand trial. At cabinet sessions Dayan maintained that the arrival of the Israeli reporters had embarrassed the Egyptians. For two days a flurry of discussions, strike threats, pressure, and counterpressure followed in Jerusalem. It was a strange argument. The Egyptians did everything to facilitate direct broadcasts from Cairo while in Israel the government objected. In the end the government backed down. The first TV images from Cairo were watched by record audiences; the arches of honor, the carpets and palm branches, and the organized demonstrations made a strong impression on Israeli viewers. Most of the demonstrations ended in the square facing the window of President Sadat's office. More than a million people participated in the largest demonstration, during the course of which an Israeli reporter was carried on the shoulders of the crowd.

The demonstrations were not spontaneous but were organized at places where people worked. Clerks were not literally obliged to participate in them, but chose to do so when senior managers took part. Nevertheless, there was a kernel of sincerity and true joy in the mass demonstrations; not everything was staged. The idea of peace appealed to the average Egyptian, though it did not fire his imagination. The national propaganda machine worked full steam at its task of mass brainwashing. Through interminable repetition in a monotonous style, it drove Sadat's idea of peace into the minds of the populace. The Israelis' first impression in Cairo was that Sadat enjoyed genuine popular support. Sometimes it seemed that rather than the president drawing the public after him, he was guided by its secret emotions. In an authoritarian regime such as Egypt's the population obeys the dictates of the authorities out of an instinctive caution. However, the Israelis believed Sadat could not manage to alter opinion on a large scale merely by pressing a button. The shift in public opinion was too sharp for it to have been dictated by an educated minority.

Peace as a moral value, as the end of an exhausting war, and the hope for economic salvation won a tremendous response in Egypt. The Israeli newsmen sometimes had the impression that "peace" had nothing to do with Israel. The conclusion was that despite the warm welcome and the peace demonstrations, there were still many reservations when it came to Israel and the Israelis.

This was also the outcome of the propaganda method. Sadat took care not to defend Israel; he never mentioned Zionism. He was not prepared to change Israel's image or accord it respectability. The opportunity he was giving Israel did not include immediate rehabilitation. There was a clear distinction between Israel and peace.

The Israeli journalists were much in demand for interviews by Egyptians reporters, who were primarily interested in obtaining confirmation from the Israelis of the positive response in Israel to President Sadat's initiative. The answers given by the Israeli newsmen were usually rewritten before publication, if not omitted completely. Radio recordings were "cooked" before being broadcast. Any Israeli mention of the need for mutual concessions was excised. The rule in the press was: Israel is as Egypt wishes to portray it, not as it really is. Israel was presented to the Egyptian reader as a country that had grown tired of war and that had experienced an earthquake after Sadat had come to power. It was described as a country where the people had put pressure on its government to change its evil ways.

The Egyptians spared no effort to prevent the Israelis from seeing the unsightly side of Cairo, seeking to ensure that Egypt was depicted in Israel in a positive light. It was important that Egypt should not be portrayed as a country begging for peace. Sadat stressed this in every speech, and the Egyptians beseeched the Israeli reporters to believe him. The Egyptians had offered Israel peace out of generosity, self-confidence, and moral superiority.

Some of the Egyptian security personnel who accompanied the Israeli newsmen in Cairo considered the Israelis' interest in the darker side of life in Egypt as tactless. "When someone gives you their hand to shake," an official of the Ministry of Information said to one reporter, "you don't check to see if his nails are trimmed."

This approach was bound to fail. The Israelis had not

come solely to report on the peace initiative but to open Egypt to the closer observation of the Israeli public. They refused to be fobbed off by guided trips to tourist sites. They had many opportunities of getting to know the country. The process which the Egyptian guides feared occurred quickly. The Israelis were shocked by the extent of poverty, the bureaucratic cumbersomeness, and the backwardness. Some of them refused to believe that this was the same nation whose army had crossed the Suez Canal, taking the Israelis by surprise in 1973.

Their impressions were very depressing. Among the ancient tombs of the Mamluk sultans hundreds of thousands of people lived in conditions of poverty unlike anything that had ever been seen in Israel. Streets were inundated with sewage water. Buses were packed with masses of people. People, fighting against the cold wind, sat on the roofs of the trains which made their way at top speed along the delta. The roads were incredibly overcrowded. The telephones did not work. Cairo was contending with a multitude of people seeking homes and employment.

The encounter did not eliminate the mental gap. The Israelis were favorably impressed by the Egyptian's willingness to let bygones be bygones, his generosity, his love of humor, and his patience. At the same time they recoiled from his fatalism, his indifference to the suffering of others, and his submissiveness to authority.

The reports of the Israeli journalists did not engender a sense of respect for Egypt, which came across as an alien, wretched country. This was an inevitable stage of the process of rapprochement, though not necessarily the best one.

The Egyptians, wishing to prevent the Israeli journalists from seeing the bleaker side of Egypt, restricted their movements outside the hotel, while doing everything to make Mena House pleasant and attractive. Everything was paid for by the government: the Israelis received European meals in return for chits. In the evening entertainment was laid on, including belly dancers. Security personnel prevented the Israeli journalists from going to Cairo without a suitable escort.

The Cairo conference had no political significance. The thousand journalists, Israeli and other, realized this almost from the first so they began reporting about minor events, and even incidents of minimal importance were given blazing headlines.

For example, while the Egyptians were preparing the seating of the delegations to the conference, in the Rubáiyát Hall built by an eccentric English couple who had decided to live facing the pyramids, among the place names on the round table the Israelis noticed one bearing the title of the Palestine Liberation Organization. Ben-Elissar asked that it be removed. The Egyptians refused. Ben-Elissar was unrelenting. The Egyptians suggested to compromise: the place name would be changed to one bearing just one word, "Palestine."

"If you put that sign on the table," Ben-Elissar said, "we are not going to enter the hall."

The conference was on the point of breaking up before it had begun. Reports of the crisis reached President Sadat. Both sides were eager to avoid a confrontation. Ben-Elissar proposed using a sign bearing the words "Palestinian Arabs," the term used by Begin. The Egyptians refused. The argument continued for a whole day and in the end no sign was placed on the round table in the wood-paneled, carpeted hall whose walls were hung with verses from the *Rubáiyát* of Omar Khayyám.

The argument had hardly died down when a new controversy arose. One of the hotel boys placed flags at the entrance to the main building, apparently on instructions of the authorities. Along with the UN flag and those of other countries he raised the flag of Gaza, which resembles the Palestinian flag.

The Israeli delegation used a diplomatic approach. "We can see a flag which is unfamiliar to us and which does not belong to any of the countries which are invited to the conference or which are members of the UN," they said to their Egyptian hosts. The Egyptians did not react. Ben-Elissar spoke more sharply. "The Cairo conference will not open until the unfamiliar flag has been removed," he insisted. The Egyptians tried to sidestep their responsibility. "The hotel is in charge of dealing with flags," they said. In the end they solved the problem by having all the flags removed.

The Egyptians made the journalists feel a sense of urgency. Egyptian spokesmen spread it about that the peace negotiations would take a few days or maybe weeks. The general feeling was that things had to be brought to a rapid conclusion. The conference opened in a relaxed, much-photographed atmosphere. The heads of the delegations spoke to the television cameras and to hundreds of millions of viewers.

The head of the Egyptian delegation, Ismet Abd-el-Magid, said, "Tangible results should become clear without delay," The head of the American delegation, Alfred Atherton, said, "Israel will doubtless not let an opportunity of this nature slip away."

Each of the three parties had reasons to keep a low profile. Sadat was angry that the Israelis had sent low-echelon representatives. The Americans had tried to postpone the date of the conference, among other reasons because they neither knew nor could assess how and when its deliberations would end. The Israelis were under orders not to conclude any agreements.

The Israelis learned from the conference that the Egyptian Foreign Ministry represented the hard line. The representatives of the ministry caused the head of the Egyptian delegation to stress the Palestinian question and the desire for an overall settlement. The Israelis had the impression that the officials from the president's office were more moderate.

The conference proved that the Israelis were very stubborn. Both sides tended to get involved in lengthy discussions of minutiae. When they sought a formula, they found they could not agree on any point. Every Israeli suggestion was immediately countered by an Egyptian one, and vice versa.

The main achievement of the Cairo conference was psychological in that it was the first encounter between Israelis and Egyptian people. Some members of the Israeli delegation said that the Egyptian leaders had also been astonished by how much the population yearned for peace. This was not from love for Israel. The Egyptians believed that peace would bring in its wake an immediate improvement in their standard of living. Peace with the Israelis embodied the dream of a roof over their heads, enough food, and decent clothes. The Israeli-Egyptian meetings ranged from restrained to enthusiastic. In the souvenir shops the visitors were accorded a warm welcome and large price reductions. The members of the Israeli delegation received a demonstration of support: shouts of approval for Sadat and Begin, all well organized by the professionals of Cairo.

The Israelis, led by Eliahu Ben-Elissar, made every effort to please their Egyptian hosts. In a meeting with Sadat's bureau chief, Hassan Ahmed Kamel, Ben-Elissar asked that his delegation be allowed to visit the village where Sadat had been born. Ben-Elissar knew that Sadat was very attached to this village. Kamel's reply was immediate and positive. The delegation visited Mit abu al-Kum, accompanied by an army of news photographers.

Ben-Elissar also had the cheerless mission of making an unconventional request to the president's bureau chief: "Mr. Kamel, you know that we are very comfortable here, but I would like to ask for something. Before I left for Egypt several of the men who were prisoners of war here during the Yom Kippur War came to me. They asked me to secure the return of the Torah scroll which they had with them when they were captured."

"Is it so important to them?" Kamel asked.

Ben-Elissar replied: "This is a purely humanitarian act, and has no political connotations. Naturally, deep religious feelings are involved."

Ben-Elissar is a survivor of the Holocaust and a graduate of a religious school in Tel Aviv. Like his Egyptian counterpart, he dresses elegantly—and has had experience in his country's secret service. Kamel's face was expressionless.

"We will look for the scroll, and if we find it we'll return it to you," he said.

The Torah scroll was not found.

The Yom Kippur War was often discussed by the military representatives at the Cairo conference. The men in both uniforms found a common language more readily than did the civilian representatives.

The Israeli army representative was the head of the planning division, Brigadier Avraham Tamir. This was not his first encounter with the Egyptian army. He had been a prisoner of war in 1948 in Jordan, and had also sat on the Israeli side of the table during the talks at Geneva. He had been responsible for drawing up the settlement arrangements of the Israeli army's general staff.

On the Egyptian side were two generals who had played

95

important roles in past settlement talks. General Taha Magdub, friend and aide of Minister of War Gamassi, had helped plan the 1973 war, and then had been appointed secretary of the national security council, of which Sadat was chairman. Magdub had headed the Egyptian delegation to the military talks in the framework of the interim agreement at Geneva. His experience in talks with the Israelis had taken him to Syria, where he had been an adviser on the talks before the separation of forces in the Golan Heights. Brigadier Muhammad Huweidi was brilliant, efficient, and a good conversationalist. He was from the intelligence service and showed considerable knowledge about Israel. He had been an infantry officer and had participated in several wars against Israel. The Israelis were always afraid that he spoke Hebrew and could overhear them.

The talks between the military delegations went forward smoothly, though cautiously. Both sides were putting out feelers: they wanted to know the peace map and conditions, primarily in the military sphere, of the other side. They did not show too great an interest in the political question, the Palestinian problem, or the other Arab countries.

The Egyptians had prepared detailed proposals for the Israeli forces' withdrawal from the Sinai peninsula. The two Egyptian officers hinted that they had even prepared proposals for interim lines. They told Tamir that they were interested in as rapid an Israeli pullback as possible: they wanted to show tangible results, and fast. Not for a moment did they think that Egypt should relinquish anything. "It is a matter of honor and prestige, therefore we cannot concede anything," they said. "We could not permit ourselves to do so."

The Egyptian generals were not carried away by the enthusiasm which enveloped the guests at the hotel. Tamir discovered that their ideas about peace between Israel and Egypt were very different from those entertained by him and his Israeli colleagues. Magdub and Huweidi saw peace between the nations as a slow and gradual process. "It is like building a house," Magdub said. "First you decide to start the construction. Then you lay the foundations, continue building, erect the roof, put in doors and windows—and only at the end do you move into the house.

The same applies to peace. We'll begin by signing, you will withdraw, and only at the end of the process will there be full, genuine peace."

There were sad moments in the Israelis' tour of Egypt. In Cairo and Alexandria the Israeli journalists met the remnants of what had been thriving Jewish communities. There are only 300 Jews left in Egypt, where they once numbered 100,000. Some of the reporters could not stop the tears when they met small groups of old, sick Jews who were afraid to speak freely lest they suffer for it. A few of the old Jews slipped notes into the hands of the Israeli newsmen, sending regards from a dying community to relatives in Tel Aviv.

The Israeli journalists, like their colleagues from other countries, were dumbstruck late one afternoon when Cairo radio announced that Israel's Minister of Defense Ezer Weizman had met President Sadat at Ismailia.

While in Jerusalem, Sadat had promised Weizman that he would organize a meeting between him and Egyptian Minister of War Abd-el-Ghani Gamassi. Shortly after his return to Cairo, Sadat had sent an invitation to Weizman, who could not accept the invitation, which reached him via the American embassy in Tel Aviv, because his leg was still in a cast and he did not want to appear on Egyptian soil for the first time in that condition. Through American mediation a date was fixed in December, when battalions of newspaper reporters had flooded into Cairo and were expecting some kind of outcome from the Mena House conference.

At age 53 Weizman had reached a peak; his appointment as minister of defense was an unexpected climax to his military and political career. He is a member of one of the oldest-established, best-known families in Israel. His uncle, Dr. Chaim Weizmann, had been one of the leaders of the Zionist movement and later the first president of Israel.

During the Second World War Ezer Weizman enlisted in the RAF, becoming one of the few Israelis to be awarded wings by the British. On his return home he was one of the small Israeli air force's first pilots.

For eight years he had been commander of the air force. He was considered the architect of the force, which had become the elite corps of the Israeli army. His personal leadership had paved the way for the air force's tremendous victory in the Six-Day War. During the war he had been chief of headquarters in the general staff, the second most important post in the military hierarchy. Some claimed that his hawkish political views had eliminated him from the running for the position of chief of staff. At the end of the sixties he joined Begin's Herut party; he was minister of transport in Golda Meir's unity government. After Herut left the government Weizman was one of the few who tried to rebel against Begin's leadership of the party. He failed, and diverted his interest to business. On the eve of the 1977 elections he became active in the Likud party and ran the election campaign. Begin was bedridden because of heart disease, and Weizman conducted the campaign alone, leading the party to victory.

Weizman was popular, even more so than Begin. He was known for his immense personal charm, gaiety, and straightforward, sometimes coarse way of speaking.

The Egyptians asked the Israelis to keep the meeting between Weizman and Sadat secret. Weizman told only a few of his closest friends and asked one of them, David Kollitz, to prepare a fitting gift for Sadat, on the assumption that he would meet him during the meeting with Gamassi. Kollitz and his wife went to the shops in Allenby Street, Tel Aviv, and bought a clock for approximately $125. The following message was engraved on it: "To President Sadat, the leader who moved the hands of time forward." Weizman also phoned his friend, El Al director general Mordechai Hod, who had succeeded him as commander of the air force. Hod was in London and brought back a pipe of the best quality, as Weizman requested.

The Americans offered to fly Weizman and his entourage to Cairo. On the morning of December 20, 1977, a U.S. Air Force DC-9 from Frankfurt landed at a military airfield in the center of Israel, and Weizman and his party disappeared inside it. He took with him Brigadier Herzl Shapir, chief of the general staff, and Brigadier Shlomo Gazit, chief of intelligence. The plane landed at Cairo West's International Airport. Gamassi was waiting. "I have heard a great deal about you from President Sadat," he said.

"You have a great president," said Weizman.

Gamassi informed him that the talks would be held at a large estate in the Alexandria region.

Gamassi is a veteran armored corps officer, a closed and pedantic man—with, however, good manners and a fine sense of humor. The Israelis had met him at Kilometer 101 at the end of 1973. He had resigned from the army after the defeat in 1967, disgusted and angry at the stupidity of his commanding officers, but returned at the end of the year, first as commander of the Suez Canal front and later as commander of campaigns branch and chief of staff. After the death of his patron and friend General Ahmed Ismaili Ali, Gamassi replaced him as minister of war.

"Before we start the talks," Gamassi said, surprising Weizman, "we'll fly together to Ismailia. The president wishes to see you."

The encounter in Jerusalem had established a personal tie between Sadat and Weizman. Sadat feared the aggressiveness of Israel's hawks more than anything else. He had regarded Israel's defense establishment, and Weizman at its head, as the focal point of hawkish views in Israel, but the discussions in Jerusalem between Weizman, the president's aides, and Sadat himself made it clear that this was not so: Weizman was far more moderate than he had been portrayed in Israel and the Arab world.

Sadat received Weizman with obvious joy. "I am hoping and waiting for a true peace," he said at the outset. "The Israelis must believe me." But almost from the beginning the conversation became heated. Weizman was taken aback by Sadat's stubborn decisiveness. He stated plainly that Israel had to be aware that he could not make peace "as long as Israel holds on to Arab lands. . . . I know what the Egyptian people can accept and what it will reject," Sadat said. "If I force it to accept something illogical it will react aggressively in the future."

The conversation took place in the courtyard of Sadat's residence in Ismailia. Only two other Egyptians, Vice-President Mubarak and Minister of War Gamassi, were present.

Sadat put his demands on the table: a complete withdrawal to the 1967 borders and the gradual evacuation of the Israeli settlements in the Rafa salient. Weizman was not surprised by these demands, which repeated what Sadat

99

had declared in the Knesset, but was disappointed by Sadat's aggressive tone. He had expected Sadat to take a more moderate line, at least in private.

The conversation with Gamassi near Alexandria was more pleasant. Gamassi began by stressing his gratitude to Weizman for having come to Egypt. He told Weizman and his aides what a deep impression the warm welcome accorded to Sadat in Jerusalem had made on the Egyptians. "You should know that we look forward to peace and that we come to you with open hearts."

"I believe in your frankness and in your desire for peace," Weizman began, presenting the Israeli stand. "I must tell you that we are a small nation. You attacked us in the Yom Kippur War before we managed to mobilize our reserves. You deserve respect for the surprise of 1973. Our army is small, though good, but if we lose a war we lose everything. I told President Sadat that we have a large air force but only five or six airfields. You Egyptians, together with the Syrians and the Jordanians, have forty airfields."

Weizman decided to repeat some of the things Sadat had said in Jerusalem. He complimented the Egyptians on Sadat's initiative and stated that he realized the difficulties he was facing in the Arab world; but Begin's difficulties should also be taken into account. "It should be remembered that peace agreements are made between nations, not leaders," he said. "The individuals disappear with time."

Weizman was not sure that his hosts had taken his hint. He wanted to make it clear to the Egyptians that Israel had to guarantee its security and that this was not a matter of a few years. Peace would have to be tenable long after Sadat was no longer president of Egypt.

Gamassi said: "We are aware of the security problems confronting you. When the president returned from Jerusalem he told us about them. But I must emphasize that both sides have this problem. In security there has to be mutuality. Mr. Weizman, you mentioned your great air force. It is obvious that we need to be secure against it too." He went on: "We cannot accept your suggestion of border changes—certainly not today. If the question were to be raised thirty years after peace is signed things might be different. A change in the borders today would be interpreted as annexation, as Israeli appropriation of Egyptian territory."

Weizman was disappointed. He was not satisfied with a vague promise; he wanted to go into details. He raised an issue that had been of foremost concern to the army general staff, the need to ensure that most of the Egyptian army would be stationed as far away as possible from the border with Israel. He also wanted to know if there was any intention of reducing the size of the Egyptian army. If that were so, every movement of the Egyptian army or expansion of its forces could serve as a warning for Israel. "Until 1967 most of your army was deployed around Cairo," he said. "Today you are stationed in the Suez Canal area. Why don't we decide to move those large forces to the rear?"

"Since 1967 the Egyptian army has been on full alert," Gamassi answered. "But if there is peace we will not keep large forces near the canal. I can inform you officially that once the peace agreement has been signed our army will be reduced in size and its strategic deployment altered."

Weizman: "May I convey that information officially to my government?"

Gamassi: "Yes, but it will require an official treaty."

Weizman: "Will it involve a significant reduction of the Egyptian army?"

Gamassi: "Of course. Some forces will remain along the canal, but with time we will move them to the Cairo area. The deployment will be toward Africa."

This constituted an important assurance on a sensitive subject. Similarly, the Egyptian minister of war again asked for Israel's agreement to the stationing of Egyptian forces in Al-'Arish and of a squadron or two of planes in Sinai.

Weizman: "We will have to discuss again the airfields we need in Sinai. In addition, I must remind you that President Sadat promised Prime Minister Begin that the army would not be moved west of the passes."

Gamassi: "It is true that President Sadat made that promise, but he is not a military man. The question is, how can I defend my country?"

Weizman suggested that Brigadier Shapir reply to Gamassi about the best way for the Egyptians to guarantee the security of the Suez Canal and their country in the

101

face of an attack from the direction of Sinai. Shapir did as asked. From his answer Gamassi understood that even after the signing of a peace treaty Israel intended to limit the size of the military forces and the nature of the weapons the Egyptians could maintain in the canal area.

Gamassi said he would oppose thinning out the Egyptian forces along the Suez Canal. He would not agree to areas of attenuation. Israel would have to be satisfied with Egypt's promise that large forces would not be stationed there. "I also object to demilitarization," he said. "Demilitarization damages Egypt's sovereignty."

"Would you Israelis agree to the demilitarization of Elath and Beersheba?" interrupted General el-Greidli, referring to the reduction in size of the Egyptian army after a peace treaty had been signed. "We hope to be able to organize our reserves like you. Until now we have not succeeded."

Weizman: "We will help you."

Greidli: "But until then you must know that every restriction raises psychological problems for us."

During the course of the discussion Gamassi surprised Weizman by saying that he had no objection to leaving the Israeli settlements in the Rafa salient, in Sinai, and along the Gulf of Elath, "if the inhabitants wish it and provided it is clear both to you and to them that they will be living in Egyptian territory, under Egyptian rule, like the Jews of Cairo." Gamassi's attitude was different from Sadat's; it was assumed at the time that this arose from lack of coordination between them.

At least one of the Israeli aides thought that Sadat and Gamassi were playing assigned roles, with Sadat as the "bad guy" and Gamassi as the "good guy." Anyway, there was no point in basing decisions on Gamassi's positive attitude, because in Egypt only the president makes decisions.

After seven hours Gamassi raised an important issue. "We have not mentioned the nuclear threat in the region," he said. "You have nuclear weapons, or an option to manufacture them. We must think about signing an agreement limiting the distribution of these weapons."

Gamassi looked Weizman straight in the eye. He wanted to read in his face whether what he had just said was true. Weizman's face was a mask.

Weizman: "I suggest that you talk to Iraq and Libya about it."

Gamassi: "They don't have nuclear arms."

This was not the first time that the question had been raised in a meeting between Israelis and Egyptians. When Sadat visited Jerusalem, a comment had been made during a conversation among Weizman, Yadin, Khalil, and Ghali.

For many years this has been bothering the Arab countries: the possibility that Israel might possess nuclear arms gave them no rest, making it apparent that the chances of conquering Israel are very slim. The general consensus has been that the Jews must not be pushed too far, as in desperation they may resort to nuclear weapons. It was also feared that the Israelis might use atomic weapons for political blackmail. However, some elements in the Arab world have claimed that nuclear arms give Israel no advantage because it will never be able to use them. Israel will finally be defeated, they say, by popular guerrilla warfare, not by regular forces. Other elements in the Arab world maintain that the Arab countries should make a collective effort to produce nuclear arms. The Arabs have the requisite financial and other resources.

In practical terms the Arabs are far removed from a nuclear option. The Libyan ruler, Qaddafi, has tried to purchase nuclear weaponry but was unsuccessful. The Iraqis have advanced more than any other Arab country in the field of nuclear research, but have not been able to produce nuclear arms. The Egyptians signed an international agreement to prevent the distribution of nuclear arms but did not ratify it, claiming that Israel had to do so first.

Late in the afternoon, at the end of the discussions, Weizman and his colleagues were surprised to hear an announcement of the talks on Radio Cairo's news broadcast. The Egyptians had asked that the meetings be kept secret, and now they were advertising them. The Israelis wondered why.

A second meeting between Weizman and Sadat the next day was even more difficult. Sadat was more rigid, leaving no doubts in Weizman's mind: "The Israeli settlements must leave. Their remaining will constitute an infringement of Egypt's sovereignty, and I will not agree to it."

Sadat would not agree to a gradual withdrawal from Sinai either. It had to be done at one stroke, quickly. He objected to stationing UN troops in the Sinai peninsula. "This would be an infringement of Egyptian sovereignty," he repeated.

The members of the Israeli party did not know what had caused this sudden swing in Sadat's mood. One assessment was that the American ambassador to Egypt, Hermann Eilts, had met Sadat earlier and informed him of Begin's new plan, which had previously been submitted to the Americans. Sadat may have wanted to send a firm message to Begin through this meeting with Weizman.

12 A PLAN IN A YELLOW NOTEBOOK

Weizman was gloomy on his arrival at Begin's residence in Jerusalem to report on his talks with Sadat. He had been taken aback by Egyptian inflexibility. "It won't be an easy negotiation," he said. "We'll be facing an unbending Egyptian position."

For decades Begin had dreamed and fought for the idea of an indivisible land of Israel as more than a utopian vision. The voters who elected him believed he might finally realize his ambition to bring the West Bank and the Gaza Strip under Israeli jurisdiction. But there were many, even among Begin's followers, who feared that annexation of the West Bank could bring much bloodshed.

The realities of international politics awakened Begin from his dream almost as soon as he took office. The outraged reaction to his election all over the world, Sadat's visit to Israel, and international pressure opened a chasm between Begin and his ideals. He saw that the moment of truth, the one all previous Israeli prime ministers had successfully avoided, was at hand: it was "peace or territories."

Begin sought a way out. He wished to hold on to the West Bank, which was so precious to him, while finding a solution for the Palestinian problem and Israel's defense needs. He called in two close aides, Bureau Chief Yehiel Kadishai and Military Secretary Ephraim Poran.

"The only possible answer," he said, "is self-rule. It will give us security and then autonomy." Kadishai pulled out a yellow notebook, and Begin paced up and down dictating section after section.

Begin had always believed in the right of Jews to settle anywhere in Eretz Israel, and certainly in the West Bank, which had been occupied by the Israeli army since the Six-Day War. Until he came to power he supported the establishment of settlements all over the historical land of Israel in order to make clear the right of the people of Israel to the land. But his party, because of a severe manpower shortage, had succeeded in founding only a small number of settlements in the occupied territories. The more moderate ruling party had managed to establish more than seventy settlements in the territories. The Arabs in the occupied territories, and the leaders of Arab states, were furious over the settlements in the Jordan Valley, the West Bank, and the Gaza Strip, which became in their eyes the symbol of Israeli occupation.

The idea of self-rule for the occupied territories was not new. Dayan, as minister of defense in the previous government, had taken care to interfere as little as possible in the internal affairs of the million local inhabitants, and his successor, Shimon Peres, had continued the policy, even trying to decrease tensions by "Arabization"—the reduction of the number of Jewish officials in the military government. Most of the administration was already in Arab hands.

Begin had raised the idea of self-rule in 1975, but as an opposition leader he did not have to carry out his promises. "The Arab nation in the land of Israel, which we recognize, should be given cultural autonomy," he had said then. "We Jews, when we were a minority in different countries, always demanded cultural autonomy for ourselves. We must give them cultural autonomy—in other words, the education of their children in their tradition, in their tongue, and according to their religious precepts."

Begin had in the past translated the autonomy idea into political language, saying that a "Likud government would guarantee to the Arab nation in the land of Israel a cultural autonomy, a fostering of the values of their national culture, their religion and heritage." Not many Israeli voters, including Begin's supporters, read party manifestos, and few if any paid heed to that section.

In the plan he conceived following Sadat's visit, Begin did not entirely give up the right to impose Israeli law on the historical land of Israel. He was postponing it, it was said; Israel continued to insist on this right, but it recognized that the other side had similar demands, and for the sake of peace it was willing to leave the question open, to be reviewed in five years.

The intention was clear: the self-rule plan would enable Israel to continue to control the West Bank but would grant the Palestinians a degree of self-government. Israel still had the option of purchasing land and settling on it inside the area of autonomy, but Begin would allow the inhabitants of the occupied territories the same right to purchase land and settle it inside Israel.

Begin, in his self-rule plan, left the Arabs of the West Bank free to take or retain Jordanian citizenship. Those who elected to be Jordanian citizens would be able to vote for and be elected to the Jordanian parliament, to move freely inside Israel, and to develop free economic systems of their own. He left the management of internal affairs almost exclusively in the hands of the residents, through an administrative council of eleven members chosen in free elections. Begin's plan was fully detailed. The administrative council would be in Bethlehem or Ramallah—not in Jerusalem—and would hold the reins of internal rule through various departments.

Like many other Israelis, the demographic problem was a great worry to Begin. He was afraid of the creation of an Arab majority in Eretz Israel as a result of the Arab population explosion and immigration. His greatest anxiety was the Arab refugees who had fled from Israel in the 1948 War of Independence. He was afraid that, now living in Arab states, they would interpret autonomy to mean that they could return freely to the land of their fathers, so he decided that an Israeli-Jordanian joint committee and the administrative council would supervise the return of refugees.

From Begin's point of view, the self-rule plan had great advantages. It did not allow Jordan to gain a strong foothold in the occupied territories; it left Israel with exclusive authority in the areas of defense and policy, and shifted the focus from the PLO to the local Palestinian inhabitants. The disadvantages were apparent: the Palestinians of the occupied territories would not be their own masters. They could determine the placing of sewer pipes in Hebron, but could not build an army, hoist a flag, compose a new anthem, or print money.

Begin's proposal for a settlement with Egypt in the Sinai was less complicated. He recognized Egyptian sovereignty over the entire peninsula and agreed to a withdrawal to the international borders. He thought withdrawal could take place in two stages. The first had to satisfy the Egyptians and compensate the Israelis. Thus the first withdrawal line would pass from the town of Al-'Arish to the area of Ras Muhammad. He would give Egypt an important town of the Sinai (Al-'Arish), to prove practical control of the area, and leave Israel Sharm al-Sheikh to guarantee free passage for Israeli ships on their way to the Gulf of Elath.

The second stage of the military evacuation would be slightly more complex, involving difficult problems that would arise when the Israeli army was ordered to return to its old border. He intended to keep the settlements of the Rafa approaches and the three Israeli military airports until the year 2001, in an area wholly under UN supervision. He thought that, since he had never failed to credit Egypt with the right to rule over the peninsula, Sadat would agree to this. Two of the three military airports would be turned into civilian auxiliaries, but one would remain under Israeli army control. The Israeli settlements and the airports would be permitted to keep a local defense force. In Begin's plan the first stage would take three to five years from the signing of the agreement and the principles of the agreement would be reviewed in 2001.

The following days were devoted to discreet consultations with friends, advisers, and some officials on the self-rule plan, until it emerged in polished form. Most government ministers were kept in the dark. In general, Begin believed that prior coordination with the U.S. could bring undue pressure, but this time it seemed right to him to present the plan to President Carter first. He conferred with Ambassador to the U.S. Simcha Dinitz while Begin was on a state visit in London.

Dinitz said: "I don't believe that a settlement can be reached without the support of the United States. That is why it is better to present the plan to President Carter first and receive his blessing. It will also make it easier for him to dismiss the idea of a Geneva convention, which is still at the back of his mind." Begin decided to go to Washington.

On the eve of his departure he presented the peace plan to his ministers, none of whom except Dayan had seen it before. Begin did not hand them a written version, but merely gave them a general oral outline. The Sinai settlement plan was not discussed.

As the cabinet had not been warned of the subject of the meeting, it was clear that they could do little: Begin had presented them with a fait accompli. Weizman had immediate reservations. Yadin said: "Autonomy is a brilliant idea. I support it one hundred percent, but I can't speak for my party. I must consult with my colleagues." The meeting lasted for seven hours and ended with a warning from Begin: "I want absolute secrecy to be maintained until I come to Carter and give him Israel's proposals. I know that there may be a risk in the plan," he concluded. "But for peace, we must take risks." He too thought it was not an ideal solution, but it was better than any other. It would allow peace with Egypt, perhaps, without a final decision about the West Bank.

The news of Begin's peace plan reached the Israel chief of staff very late, as Begin had not consulted Major General Gur, just as he had not spoken to Gur's superior, Defense Minister Weizman. Gur wanted to accompany Begin to Washington as a military consultant in the talks with Carter.

Weizman rejected Gur's request, with Begin's tacit approval. Gur did not take it well, seeing in it a personal insult and perhaps even revenge for his remarks made on the eve of Sadat's visit to Israel.

Gur did not keep his opinions to himself. He complained privately that the decision-making process on Sadat's visit and the peace negotiations in general was deficient. In the present situation there was no chance of a lasting peace, as the Palestinian problem remained open.

What was needed, therefore, was a partial settlement with Egypt that would leave Israel in control of the Sinai. Then the Israeli army would retain its maneuvering power in case of war. Gur's words did not please the new leaders responsible for Israel's defense system. "I would like it to be understood once and for all that this country is not run by generals," retorted Deputy Defense Minister Mordechai Zippori.

Begin presented Carter with his peace plan on paper with some typewriting and some handwriting, and discoursed at length on self-rule. For the first time Israel had presented the American government with an inclusive peace plan.

Carter listened closely. From time to time he reacted with an "I agree." He and his aides voiced no reservations when Begin presented his Sinai settlement plan. The reactions about self-rule in the West Bank and Gaza were more moderate: "An important contribution"; "An important advance."

Carter flooded Begin with questions: "Will the Israeli defense forces remain in the area? What about the settlements?"

Begin answered: "I don't want friction with the population of the occupied territories, so I will remove the army from the towns to a few bases."

Dayan added: "Even now the army is not in the town proper." As for Israeli settlements, Begin said, "They will remain in the area. We want to live together." Carter's national security special adviser, Zbigniew Brzezinski, persisted with questions that annoyed the Israelis.

Brzezinski: "What citizenship will territory residents have?"

Begin: "Whatever they like: Jordanian, Israeli, or local."

Brzezinski: "Will they be able to vote and be elected to the Knesset?"

Begin: "No, only those who choose Israeli citizenship."

Brzezinski: "But that's like South Africa. You are taking away the right to vote from the people."

Begin was outraged by the comparison. "Can the blacks in South Africa choose among citizenships, or be elected? We say that anyone who so chooses can become an Israeli citizen with full rights. We are not imposing anything."

110

Secretary of State Vance suggested emphasizing the linkage to Jordan in the autonomy plan, so that King Hussein would have an interest in joining the discussions.

Begin boasted that this was the first time Palestinian Arabs had been offered an entity of their own. He refused to use the term "Palestinian people."

The protacted discussion ended with a Begin question: "Mr. President, don't you think this is a fair basis for negotiations?"

Carter said: "Sure, sure."

From the reactions of the president and the comments of others present, Begin concluded that the plan was acceptable to Washington. He did not attempt to hide that it still needed ratification by the Israeli government.

The next day Begin met with four important senators and told them that President Carter had said his plan was "a fair basis for negotiation." The principles of the plan were sent from the White House to President Sadat.

In the end it was Brzezinski who seemed most amenable to Begin's proposals. "It is a good beginning," he said to his aides. "It fits my own plan and I'm glad that it was Begin who proposed it. In the second stage, the self-rule will become a Palestinian state." Begin presented his plan to other western leaders and afterward claimed that "they all praised it to the skies."

But back home, when parts of the plan were leaked, even some of Begin's best friends were against it. Members of the Labor party, who did not espouse the establishment of a Palestinian state, were sharply critical. They felt that Begin's plan was an "arm for a Palestinian state." They preferred a safer formula: a territorial compromise with Jordan.

The plan was discussed for seven hours at a cabinet meeting in the last week of December with Gur and Weizman present. Weizman objected strenuously, pointed to defects, but finally capitulated. In the absence of orderly teamwork on the part of the government, Begin's plan contained glaring loopholes. Among other things, it did not mention Israel's sources of water, which were mainly in the West Bank. At the end of the cabinet meeting an urgent cable went out to Simcha Dinitz: Israel wished to add eleven amendments to the plan presented to Carter, some of them fundamental, and ten of them

111

related to self-rule on the West Bank. Five sections were put forth that had not appeared in the original plan. Begin's peace plan reached twenty-six sections before it was ratified by the government of Israel on December 23, 1977—after it had been laid before Carter and Sadat.

The amendments contained declarations that Israel would assume responsibility not only for peace in the area of the autonomy, but also for public law and order; refugees would be allowed to return only in reasonable numbers by a unanimous decision of a joint committee; a committee to decide legislative authority would be established, its decisions also unanimous. Only Israeli citizens or Arabs who had assumed Israeli citizenship would be entitled to purchase land. Furthermore, it was emphasized that the plan was conditional on the establishment of peace.

As for Sinai, the amendments stated that the new Israeli settlements in the Rafa approaches would be under Israeli administration and Israeli law. The amendments curtailed the degree of self-rule, and increased the veto power to be maintained by Israel even in the transitional period.

Washington was indignant. The White House and State Department officials had been made to look like fools in the eyes of President Sadat, who was already familiar with Begin's original plan. It was the first of a chain of misunderstandings between Begin and Carter.

While still in Washington, Begin had expressed his desire to present the plan to Sadat. A telephone connection was established between the White House and the presidential palace in Cairo. It was decided that Begin and Sadat would meet in Ismailia. Sadat agreed to this after it became clear that the Mena House conference had reached a dead end. The American ambassador in Cairo, Hermann Eilts, put pressure on him to recognize that fact.

Eilts had a fairly strong influence on Sadat. He had been a close confidant of Kissinger, and was a professional diplomat who had served in Saudi Arabia and Lebanon. Tall, with a thin mustache and a constant smile, he was good-natured but very reserved. During his service in Cairo he never talked to the press. He was liked by Sadat and generally spoke with him daily on a special telephone line which followed the two men wherever they went.

Eilts always answered Sadat's questions immediately, even if the response would not be welcome.

Since his appointment as ambassador to Cairo, Eilts saw himself as an active partner in the peace-building process. "I shall stay here," he said once, "until after the peace." He chose to stay in Cairo even after being offered promotion to assistant secretary of state for Middle Eastern affairs.

Eilts had initially concluded that Sadat needed a "fig leaf" and not a "fig tree" to reach a settlement with Israel, as the American commentator Joseph Kraft would later put it. The ambassador believed that the meeting at Ismailia would bring about general declarations of principle, after which the peace ball could be set rolling.

Eilts saw Sadat's main weakness as not planning his moves down to the last detail. Sadat would outline his plans and allowing his aides to fill in the details. Then they often did what Sadat did not like. Sadat believed that the unexpectedness of his journey to Jerusalem would generate a shock that would bring about an immediate radical change.

Eilts was very critical of Israel, which, to his mind it had not done enough to rally support for Sadat among the leaders of the occupied territories. Two small delegations—one from Gaza and another from Hebron—had arrived in Cairo and were hardly impressive, led as they were by second- and third-rank men.

The meeting between Sadat and Begin was set for Christmas Day at Gazirat El-Fursan, the Cavalry island in the Suez Canal. Finally it was moved to Sadat's summer residence in Ismailia, which had been rebuilt since the war of attrition.

Excitement in Israel about the Ismailia meeting ran high. In Egypt, on the other hand, it was quiet. The streets of Ismailia were decorated with Egyptian flags, arches of honor, and giant pictures of Sadat in uniform. Not a single picture of Begin was to be seen, nor a single message of good wishes. Tensions were high. "Sadat and Begin are unguided missiles," said a State Department official to a *New York Times* reporter. "It is difficult to predict the results of such a meeting."

13 CRISIS ON THE BANKS OF THE SUEZ

Prime Minister Menachem Begin was tired but in good spirits as his plane headed out over the Mediterranean on the flight from Ben-Gurion Airport to Ismailia. As they flew toward the Egyptian harbor of Port Said, a stewardess came up to him and said in a low, melancholy voice: "Today would have been my husband's birthday. He died in Egypt in the Yom Kippur War." Her eyes brimmed with tears and Begin, sentimental by nature, patted her shoulders. When the young woman had regained her composure, she said, "The nation looks up to you. We hope you bring peace."

As the plane entered Egyptian airspace, Begin reminded his entourage: "Moses made this same trip thirty-five hundred years ago. Today we are retracing his steps, but at a much faster pace, and in the opposite direction."

After a forty-minute flight, the El Al plane landed at Abu Sweir Air Base near Ismailia and the banks of the Suez Canal. During and since the Six-Day War the airfield had been heavily bombed, and as a result of its proximity to the front lines, the Egyptians had kept it out of commission until the 1973 war.

Begin stepped off the plane a weary man. The intense

activity of recent weeks had begun to take its toll. The night before, he had had time for only a short nap. Even President Carter called, urging him to rest.

The reception at the Egyptian airfield was cool. There were no flags, no national anthems, no gun salvos, no speeches. The ceremony was hurried. To make matters worse, an Egyptian television technician had apparently fused the sound cables and no live broadcasts could be transmitted to television stations around the world.

In Ismailia the scene was more festive, with thousands of colorful arches, Egyptian flags, and giant posters proclaiming "Sadat, the Hero of the Crossing" and "Sadat, the Hero of Peace" fluttering in the breeze. The Israelis were puzzled. "There isn't a single sign to welcome us," Dayan commented to Begin.

Sadat awaited his guests on the terrace of his two-story villa on the outskirts of Ismailia, which had once served officials of the Suez Canal Authority. Hundreds of Egyptian policemen and security guards milled about beyond the low fence that separated the house from the street.

Sadat, elegantly dressed in a dark suit, came out to shake Begin's hand. Begin looked at his host and said, "Mr. President, you look well. Do you feel well?"

"Yes," Sadat replied. "But we shall see how things develop."

"What will develop?" was a question that had been haunting Dayan for some time. He had posed it to Begin in just those words at the government meeting that preceded their trip. Dayan had been pessimistic during Sadat's visit to Jerusalem, and was even more so later on. He was worried about facing the moment of truth. Almost from the start, Dayan had felt certain the Israeli position would be unacceptable to Egypt and the United States, and that Israel would be asked to pay a steep price. He was somber.

Weizman, who had not expected to be invited to join Begin on this trip, was also worried. When he reported to Begin on his meetings with Sadat and Gamassi, his pessimism had been tinged with rays of hope. "In Ismailia," he had said, "it will be decided whether our negotiations with Egypt will continue. I hope there will be a continuation." He had instructed his aides in the Defense Ministry to prepare orderly files for the trip, including options for withdrawals, mutual arrangements, and the security significance of withdrawals and their costs.

Begin believed the compliments showered on his peace plan; but even before he left for Ismailia, the first cracks in his faith in his autonomy plan had begun to show. U.S. Ambassador Samuel Lewis, in a briefing to the members of the American legation in Tel Aviv, was skeptical about whether Egypt would accept the peace plan. Begin, on learning of this, fumed quietly. From Egypt too came winds unsettling to the Israeli prime minister. Sadat had been even tougher than Lewis. Even before Begin arrived in Ismailia, Sadat declared that he would not consent to an Israeli military presence in the autonomous areas. His public statements corresponded with the report that Weizman had submitted following his meetings with Sadat and Gamassi. Nevertheless, Begin left for Ismailia convinced that the discussions would be conducted mainly on the basis of his peace plan. Sadat had a surprise in store.

The two leaders were in good spirits. Begin joked about his personal physician, Dr. Lewis Gutesmann: "This is my cardiologist. Every morning I ask him: 'How do you feel?'" Sadat smiled politely. Then Begin was surprised to find himself in an adjacent room in purely Egyptian company, a guest at the swearing-in ceremony of Muhammad Ibrahim Kamel, the new Egyptian foreign minister and successor to Ismail Fahmi.

After the ceremony Sadat and Begin closeted themselves for twenty-two minutes as their aides waited outside. Hundreds of journalists were gathered in a large communications center set up in a building that belonged to the Suez Canal Authority. When the door of the side room opened, Begin stepped out, beaming. Sadat's face was expressionless. Begin announced, "We have agreed on the establishment of two committees, a political and a military . . ."

Journalists mobbed the nonfunctioning telephones to try to relay the news. The atmosphere improved. The announcement seemed to many like an auspicious start.

The two delegations crowded around a long table in a rectangular hall. Sadat clapped his hands twice and a waiter wearing white gloves sprang to his side and poured green tea for the Egyptian president and his Israeli guests.

Sadat sipped from his cup and said, "In Jerusalem I drank better tea." Begin enjoyed the compliment.

Sadat rose and began to speak. "In the name of my people, my government, and my own name, I welcome you warmly. It is more than happiness for us to receive you here. I must say that these are the best days of my life. We must eliminate the disagreements between our two peoples. My people have already expressed their feelings and their wishes for peace based on justice . . ."

Sadat's drawing room was crowded and stiflingly hot. He motioned toward the window and pointed beyond it: "Not since Moses crossed the sea, not far from here, have representatives of our two peoples met. We shall work together here for peace. No more of the hatred that has existed for thirty years. The world is watching us. Let us show them a new way of reaching peace."

Sadat pointed to the Israeli defense minister and said: "Weizman and I had fruitful talks. We agreed on some points and disagreed on others . . ."

It was Begin's turn to speak. He stood up and said, "I wish to use this opportunity to congratulate you on your fifty-ninth birthday . . ."

Begin had done his homework well. Sadat glowed. "You were born in a small village and rose by struggle and sacrifice to a most highly respected national and international position," Begin continued. "We have a profound appreciation of you as a leader. Moses lived to be one hundred and twenty years old and today we wish you as long a life, so you are still in the middle of your way. When Moses went into the desert, his journey lasted forty years. When we came to you today, it hardly took us forty minutes to agree about the continuation of the negotiations.

"Egypt and the world need you, and I hope that we shall attain peace before you are sixty years old," Begin said. "We have come to you with an open and trusting heart. We want a comprehensive peace. We want all our neighbors to join the circle of trust. You have rightly said that the whole world is watching us. This is a great moment! In our hearts we believe that there will be no more war, no more hatred, no more bloodshed. Let us be friends . . ."

117

He added: "We have started with the right foot forward. It's a good omen for the future."

Begin then turned to the business at hand, saying, "I've brought you Israel's peace plan." Sadat of course knew its main points and showed no interest in the petty details.

For an hour Begin read his peace plan to Sadat and his aides. He read every sentence in a clear voice, slowly and emphatically. The participants became bored; people began shuffling about the room; Weizman was obviously restless; Dayan whispered to his neighbors, "I can't understand why he's reciting all this rigmarole." But Begin continued undaunted.

Begin tried to call Sadat's attention to the extent of his concessions: "We have decided, in effect, to nullify the decisions of the post-1968 governments with regard to the Sinai. We do not intend to ask you to sign a peace treaty while any part of the Sinai is still under our control . . . this is a peace treaty which will be perpetuated for generations . . . I proposed that it extend to the year 2001 and then be reexamined . . ."

Sadat asked one of the waiters to fill his pipe with tobacco. He sipped the green tea. His expression betrayed a growing impatience.

"We are undertaking risks," Begin concluded, "but we trust you and your promises. We consent to undertake these security risks, trusting that our children will live with smiles on their faces . . ."

The ministers and aides sighed with relief as Begin finally seemed to be drawing his lecture to a close. Sadat raised his hands over his head. An aide hurried to his side and lit the president's pipe. The table was laden with cookies and oranges. A cream cake sent by the Suez Canal Authority in honor of Sadat's birthday remained untouched.

"Mr. President," Begin said, "would you like to comment on my proposals for the Sinai now, or would you prefer to hear about the second plan?"

Sadat showed surprise. "A second plan? What does it refer to?"

"Our proposals for self-administration in Judea and Samaria, and the Gaza strip . . ." Begin responded.

"Please continue," said Sadat. "Let's hear what you have to say on the second subject too."

Begin seemed to start from the beginning: "Israel has

claims of sovereignty over Judea and Samaria, and Gaza," he said. "This is the land of our forefathers. But . . ."

Dayan held his head in his hands. Weizman scanned the people present for the thousandth time. But the representatives of the Egyptian Foreign Ministry came to life. This was the subject that interested them most. "As others have similar claims of sovereignty," Begin continued, "I suggest that we leave this subject open . . ."

Begin spoke with great assurance. "If this plan is accepted," he said, emphasizing every word, "it will be the first time in history that the Arabs of the territories have enjoyed self-administration, and we shall have security."

Sadat clapped his hands. A servant rushed to his side, and at the president's command hurried to open the windows. Tobacco smoke had clouded the room.

Begin, after concluding his presentation of the plan, added: "I wish to inform you that I have also submitted this plan to President Carter, Vice-President Mondale, and Secretary of State Vance. They, and many American senators, have assured me that it is a most fair plan. But it was not so received in Israel. They rebel against my proposals. They demonstrate against it around my office and my home."

"Yes," Weizman interjected in support of Begin, "a delegation came to me to express its firm opposition to this plan."

Begin did not seem particularly impressed by Weizman's attempted assistance. "You're lucky, Ezer," he said. "To you they send delegations; with me they demonstrate . . ."

It was noon. The Egyptian delegation were anxious, seeming to feel psychologically pressed because of Begin's visit to the U.S. They suspected he might have succeeded in mobilizing the support of Carter and others for his peace plan.

Sadat feared that a joint Israeli-American front had been formed against him. He was obviously displeased with what he had just heard. "I am disappointed, Mr. Prime Minister," he said.

"Don't be annoyed," Begin responded, "these are negotiations."

"Prime Minister Begin has spoken frankly and we have heard his proposals," Sadat began his reply, "but we shall submit counterproposals in the course of the negotiations.

We differ on several subjects, but I consider today's meeting to be a great success, whatever the differences between us . . ."

There was a sigh of relief from the Israeli side of the table. Begin and his colleagues were pleased. Sadat noticed the effect of his remarks on the Israeli delegation. "You have spoken about your difficulties, Mr. Begin," he continued. "But I too face difficulties. Egypt has certain obligations toward the Arab world, like the resolution that Israel must retreat to the 1967 borders, and the need to solve the Palestinian problem. This must be discussed at length. We shall discuss it when we deal with a draft of a declaration of principles."

The Israeli delegation were caught by surprise. Before leaving for Ismailia they had hints of Sadat's intention to discuss a declaration of principles, but none had expected him upset the whole plan of the meeting and to impose its central theme. A confrontation between the two sides was unavoidable: the Israelis wanted to discuss Begin's peace plan, but the Egyptians wanted to draft a declaration of principles. It would be difficult to compromise between the two goals.

Sadat went on to say that the declaration of principles would reinforce the Cairo conference; everything would have to be prepared thoroughly; the essence, not the procedures, would have to be discussed; it would be possible to go to Geneva, but it would also be possible to move the discussions to Cairo. The visit to Jerusalem had been an effort to get at the essential problems.

Sadat betrayed his impatience: "I propose that the two delegations exchange views about the declaration of principles. We shall meet again in the late afternoon and continue our discussions," he concluded, beginning to rise from his chair. It was obvious to the Israelis that Sadat intended to have the last word at this meeting.

But the Israelis had no intention of discussing a declaration of principles. It was Moshe Dayan who brought the Egyptian president back to his seat: "Mr. President," he said, "would you agree that in regard to the Palestinian issue we have, in principle, reached an agreement to discuss the matter, but that we will not discuss it here? In my opinion, it is better that we should not discuss this matter in Ismailia."

"I intend," Sadat responded, "that we achieve only a general agreement about principles. There are matters that we do not have to go into here. The security arrangements in the West Bank, for instance, or arrangements in the Golan—this is the Syrians' business. But with regard to the Palestinians—that is a different matter altogether! I intend to reach an agreement in principle on the matter here. That is important!"

"When should the committees begin their sessions?" Dayan asked.

"As soon as we agree about the declaration of principles, we can immediately activate the two committees," Sadat responded.

Everyone felt trapped. The establishment of the two committees had seemed like a great achievement by Begin, but now it appeared to fade away in the smoke of the Egyptian president's pipe. It was clear that Sadat had presented a veiled ultimatum: no declaration of principles, no committees.

Weizman tried to move the discussion to another subject, and succeeded. "From my conversation with General Gamassi," he said, "I gathered that you wish to maintain military forces east of the Sinai passes. General Gamassi told me he wants this in order to defend the Suez Canal . . . We need the airfields in the Sinai."

Sadat: "Why do you need the airfields?"

Weizman: "To defend ourselves."

Sadat: "Aren't we making peace?"

Weizman: "So why do you need an army east of the canal?"

Sadat: "To defend the Suez Canal."

Weizman: "Against whom?"

Sadat: "Against you!"

Weizman: "But we are making peace . . ."

Sadat: "You are right. It costs me a lot of money. I don't need more than a brigade. I don't want the extra expenses involved in maintaining a large army there. Before 1967 we didn't have a single division in all of Sinai. If we achieve peace we won't need a single soldier in the area."

The conversation was interrupted by an aide who whispered in the president's ear. Sadat's normally impassive face betrayed excitement: the president of the United States was on the telephone.

Sadat raised the receiver to his ear but heard nothing. He called into the mouthpiece, but there was no response. A moment of discomfort. The Egyptian telephone system had long been in a state of disrepair. An embarrassed Sadat replaced the receiver.

Lunch was served and the tension that had built up between the two delegations disappeared. The conversation over the mushroom salad, stuffed vine leaves, veal, and cider was easy and relaxed. Ben-Elissar, who had come from Cairo, and Weizman, who had previously visited Ismailia, joked about the mysteries of the Egyptian telephone system. Some of those present tried to guess at the message Carter wished to transmit to Sadat and Begin.

Outside, hundreds of journalists cursed the two leaders: the Ismailia conference had spoiled their Christmas holidays. Their grumbling turned to fury when it became obvious that there was nothing to wire home. The newsmen were locked in the Suez Canal Authority building and were prevented from approaching the villa where the negotiations were being held.

Suddenly the press photographers were galvanized into action as Sadat entered his big, armored black car. "Mr. Prime Minister, please sit next to me," he told Begin. "Moshe and 'Ezra,' you sit in the back." Sadat settled behind the steering wheel and drove the car into the streets of Ismailia. The stunned security men raced after him. The excited press photographers ran with all their might to catch up with the security men, the Egyptian president, and his Israeli guests.

The afternoon hours in Ismailia were devoted to an interim summation. The members of the Israeli delegation were convinced that Sadat had intended from the start to press for a declaration of principles, and they realized what lay behind Sadat's ostensibly innocent aim. Sadat had been accused by the Arab world of moving toward a separate treaty with Israel; he had vehemently denied this, promising to present the Arab world with his own formula for a comprehensive settlement; whoever later wished to participate in peace talks with Israel could do so on his own. He had committed himself to the solution of the Palestinian problem. The declaration of principles he hoped to extract from the Israelis was meant to rid him of his burden, but Begin and the Israelis were unable to provide him with a formula that would satisfy the Arab world. Begin maintained that a Palestinian state between Israel and Jordan would be a powder keg which would wreak havoc in Israel. No declaration of principles could be elicited from Begin on the Palestinian issue, even if this risked the breakdown of peace negotiations. As a result, a sense of imminent failure permeated the atmosphere.

Begin consoled himself with his personal achievement, the establishment of the political and military committees. He reviewed again to his aides why he considered it an achievement.

First, Jerusalem, the capital of Israel, had been chosen as the seat of the political committee. The Egyptian readiness to conduct political negotiations in Jerusalem was something Israel was not used to even from friendly governments. It could be interpreted as recognition of Jerusalem as the capital of Israel.

Second, the proposed setup of the talks was tantamount to direct negotiations, free of external pressure, in the framework of which both sides would try to settle the differences between them. Israel had thus achieved a demand it had raised from the first: direct negotiations with its neighbors, or at least with one of them.

A solution seemed to emerge early in the afternoon. Begin proposed his version of the declaration of principles on the Palestinian issue. It contained little substance, but he hoped that Sadat would be satisfied with it: "The issues of the West Bank and Gaza will be discussed in a working group consisting of the representatives of Israel, Egypt, Jordan, and Palestinian Arabs, with the aim of finding a just solution to the Palestinian problem."

Surprisingly, Sadat's initial reaction to Begin's lukewarm, colorless formulation was favorable; it seemed a solution had been found to the time bomb that threatened to blow up the Ismailia conference. But before the evening session, which was to be the concluding one, Begin learned that the officials of the Egyptian Foreign Ministry had prevailed on Sadat to reject Begin's version of the declaration of principles. During the morning session Begin and his entourage had gathered that Foreign Ministry officials had pressured Sadat to extract satisfactory terminology. He was in the habit of watching their reactions during his speech, and they continually whispered in his ears during

Begin's remarks. They interfered in the bilateral talks much more than the other Egyptian participants.

Sadat was tense as he opened the evening session. "Let us speak openly and frankly, as there is nothing to hide . . ."

The sense of imminent failure weighed heavily in the air; people were openly anxious. Green tea was again served. Sadat said, "I must mention again that when I journeyed to Jerusalem I intended to remove all barriers of mistrust. This I also hoped to find here . . . I wish you to realize that my people stand behind me and against all the world. Five million Egyptians cheered me when I returned from Jerusalem to Cairo. When I saw it, I told my deputy, Mubarek, and the prime minister, Mamduk Salem: 'Something happened here. It is impossible that the masses would react so enthusiastically. Even in the great and brilliant days of Nasser, when he nationalized the Suez Canal, nothing like this happened. Mass reaction was not so enthusiastic even when Nasser was the national hero of Egypt and of the third world.' "

Sadat's voice became harsher: "But these people, my people, will not consent to unacceptable conditions. I have already told Ezra Weizman that my people will accept no conditions about the return of the Sinai. We shall discuss everything, but without conditions . . ."

Sadat evoked the past: "We are today in conflict because of what Ben-Gurion initiated and did. He tried to impose peace on the Arabs. When I was a journalist during the fifties I founded a newspaper in Cairo and wrote about this subject. We have always been apprehensive of you, while Ben-Gurion was apprehensive of peace. He opposed peace."

Sadat now complimented both Jews and Egyptians: "I was told that when your people visited the Cairo synagogue, there was a military officer among them. The Egyptians hugged him from all sides and practically suffocated him. This is a clear sign of the friendship of the Egyptian people! We are all descendants of Abraham. We are cousins. Our peoples have a cultural tradition thousands of years old. After many years Egypt has become a democracy like Israel. We have established newspapers which publish anything that they want. All Arab countries except Egypt are monarchies and dictatorships . . ."

But the compliments were followed by more harsh words: "If I tell my people that Begin wants to leave his settlements in the Sinai and that the Israeli army will protect them, they will stone me! Begin's proposal is not enough for me, especially when I face the whole Arab world. Egypt is the leader of the Arab world. Therefore, it cannot, even if it wished, make a separate peace with Israel. Nevertheless, we shall discuss your and our proposals."

Sadat reverted to his original proposal: "What we requested from you, through the United States, is a declaration of principles. I don't want to discuss issues which do not concern us. I have told my aides that Begin is apt to put me in a difficult position if and when he asks me how he is to solve his security problems in the West Bank. I have no satisfactory answer to this problem. We can discuss our problems in a civilized manner and there is no need for the great powers to conduct the negotiations on our behalf. I want our declaration of principles to contain an explicit statement about the termination of the occupation of Arab lands and the solution of all aspects of the Palestinian problem. Any side involved in the conflict, apart from Israel and Egypt, can negotiate later on with Israel about security problems. I definitely agree that you have the right, Mr. Begin, to demand security from me. I am interested in a declaration of principles which will satisfy the minimum that our people feel they are entitled to."

Sadat's speech was beautifully constructed. After the harsh demands presented to Israel, he made tempting offers to the Israeli leaders facing him: "Ezra asked me about diplomatic relations. President Carter also talked with me about the contents of a Middle East peace. I told Ezra that not only am I in favor of normalization and diplomatic relations, but I am also in favor of open economic relations. We must open an air corridor between us. The whole world is focusing its attention on us. I am determined that we have had enough of wars and bloodshed. That is what I said to my advisers before coming here. I am ready for diplomatic relations and normalization, for anything! I told Ezra that I have no desire or need for the UN force in Sinai. On the contrary, let us have joint Israeli-Egyptian patrols on both sides of the border."

He reverted to the harsh tone: "What I have heard hitherto from your side disappoints me. I think that the proposals should be passed to the committee for discussion. Don't try to force anything on our people. That would be an error. With a good declaration of principles I shall be able to win in my struggle against the rejectionist front. Even if I lose, I shall be able to say that it was for the good of the Egyptian people."

The concluding remarks were warm—a good ending to a long speech spiced with a defense of his tough stand on the question of withdrawal and the Palestinians: "Our people will be your good friends! I told Ezra: 'You must try and win the support of the Egyptian people. If you succeed, it will be a great achievement.' I shall never forget your courtesy and the friendship that the Israeli people have displayed toward me. The Egyptians know it and they will become your good friends, I am sure of it. There is no way but the way of friendship, for this and the coming generations. I shall say so and say it again, even if I am forced to resign."

Begin wanted to answer Sadat in the same coin. He understood the veiled hints, the tough demands, and the expression of warm friendship, and walked the trail opened before him by the Egyptian president: "You were right to say that we are now facing one of the gravest moments of our lives. We have fought for our independence. Nobody handed it to us on a platter. We are two ancient peoples, and it is a great opportunity to make peace between these two peoples. Personally, I am prepared to leave tomorrow for Damascus to meet with President Assad; but you must realize that we cannot negotiate with Syria while it refuses to negotiate and to come to the conference table . . ."

Begin's hint should have been clear: he proposed that Sadat think about the possibility of a separate settlement with Israel—which Sadat had always wished to avoid. In effect, Begin implied that Sadat had no other course. Sadat knew that Israel would not negotiate with the PLO, and that Syria and Jordan were not inclined to join the negotiations.

Begin also evoked the past. He referred to Sadat's remarks: "You are surely aware that David Ben-Gurion and

I were sharp opponents, but it is a grave and utter error to say that he wished to impose solutions on the Arabs. You and we should remember the era Ben-Gurion lived in. We had just come through the horrible Holocaust in Europe. A day after our Declaration of Independence, in May 1948, we were being attacked on all sides. All our neighbors attacked us, including King Farouk's Egypt. We had hardly any weapons or defenses; we faced extermination again. We lost one whole percent of our population in that war. It is true that there were retaliatory actions in Ben-Gurion's time, but there was no alternative. I want you to know that Ben-Gurion never wished to impose a peace on you. He craved peace with all his being. He asked Nasser, your predecessor, to meet with him, but he was rejected."

It was a chivalrous gesture on Begin's part to the memory of his greatest opponent, Israel's first prime minister and minister of defense, who had practically excommunicated Begin. For a generation Begin bore on his shoulders the burden of Ben-Gurion's hostility. Upon assuming the prime ministership after Ben-Gurion's death Begin forgave him. Now, in Ismailia, he became Ben-Gurion's loyal advocate.

Begin feared for the failure of the Ismailia conference: "We have come here in goodwill, intending cooperation. But we cannot risk the safety of the citizens of Israel. We must maintain the momentum. Let us pass the issues on which we disagree to the committees. I, personally, am prepared to meet with you, Mr. President, at any place, at any time."

Begin did not evade the subject of the agenda: "I proposed to you today a good draft for a declaration of principles. The draft speaks of the need to find a just solution to the Palestinian problem, and suggests that the issue be discussed in a joint work group consisting of Egypt, Israel, Jordan, and a representative of the Palestinian Arabs . . ."

Sadat interjected: "That is correct. That's what we talked about, but my people . . ."

There was an air of excitement in the conference room. The Egyptian ambassador to the United Nations, Ismet Abd-el-Magid, jumped from his seat, saying, "It's unacceptable, totally unacceptable."

The managing director of the Foreign Ministry, Dr.

Osama al-Baz, also rose from his seat: "Unacceptable. Totally unacceptable."

The third Foreign Ministry representative was not quiet either. Secretary of State Boutros Ghali commented excitedly, but his words were lost in the commotion which ensued.

Begin: "You want an Arafat Palestinian state."

Sadat: "I am not talking about Arafat. The subject is self-determination for the Palestinians."

Begin: "Self-determination means a Palestinian state, but I cannot consent to that."

Sadat: "It is in your interest that I continue to be the leader of the Arab world. I can finish Arafat off in two weeks. We must have something in hand, otherwise they are going to stone me."

Begin: "I am under pressure too."

The atmosphere became heated. The Foreign Ministry officials leaned toward Sadat and whispered in his ear.

Begin: "Look, there was not a single inhabited place in Palestine whose original name was not Hebrew. Are you familiar with the village Batir, close to Jerusalem?"

Sadat: "No, no."

Begin: "Batir is Bethar."

Begin described at length the story of the Bar Cocheba rebellion against the Romans after the destruction of the Second Temple, how they had been encouraged by Rabbi Akiba to conquer Jerusalem, how they had minted coins and established self-rule until they were overwhelmed in the fortress of Bethar by the Roman General Severus, and how Palestine had subsequently been devastated.

Sadat sucked on his pipe and made no comment. From time to time he smiled and nodded, listening patiently to Begin's long dissertation. At times he interrupted to order drinks. Once or twice he sent the Foreign Ministry man, Abd-el-Magid, to order drinks, putting him in the role of errand boy.

Abd-el-Magid presented Begin with a sheet of paper. "This is our draft declaration of principles."

Sadat seconded him: "Mr. Prime Minister, I suggest that Abd-el-Magid explain our proposal. The Foreign Ministry people are my lawyers."

Abd-el-Magid read aloud the draft declaration prepared by the Egyptians, with explications. From the first sentence it was obvious to the Israelis that the Egyptian proposal was unacceptable. It called for an Israeli withdrawal from the Sinai, the Golan, the West Bank, and Gaza, according to UN Resolution 242 which established in its preamble that territories cannot be acquired by force. It further stipulated a just settlement of all the aspects of the Palestinian problem, on the basis of the right to self-determination, by means of joint talks among Egypt, Jordan, Israel, and the representatives of the Palestinian people.

Begin: "We are prepared to accept the text of Resolution 242 without the preamble, as an introduction to a peace treaty between us and Egypt."

Sadat: "No, no! The preamble is important: it establishes the principle of nonacquisition of territory by force."

Begin: "The question is what kind of war you refer to. A defensive or an offensive war?"

Sadat: "You attacked us in 1967."

Begin: "You had better look up what was written at the time in your newspapers and what you did in the Strait of Tiran and with the UN Emergency Force. Your predecessor, Nasser, sent great military forces to the Sinai against Israel. Syria and Jordan also attacked us. We consider it to have been a defensive war."

Sadat: "I know, I know."

Begin: "Our presence in the Sinai is also legitimate from the point of view of international law, which permits the occupation of territories until a peace agreement is reached."

The mood became more heated. Sadat was irritated: "But all this took place before my visit to Jerusalem, before November 19. Now everything has changed. A new era has begun."

Begin: "True, but we cannot abandon safety measures."

Sadat: "You should also remember that I must lead Egypt in the Arab world."

Begin was inexorable. He quoted passages he had prepared in advance from the classics of international law, from the works of Lauterpach and Oppenheim. The two discussed the distinctions between a defensive war and a war of conquest.

The lengthy quotations made Sadat, who has never liked learned quotations, and definitely not at a late hour, weary. Weizman noticed it. "Oppenheim? Let's open the window. It's getting hot in here," he said.

Sadat is known as an exemplary host. He is extremely polite and courteous, though somewhat cool and reserved. His expression was a clear indication to the people in the room that the conversation should end quickly.

Begin took up the draft declaration of principles submitted by the Egyptians. He began to expostulate on how the purpose of negotiations was to achieve a peace treaty and not a peace agreement.

Loud whispers were heard in the conference room. The representatives of the Egyptian Foreign Ministry were conversing among themselves.

Begin remarked: "The gentlemen of the Foreign Ministry may not agree, but there is a difference between a peace treaty and a peace agreement."

While in fact there is no essential legal difference in international law between a peace treaty and a peace agreement, in the Cairo conference held at the Mena House hotel, the Egyptians insisted for days on end of talking about a peace agreement and had rejected out of hand the definition of the subject under discussion as a peace treaty. The reason: under the Egyptian constitution, a treaty calls for ratification by the Egyptian parliament, while an agreement calls only for approval by the president.

Sadat was fed up with the senseless argument. He was aware of the bargaining on this issue that had gone on for two weeks at the Cairo conference. His face revealed impatience. "Yes, treaty, no treaty. I agree: a treaty!"

There was confusion. The Egyptian Foreign Ministry people became silent and sour. The person who seemed most disappointed was the French-educated Ismet Abd-el-Magid. Formerly minister of information and state secretary for foreign affairs, he is considered one of Egypt's most brilliant diplomats. The tall, plump, well-manicured and elegant ambassador to the UN had had secret contacts with the Israeli ambassador to the UN, Chaim Herzog, long before the peace initiative. He had expected to become foreign minister but had been forced to limit his ambitions. His two-week struggle at Mena House had ended in failure.

It was late at night. The legal counsel of the Israeli Foreign Ministry explained to the assembly the meaning of

Security Council Resolution 242, which also referred to the subject of peace.

Dayan snapped: "Stop lecturing. President Sadat has already accepted it."

Sadat then said: "I propose that two people be chosen by each side, and they will reformulate the matter of withdrawal which appears in the declaration of principles. With regard to the Palestinian issue, I insist on the matter of self-determination. I agree that neither Arafat nor Kuddoumy shall represent the Palestinian side. I have always been of the opinion that there must be an affinity between the Palestinians and Jordan. You have to accept this, otherwise I shall be accused of having sold out the Palestinians! All my efforts are at getting a declaration of principles which will enable me to face my opponents in the rejectionist front and in the Arab world."

Members of the Israeli side exchanged remarks. At his colleagues' urging, Begin requested a short intermission for consultation. At the consultation it was decided not to agree to Sadat's request on the matter of Palestinian self-determination. They returned to the conference table.

The colloquy went this way:

Dayan: "The acceptance of this proposal contains a grave danger to Israel. Its practical meaning is, in effect, an attack in stages on Israel."

Sadat: "I agree with you that the extremists should not be permitted a toehold. I also agree with you that Israel has security considerations. It is also true that the extremists are liable to make trouble for all of us, for the whole region, particularly after the Tripoli conference. George Habbash has declared himself a Marxist-Leninist. For that very reason one must work for the right of self-determination which is so absent for the Palestinians."

Begin: "A thing like that, which means the establishment of a Palestinian state, will be accepted by only the five representatives of the Communist party in the Knesset."

Sadat was tired. He held his head between his hands. He was clearly very agitated. "I don't wish to reach an agreement with your five Communists in the Knesset," he said.

Begin: "Mr. President, you must understand. With us it

131

is not a verbal matter, not a matter of definitions. For us it means facing a mortal danger."

The clock pointed to 10:00 p.m., and the atmosphere was heavy. It was clear to the weary delegations on both sides of the table that no agreement would be reached and no declaration of principles would be published. The discussion veered to paragraphs bearing on the network of peace relations. These were no problem. Every paragraph suggested by Begin was received by Sadat with a gesture meaning "Fine." It was agreed that Security Council Resolution 242, including the preamble, would be included as an appendix to the peace treaty. The conferees were exhausted.

Begin: "Mr. President. Let me tell you a story. I have a friend whose watch is always out of order, but nevertheless he always knows what time it is."

Sadat: "How?"

Begin: "He has to eat every three hours."

Sadat: "All right, Mr. Prime Minister. Let's stop now. We must eat. We shall meet again tomorrow morning."

Begin lay down to sleep. He failed to find the electric switch and the light burned all night. He could not close his eyes. Nor did the other Israelis, who spent the night in the de Lesseps building, sleep. They continued their consultations without respite. Three members of the Israeli team, Moshe Dayan, Meir Rosenne, and Yehuda Avner, met with Boutros Ghali and Ismet Abd-el-Magid late into the night. The five tried to draft a joint communiqué in anticipation of the mammoth press conference that was to take place the next day. This failed, too, and it was finally decided that each side would issue its own communiqué.

In the de Lesseps guest house, in the center of Ismailia, the Israelis joked among themselves in order to discharge the tension accumulated during the day. An out-of-order telephone rang incessantly, its metallic clangor resounding in the large, high-ceilinged rooms of the building, until someone finally took it off the hook.

The Egyptian team did not go to sleep either. The Foreign Ministry people sat up until 4:00 a.m. in an attempt to find a solution. At dawn they still had not found the magic formula. Dayan returned from his meeting with Sadat's advisers. "I couldn't move them," he said.

At breakfast the Israeli team was pensive. The press

conference was set for noon and everyone was anxious to use the precious time left to reach an agreement on a joint communiqué. It was proposed that Begin open the meeting with the Egyptian team with a subject specially prepared for him for the conference: Soviet infiltration and its dangers. Begin declined. He seemed exhausted from lack of sleep. He irritably turned down a draft proposed by his adviser on Arab affairs, Dr. Moshe Sharon, who wanted to offer Sadat the phrase he so strongly desired—"self-determination" for the Palestinians—but with qualifying terms which would not enable the Egyptian president to make much use of it. After consulting with his team, Begin began to wander around the room, deep in thought. No one dared approach him. He was depressed. He had been negatively impressed by the welcome he had received in Ismailia. While touring the streets of the city in Sadat's company, he had become even more aware of the absence of any welcome signs for the Israelis. Begin, who knows no Arabic, had asked Sharon: "What is written here? Is there even a single greeting in our honor?"

During the morning consultation Begin decided to propose to Sadat that they issue a joint declaration about the points on which an agreement had been reached, that they tell the assembled newsmen, and through them the world, that on some points no agreement had yet been reached, and that the committees would continue to work on them.

Dayan, who throughout the twenty-four hours of the state visit was in a sour mood, exploded: "Why should we? We are sitting in the Sinai, or the Suez Canal, and on the Golan Heights. If he likes it—fine and good! If not—then not! What does all this mean? There's no flag! No welcome posters! We are not invited to Cairo! Either we issue a communiqué about an agreement, or we leave without it."

Weizman weakly tried to oppose Dayan. The legal adviser, Aharon Barak, sat silently. Begin said he would offer a proposal to issue a joint communiqué with Sadat, and if the Egyptian president refused, no communiqué would be issued.

The morning session began a half hour late. The mood was tense, but the members of the two delegations tried to demonstrate goodwill.

"We made a lot of progress," Begin announced. "We have a draft declaration."

The Foreign Ministry's legal adviser, Dr. Meir Rosenne, read the paragraphs of the declaration. Sadat approved them paragraph by paragraph. Soon they arrived at the Palestinian issue.

Begin explained that the Palestinian people, for the first time in its history, would be gaining autonomy. "This is an important historical event." Sadat asked for something more concrete.

"If there is no joint communiqué," Begin said, "then each side will present its position. I propose that we announce that we reached no agreement between us on this issue. We shall declare in the communiqué that Egypt is of the opinion that a Palestinian state should be established, while Israel stands for autonomy."

This took Sadat by surprise. He had not spoken at all about a Palestinian state. He listened to Begin, nodding his head approvingly. "All right," he said.

"But it's unthinkable!" Abd-el-Magid interrupted. "What is this paper Dr. Rosenne is reading? If there is no agreement on this point, then there is no agreement at all. Without a declaration about the Palestinians it simply will not do."

He turned in consternation toward the Egyptian president. "You are risking your position," he half-shouted. "It is impossible! This would be a statement of surrender."

Pandemonium broke out. Boutros Ghali motioned to Dayan: "I told you last night that a declaration which does not contain a reference to the Palestinians' right to self-determination will not do."

Abd-el-Magid: "The declaration must be a joint one."

Ghali: "We told Dayan that without the Palestinians there will be no joint declaration—or that it must contain what Egypt has to say about the Palestinian problem."

A confused exchange ensued. Begin was talking with Egyptian Prime Minister Mamduk Salem. Abd-el-Magid was explaining something to Sadat. Everyone talked out of turn. Only one man, Egyptian Vice-President Hosni Mubarek, did not say a word.

Begin, in an angry outburst, shouted: "If it's so difficult for you, then there's no need for a joint communiqué. We shall go to the press without a communiqué, each side with its own version."

Sadat's face was expressionless. He was exhausted and disappointed. He wanted to conclude the meeting. "A declaration without the Palestinian issue is going to be feeble for us," he said. "I suggest that we announce the points we have agreed upon, the points on which we still differ, and that we have agreed about the continuation of the Cairo conference."

"I propose," Begin offered, "that we say that we have continued our efforts to reach a comprehensive peace settlement. We have agreed on several points based on Security Council Resolutions 242 and 338. In the press conference we shall present our positions on the Palestinian issue and say that the Palestinian problem will be discussed in the political committee."

Begin rose. "And of course, we shall make peace!"

Sadat also rose. "Yes, yes," he said.

The mood on the Israeli side was heavy and full of foreboding. Sharon suggested in a scribbled note that Begin retire to a side room with Sadat "to conclude the matter with him alone, face to face." Barak muttered: "What a disgrace!"

It was obvious to both sides that the Egyptians were pressed for time. Begin thought differently. He simply needed a communiqué.

Before going to the press conference, Begin presented Sadat with a birthday gift. He had him a medallion specially minted to commemorate his historic visit to Jerusalem. There were still a few minutes to go before the opening of the mass press conference and Dr. Osama al-Baz of the Egyptian Foreign Ministry moved back and forth between the Israelis and his Egyptian colleagues: "One more thing, and it will become acceptable," he said. He still insisted, speaking for his colleagues, on the principle of self-determination for the Palestinians. Many, in the Egyptian and in the Israeli delegations, felt that if they continued to bargain and play with words, a saving formula would yet be found.

Dr. Sharon said: "Let's decide that we will not leave here without an agreement."

"Let him be!" Dayan cut in. "If he doesn't want it— there's no need!"

Sadat asked Begin to spend a few minutes alone with him. Half apologetically he explained to the Israeli prime minister that it was his advisers from the Foreign Ministry who had insisted that he not yield an inch on the matter of self-determination for the Palestinian people. Later on Sadat claimed that Begin had tried to entangle him in a mesh of words.

Weizman was angry. On his way to the press conference he met some of his friends. "They screwed the peace," he said in Arabic.

"It didn't work," Begin said. "It didn't work."

At the press conference Begin surprised Sadat. He announced that both the United Nations and the United States would be made partners to the peace negotiations. The press conference, attended by hundreds of newsmen, took place in the grand hall of the Suez Canal Authority. The hall had been refurbished ahead of time and lined with carpets. Begin persuaded Sadat to read a summing-up statement in which Sadat, without noticing it, called the West Bank by its Israeli name: "Judea and Samaria."

The Egyptians were furious. They claimed that Begin took advantage of Sadat's exhaustion, since under normal conditions he would never have consented to speak such a phrase. The newsmen's questions were routine. So were the replies. It was impossible to hide the great fiasco from the journalists.

Sadat accompanied Begin to the door of the helicopter which would carry him back to the military airfield. His face seemed utterly worn. Prime Minister Salem and Minister of War Gamassi accompanied Begin to his El Al plane, and parted warmly from the Israeli team.

Depression reigned in the plane as it took off in the direction of Ben-Gurion Airport. In one corner Begin said that he was "happy." The newsmen industriously took down every word he said. Dayan, who sat next to him, gave the journalists a pessimistic interview.

Sadat closeted himself in his home in Ismailia. He had achieved nothing. The failure of the meeting oppressed him. Both Egyptians and Israelis felt they had missed the point. Both would later claim that the price of peace would have been cheaper at the time for Israel, especially since the rejectionist front was in a state of shock from things moving so quickly and had not yet gotten properly organized.

Begin thought differently: "The minimum condition in Ismailia was a retreat on all frontiers and a declaration on the Palestinian issue," he said. "We could not accept that."

14 THREE BULLETS

On the afternoon of January 4, 1979, someone came running out of the basement of the house occupied by the Arab League in London. A few minutes later the body of Said Hamami was found at his desk. Three bullets had ended the life of the PLO's representative in London. The investigation by the British police revealed little. Apparently someone who called himself Adel had phoned Hamami that morning and asked to meet him urgently. They did meet and Hamami was dead. The first shots against Sadat's initiative had been fired. The various Palestinian organizations, which tend to boast about their deeds, kept quiet this time. No individual or organization admitted this murder. However, the message of the three bullets was understood throughout Europe and the Middle East: Any Palestinian suspected of inclining toward approval of Sadat would pay for it.

Hamami, a pioneer in direct contact with the Israelis, was an appropriate target. While fulfilling the necessary quota of public reservations about Sadat's initiative, he had not concealed his personal dissatisfaction with the Palestinian leaders' lack of vision in the new situation. It was Hamami who had once compared those in the PLO who demanded "all or nothing" to the "not one inch" camp in Israel, which clamored for annexation of the West Bank. Hamami believed that extremist views could be mitigated only by furnishing unequivocal proof that moderates on both sides were acting on practical logic.

The day of Hamami's murder, Air Force 1, Carter's plane, landed at Aswan. At the end of the long journey that had taken him to five capitals, the American president had decided to lend a hand in solving the thorniest problem of the talks, the Palestinian question. Brzezinski and Vance had convinced Carter that Sadat had to be helped to achieve something on this point before proceeding to peace with Israel. During the brief stopover Sadat gave his blessing to a formula proposed by Carter, which the U.S. president read to reporters: "A solution must be found to the various aspects of the Palestinian problem. It must be recognized that this problem includes recognition of the legitimate rights of the Palestinian people, enabling them to participate in the determination of their own future." And so what the Egyptians demanded that Israel recognize, the Palestinians' right to self-determination, became the Palestinians' participation in the determination of their own future. They would not decide their fate on their own, but together with the other Arab countries involved and with Israel. Carter was pleased with his achievement: he boarded his plane to return to Washington convinced that the wheels which had previously been bogged down in the thick mire of the Palestinian dispute would now begin to move. He was wrong; words were not enough to overcome genuine differences.

The conflict in Palestine between Jews and the Zionist movement on the one hand and Palestinian Arabs on the other had changed in character over many years but had fundamentally remained the same. The Arabs of Palestine had begun to regard themselves as a special national group within the Arab world during the 1920s. The struggle between two national movements was already under way. The Jews wished to settle in the land of their forefathers, pushing the Arabs aside. In 1918 there were 700,000 Arabs in Palestine and only 56,000 Jews. Over the years the order was reversed; the Jews became the majority in Palestine and took over much of the land. The victory of the Zionist movement was bought at a high price: each day

139

there were more graves in the Arab villages and the Jewish settlements.

As a result of the Arab defeat in the 1948 war, 600,000 to 700,000 Palestinians left Israel, and their political leadership collapsed. An attempt was made to establish an all-Palestinian government in Gaza, at the instigation of the grand mufti of Jerusalem and his associates, but it failed, primarily because of the opposition of King Abdullah of Jordan, who hoped to annex the West Bank. One by one the Arab states had to relinquish the goal of Palestinian independence.

After the mid-1950s the Palestinians organized acts of infiltration into Israel with the aim of striking at the population, and were helped by some Arab governments. They did not succeed in getting organized on a large scale, and were replaced by Palestinian recruits in the service of the Egyptians. These were more successful but were destroyed during the Sinai campaign in 1956 by the Israeli army, which captured the bases of the fedayeen, the Palestinian suicide squads.

Israeli policy in Palestine was based on the principle that an attempt should be made to find understanding among the Palestinians without giving up the prime aims: immigration and independence. After the 1948 war it seemed to the Israeli leaders that the Palestinian problem could be resolved within the Arab countries which had prevented the establishment of an independent Palestinian state. The Arab countries thwarted the process, refusing to allow the refugees to be rehabilitated and settle in their midst. The wound remained open. Israel ignored the problem. During her term as prime minister, Golda Meir claimed, "There is no such thing as the Palestinians," while Begin, as leader of the opposition, ridiculed them. "The Palestinians were not a factor in the relations between the Arabs and Israel after 1948," said Brigadier Aharon Yariv, at the time chief of intelligence in the Israeli army. "We fought the Arab countries, not the Palestinians themselves, over every aspect of the Palestinian problem."

It was naively thought that the continued exacerbation of the Palestinian dispute was the result of a compact between extremists on both sides. "The fanatics on our side and the opposing one will never find a solution," wrote the

Egyptian author Abd el-Kahman el-Sharqawi. "They do not want to find a solution! It may even be that their very existence is based on increasing the tension. Balancing on the brink is their livelihood. We have made an unholy alliance with generators of tension, so that it can be used as an excuse for degrading human dignity and preserving power and crime."

After the Sinai campaign there was a strong tendency among the Palestinians to join the Nasserist stream and seek a solution for their problem through the struggle for pan-Arab unity. There were no Palestinian organizations of any importance. The idea of reviving the Palestinian entity played a significant role only beginning in 1959, but since then it has been discussed continuously at Arab League meetings. Jordan has always opposed Palestinian aims, claiming that Jordan represents the Palestinians: the majority of Jordan's population is Palestinian and Jordan has controlled most of the land which the Arabs designate as Palestine.

The basic concept of "the entity" was that the Palestinians were to serve as the vanguard of the Arab struggle against Israel; consequently, they had to emphasize their national identity and work toward establishing a state of their own within the area of Palestine controlled by the Arabs, or at least establish a representative organization which had military power. This was implemented in 1963 when the Palestine Liberation Organization was founded. There was considerable opposition on the part of Palestinian intellectuals to an organization which had been established at the initiative of the Arab governments in agreement with Jordan. They cultivated their own version of the Palestinian entity, which centered mainly on independent organizations, as well as combat, to force the Arab governments to adopt a more forceful line toward Israel. They were also characterized by undisguised suspicion and resentment of the part played by the Arab countries around 1948; they provided the kernels of the fedayeen groups, one of which was Al Fatah, which was set up in the Persian Gulf area and later moved to Beirut and Algeria. These groups took control of the PLO at the end of the sixties.

The PLO rejected every attempt to determine a territorial objective for a Palestinian entity before the destruction

141

of Israel. The organization found many supporters among the Palestinian community, which numbers about 4 million today, most of them in Jordan, Israel, Syria, and near the Persian Gulf.

In 1974, after the Yom Kippur War, the organization adopted the slogan "the independent, fighting Palestinian national authority." This authority was to be established in the occupied territories, from which Israel would withdraw before the elimination of the Zionist state. This turning point in the PLO's identity was given an all-Arab imprimatur at the Rabat summit conference in 1974, which appointed the PLO the "sole legal representative of the Palestinian nation."

The terrorist war against Israel accelerated. The war did not select its victims on either side; the fedayeen caused the deaths of women and children, in Israeli retaliatory raids on terrorist bases, women and children were also killed. The terrorists did not let up for a moment. "Palestine fell in a storm of fire and steel, and it will arise in a storm of fire and steel," said the terrorists, using a phrase taken from the Irgun Zvai Leumi under Menachem Begin's leadership: "Judea fell in blood and fire and in blood and fire it will arise."

Since 1972 Sadat had been pressing the PLO to moderate its stand so that it could participate in the political process. In particular he demanded the establishment of a government in exile and the acceptance of Security Council Resolution 242, which referred to the withdrawal of Israeli forces from territories conquered in the Six-Day War and called for an end to the state of war, respect for sovereignty, territorial compromises, the political independence of all the countries of the region, and their right to exist in peace.

Sadat sought to overcome the difficulty of Israel's refusal to talk to the PLO by finding a compromise formula; but he was alone. The organization was strongly influenced by Syria as a result of the Syrian military presence in Lebanon, where the PLO was so numerous. The more extreme Palestinian organizations had found shelter in Iraq. The Egyptians were unable to exert pressure. Damascus secretly fostered the dream of annexing the Palestinian problem and its solution to Greater Syria.

By 1977 the Palestinian problem was different from the

problem of ten years before. It had become "the heart of the matter," as Sadat put it, and not "a marginal issue," as Israel would have it. The most important expression of this was in the shift in the American attitude. For the first time secret contact had been established between Americans in high positions and PLO leaders. President Carter spoke of a "homeland for the Palestinians." Strong hints were sent from Washington in the direction of the PLO, urging it to accept Resolution 242 as an opening for a dialogue between the U.S. and the Palestinians. No one in authority referred anymore to the commitment given to Israel at the end of 1975 by the White House, promising not to enter into negotiations with the Palestinian organizations.

With Sadat's encouragement, moderate voices began to be heard in the PLO, saying, "We must take what is given to us, and continue demanding what has not been given." Hamami's was such a voice, but the bullets did their job.

Said Hamami, who was murdered in London, was a fitting target for attack. He had made a name for himself as a pioneer arguer for direct contact with the Israelis. He had fulfilled the necessary quota of public reservations about Sadat's initiative, but he had not concealed his personal dissatisfaction with the Palestinian leaders' lack of vision in the new situation.

The thousands who attended Hamami's funeral heard angry speeches peppered with oaths of vengeance. Henceforth there was virtually no contact with the few Israelis who had agreed to speak with PLO people. It was learned that the assassin had been sent by a tiny offshoot of fanatic Palestinians, based in Baghdad. This group, which lived in the shadow of Iraqi intelligence, was headed by Sabri el-Bana, called Abu-Nidal, a picturesque, mysterious character who kept to an underground hideout in the Habbania camp in Iraq.

Abu-Nidal was one of Yasir Arafat's oldest friends, one of the founders of the PLO. He was orthodox in religion and uncompromising in views. As Arafat's representative in Baghdad he found his opinions closer to those of his hosts than to those of the man who had sent him. He gradually transferred his allegiance to the Iraqi side. When the truth was discovered he was expelled from the ranks of the PLO and a death sentence was placed on his head.

His murder units did not operate against Israel, only against Al Fatah. Abu-Nidal wanted to stop Arafat from sitting on the fence and squinting in the direction of taking part in a settlement between the Arab countries and Israel. The assassination of Hamami was intended to prevent Arafat from moving closer to Sadat. As far as Sadat was concerned, the murder provided further proof of his conviction that the PLO had to be bypassed in attaining a Palestinian settlement.

Hamami, together with another Palestinian leader, Dr. Issam Sartawi, reached a conclusion similar to that of Acting Foreign Minister of Egypt Boutros Ghali: a peace settlement would be a suitable tool for attaining a Palestinian state on the West Bank and in the Gaza Strip, having good relations with Israel but without abandoning the dream of a "democratic, secular Palestine," without Zionists but with Jews.

Arafat was not prepared to support this openly. He remained bound to the Palestinian covenant, the PLO's founding charter, which described any connection between the Jews and the land of Israel as deception and fraud. The international recognition of Israel's right to exist is, according to the covenant, a crime.

Sadat maintained that a recalcitrant PLO was a bothersome burden, while a tamed PLO with an improved political image, a PLO which had abandoned terrorist activities, could be effective in diplomatic warfare and even a partner in a settlement which would relieve Egypt of the Palestinian incubus.

Hamami's suggestion of establishing two states in Palestine fired the imagination of some on the left in Israel. They regarded his proposal as a ray of hope, something that could lead to recognition by the Palestinians of Israel's right to exist. They grasped at the idea of partitioning western Palestine while continuing the struggle over the final result by peaceful means and led some of Israel's foremost left-wingers to call for an open dialogue with the PLO in return for recognition.

Egypt encouraged the secret meetings which had begun between a handful of doves in the PLO and left-wing doves in Israel. Egyptian emissaries kept close track of the contacts and sent continuous reports to Sadat. The go-betweens were Henri Curiel, a professional revolutionary, and Joyce Blau, a lecturer in Kurdish at the Sorbonne, both Jews who had been among the founders of the Egyptian Communist party and had gone into exile.

Matti Peled, formerly a general in the Israeli army and now a lecturer in Arabic literature, flew to Paris at the end of 1976 for a meeting with Sartawi. Peled advocated a dialogue with the PLO. He was later joined by Arieh Aliav, former secretary of the Labor party. Peled informed Foreign Minister Yigal Allon and Prime Minister Yitzhak Rabin.

Despite arguments at the meetings, both sides had the impression that there was a basis for continuing. Both sides wanted to involve a well-known international personality who would serve as a witness. They decided on Pierre Mendès-France, a Jew and former prime minister of France, who agreed.

At the next meeting, after an Israeli newspaper had published information about the contacts, Sartawi expressed his anger at the leak. He was attacked by the Palestinians. In Israel there were calls for the "traitors" who had talked with the PLO to be put on trial. There was another meeting between Peled and Sartawi, at which Peled demanded that they issue a public announcement which would save his honor and that of his friends. He prepared a draft and Sartawi amended it and agreed. When he was asked to sign it, however, he declined. At a crowded press conference in Tel Aviv the announcement was read "as agreed by the PLO." But less than an hour later the teleprinters were telling of a firm denial from Beirut. Mendès-France lost his temper. Peled and his friends were a laughingstock.

Everyone had learned his lesson. Even the moderate ones among the Israelis and the Palestinians were very far from a compromise.

When Sadat embarked on his initiative Sartawi was the only PLO activist who welcomed it publicly, and he went underground in Paris, his fears increased when Curiel was murdered.

Sadat concluded that Sartawi's courageous effort had been nothing but a passing episode. Arafat's letters did not win him over. Sadat despised Arafat for his hesitancy, his submissiveness to the Syrians, his inability to lead the Palestinians on the right path. The link Arafat was at pains to maintain with Egypt was regarded by Sadat as merely a trick, a kind of attempt on Arafat's part to hold on to an insurance policy in Cairo while at the same time fighting Egypt in the ranks of the rejectionist front.

Sadat did not know that Arafat was acting similarly with the Israelis. At least once, through a European personage, he transmitted a verbal message to Begin's government. "All I want," Arafat claimed, "is a state with a flag, a prison, and a passport. If Israel agrees to the principle of a Palestinian state on the West Bank and in the Gaza Strip we can discuss security arrangements." The Israelis were not prepared to listen to this secret message, preferring to pay attention to the very different statements he made on countless other occasions, against the existence of Israel, against the peace treaty, against compromises.

Sadat realized there was no hope of a change within the PLO. In February 1978, four months after Sadat's initiative, two Palestinians murdered his close friend Yusif el-Sibai, the chief editor of *Al Aharam*, then captured hostages at Nicosia Airport. A commando force sent by Gamassi to free the hostages failed in its mission and paid a heavy price in lives. The Cypriot police shot at the Egyptians. An Egyptian Hercules plane went up in flames. The attempt to include the PLO in the settlement had come to an end. At the funeral of the commandos in Cairo the crowd shouted: "Death to the Palestinians." Sadat decided to cross Arafat's name out. "The cabinet watchers," he called Arafat and his associates.

Ezer Weizman, Israel's minister of defense, sent a letter to his Egyptian counterpart, Abd-el-Ghani Gamassi. Through the Israeli delegation in Cairo he congratulated the Egyptians for their courage in "cutting off the arm of terrorism." He expressed his regret over the lives that had been lost.

In this atmosphere Hassan Tuhami proposed trying to create a rift with the PLO, but his effort failed. Sadat tried to entice Jordan to negotiate, using the bait of banishing the PLO. The Americans supported his approach, but Hussein decided that the difficulties of the talks outweighed the chance that they would succeed, and he noted the already worsening atmosphere between Cairo and Jerusalem over Israeli settlements.

Even before Sadat's visit to Israel in November 1977,

Dayan had instructed the chairman of the Jewish Agency's settlement department, Ra'anan Weitz, to move forward with all speed in implementing the development plans for the Rafa salient, a sandy area south of Israel which was occupied during the 1967 war. After the war the Israelis cultivated the soil, turning it into a blooming garden, partly as a result of Dayan's initiaive and encouragement. Hundreds of millions of dollars have been invested in the salient.

Since the beginning of the century settlement has been the essence of the Zionist movement in the land of Israel. "Making the desert bloom" has been one of the most popular slogans of the Jewish nation's liberation movement. The state of Israel established its position by means of hundreds of settlements scattered throughout the country. The settlement movement provided the top echelons of the Israeli administration and army with its best sons. A very large proportion of top politicians, until Begin's election, came from the settlement movement originally. Begin's rule gave hegemony back to the petit bourgeois establishment, the urban element. The settlement of the Rafa salient had an agricultural basis and a military background; its object was to erect a barrier between the Gaza Strip and Egypt.

It was generally assumed by the Israeli cabinet that, after some arguments and some changes, the Egyptians would buy the idea of Israel establishing settlements with a local defense force operating under Egyptian sovereignty or in Israel through border adjustments.

After Sadat's visit to Israel there was some consternation among the higher echelons of Israel. Should settlement be continued in areas which would eventually be handed over to Egypt? The cabinet committee on settlement affairs decided, after the Ismailia summit, to continue settling the Rafa salient and east Sinai and to prepare terrain east of the Al-'Arish–Ras Muhammad line, which crosses the Sinai Desert through the middle, to create faits accomplis. The chairman of the committee, Ariel Sharon, was given the task of preparing a plan for "thickening" the salient.

Begin was on a state visit to London, so Sharon laid before Dayan the idea of appropriating land on which to establish settlements in the Rafa salient, including areas near existing settlements. Dayan was apprehensive.

"It is vital that we do it before the [Egyptian-Israeli] committee meets," Sharon said. "If the Egyptians accept this act, then we have succeeded; if worse comes to worst we can always make a gesture and give in to them." He was thinking of inviting the Egyptian delegation to tour the area and see what had been done.

Dayan accepted Sharon's suggestion, and cabled it to Begin in London, requesting authorization for embarking on the activities required for the appropriation of the land. From London, Begin sent his approval for it as an experiment from which it would be possible to retreat if there was no alternative.

The Bedouins of the Rafa salient realized immediately that changes were being made. They reported to their operators from Egyptian intelligence that the Israelis were engaging in new undertakings. The Americans received the information a little later, through satellite photographs taken over Israel. So the American ambassador in Cairo was not telling the Egyptian leaders anything new when he informed them of the Israeli initiative.

The Egyptians reacted to the Israeli activities with heavy silence. The Israelis were more vociferous. The Friday radio newscasts of the Israel Broadcasting Authority exposed Israel's new activities in the Rafa salient, mentioning the drilling towers, apparently to establish a new fait accompli in the region. On television new facts were added. Later, jokes were made in the cabinet, noting that "the camera follows the plow."

There was a great commotion. The Americans demanded an explanation; the Egyptian press began to ask questions. With Weizman's agreement, Dayan instructed Sharon to stop certain activities and dismantle what had already been built in central Sinai.

The storm was still in its initial stages when the Israeli radio broadcast additional information: the cabinet had decided to establish twenty-three new settlements in the Rafa salient. Arieh Naor, the cabinet secretary, jumped up from his seat as if bitten by a snake when he heard the newscast. He immediately phoned the newsroom and, relying on the Broadcasting Authority Law, demanded that an announcement be made in his name that the statement was totally false. The radio acquiesced, broadcast the denial, and added: "Our reporter insists that the information is correct."

Cairo's reactions were still restrained, but President Carter was irate, and his aides incensed. The American embassy in Tel Aviv was ordered to protest. Communications media throughout the world portrayed Israel as a country which said one thing and did another, in public declaring its eagerness for peace and willingness to make concessions, while creating new faits accomplis in the territory conquered in 1967.

Dayan claimed that Sharon had acted contrary to what had been agreed between them. Begin reprimanded Sharon quietly and sent a message to the Americans stating that since he had taken office he had not established a single new settlement in the Rafa salient. The existing settlements would merely be reinforced.

There was public uproar in Israel too; many sections of the public accused the government of torpedoing the chances of peace. Public opinion was hostile to Begin and the affair was depicted as irresponsible foolishness. "You'll thank me for this one day," Arik Sharon said in response to the negative reactions. "Whatever happens, it will be a good card with which to bargain with the Egyptians." Since most of the blame was laid on his shoulders, Sharon asked Begin to publish a statement that what he had done had been with the government's knowledge. Sharon threatened to draw the obvious conclusions. After a few days' pressure Begin gave in and issued a general statement, which did not mention Sharon's name.

On Weizman's recommendation the new settlement programs were frozen for the moment; but the damage was already done. The credibility of Begin's government fell to an all-time low in the eyes of the American administration. "You had just got the Americans to grant you a modicum of credibility, after you started off with their total mistrust," Deputy Prime Minister Yadin said to Begin. "You managed to gain Sadat's trust and now you are losing your credibility with the Americans and with the Egyptians."

Members of the Egyptian administration used the affair to condemn Israel, who were depicted as unreliable cheaters. Caricatures appeared in Cairo's newspapers showing Begin stabbing the dove of peace in the back with the knife of the settlements. Sadat was beside himself with wrath. He exclaimed bitterly: "Not a single settlement will be allowed to remain in Sinai once peace has been made."

The credibility crisis between Israel and the U.S. reached new heights because of a few water towers and the rusty hulks of some old buses which Sharon had placed at the navel of the Sinai Desert. The incident had been blown out of all proportion.

15 A DIFFERENT CAIRO

When Israeli Defense Minister Ezer Weizman arrived in Cairo in January 1978, he saw something different in the expressions on people's faces. His host, Muhammad Abd-el-Ghani Gamassi, forced a smile to his lips, but his eyes were hard. He extricated Weizman from the large group that had come with him and said belligerently: "President Sadat does not understand you people at all. You are making the whole thing impossible, it is a breach of trust, you are misleading us . . ."

Gamassi pointed to a Mystère-20 executive plane warming up not far away. "You must meet with the president; he is waiting for you in Aswan." As the other members of the delegation drove into the city, Weizman headed for Aswan.

Sadat was waiting. "How was the flight?" he asked as he shook hands with demonstrative warmth. "I hope visibility was good and you managed to see something of Egypt."

Weizman said: "Mr. President, it took us an hour and a quarter to get here. I had the feeling that we were flying and flying and not coming to the end of Egypt. With us in Israel, flying eastward from Tel Aviv for an hour and a quarter, we would be in Baghdad. Everything in Israel is of such small dimensions as compared with Egypt—which is why to us the Rafa salient, for example, seems to be a large area. For you, it is not even one-half of one percent of the area of Egypt."

Sadat did not react. He wanted to lead the conversation into a personal vein, to improve the atmosphere. He thanked the Israeli defense minister for the pipe he had given him on the previous occasion. Weizman expressed surprise that Sadat had no pipe with him today. "I am fasting today because of Id el-Pitr, I am not eating, drinking, or smoking, not even the pipe you gave me."

Weizman remarked that on Id el-Pitr building comes to a standstill in Israel because most of the construction workers are Arabs from the West Bank and the Gaza area. Weizman, as in his remark about the flight to Aswan, wanted to drive home a political moral: "It is essential that any peace agreement provides that Gaza and the West Bank remain open from the economic point of view."

Sadat replied: " 'Ezra,' there can be no argument about that at all. You must understand that I am talking about real peace: commercial relations, exchange of ambassadors. You will get a true peace, but first I must get back part of my land you took from us."

"Mr. President, ambassadors are very important," Weizman said, "but not long ago I read that you recalled your ambassador from Iraq. Tomorrow you can do the same with Israel."

Sadat's face clouded.

As if unaware of the Egyptian president's reaction, Weizman went on: "First of all, we are talking about peace with security. The problem is not only between us and Egypt. We have a serious problem with Syria and Iraq. As long as those problems remain unsolved, it is impossible for Israel to give up all the Sinai airfields."

These words angered Sadat even more. He realized that Weizman had brought no new message from Israel, but was reiterating his strong opposition to abandoning the military air bases in Sinai.

Sadat: "You and President Carter talk about withdrawing from the West Bank and the Gaza Strip, but leaving security forces there. Now you are talking to me about the Sinai air bases in connection with the Syrians. What are you afraid of? The Syrians? You should have heard what Assad said after the October War. He came to tell me how in a few days you destroyed twelve hundred of his tanks. Ezra, are you worried about the Syrians?"

Weizman: "Problems related to internal security worry me no less than the fact that the Iraqis will move two thousand tanks to our border. A few days ago a bomb burst in a Jerusalem market. People were hurt. What action can I take today? I can send police into Ramallah, Nablus, wherever I want, after the murderers. My police force can search everyplace. That will be an essential condition in the future also. You too, Mr. President, would behave no differently were the security of your country at stake."

The conversation was conducted quietly, but each side was firmly entrenched. Even before the military committee gathered for its first session, failure was in the air.

Weizman said, "I suggest that you send an Egyptian military delegation to us. Choose four or five Egyptian generals, with Gamassi at their head, to come to the West Bank and Gaza Strip. We will receive them with full honors and hear what they have to say. Let us hear how they would solve the security problems of the state of Israel after, as you are suggesting, the borders are pushed back to where they were in 1967, and taking into account that a Palestinian state has risen across those borders. I should like to hear your generals! I should want to hear where they would station the tanks, where they would build the emergency supply depots."

Sadat was adamant. He would not agree to Israeli settlements remaining in the Rafa salient and the Sinai peninsula. He objected strongly. "If we leave those settlements," he said, "we will be sowing the seeds of future war."

It was clear to Weizman that the Egyptian position had hardened. He thought that the noisy publicity emanating from Israel about plans for new settlements had made the Egyptians more intransigent. The new settlements were to Sadat like a red flag to a bull. Weizman felt that in Cairo he would not be able to even suggest that the Israeli settlements remain where they are.

Weizman went on: "We have made big concessions. When we came to power we were considered a hawkish government, but we are the ones who took the great step

153

forward that nobody believed we would take. My suggestion to you is, do not tighten the rope, because there is a growing feeling in Israel that your position is becoming more intransigent. Mr. President, do you know what they are saying in Israel? People are asking whether Sadat can now do whatever he likes just because he came to Jerusalem.

"Mr. President, you are a courageous man, you can take decisions and explain them to your people."

"I know my people and know what concessions they are ready to make and those they cannot make," Sadat declared. "They will not agree to Israeli settlements in the Rafa salient."

But Weizman pressed on. "You say your people cannot compromise on this. You must bear in mind that in the course of a few decades the Jewish people lost more than a third of its sons. The Israelis are more burdened by security problems than the citizens of any other country in modern history. You tried to annihilate the state of Israel at the time of its establishment: Egyptian planes bombed Tel Aviv. In 1948 I myself tried to down an Egyptian plane south of Tel Aviv. I was also the man who in 1967 gave the first order to move Israeli troops, when the information came that Nasser had brought troops into Sinai. I did not believe war would break out, but it did, and now Gamassi tells me that the war in 1967 was the result of a political error.

"What are we talking about?" Weizman continued. "We're talking about an area that does not exceed four percent of Sinai and is not even half a percent of the area of all of Egypt! Because of that, are we going to break relationships that we have begun to formulate at your initiative, Mr. President?"

It was no use. Sadat was immovable. He made it clear that he would not have Israeli settlements and military air bases in Sinai. After fifty minutes of conversation, each side continued to hold fast to the position it had started from. Before leaving, Weizman sought to reestablish the cordial relationship between himself and Sadat: "Only yesterday I saw your picture together with that of Begin in a Tel Aviv shop window. The name of the shop is Sadat Fashions."

In Cairo, meanwhile, the Israeli and Egyptian military delegations were waiting for Weizman in the Tahara Palace, which was built forty years ago by King Farouk for his first wife, Farida, and consists of a series of buildings surrounded by a wall. The Egyptian minister of war and Israeli minister of defense, the chiefs of staff of both armies, several generals and their advisers, as well as representatives of the Foreign Ministry, held their meetings here, in an oak-paneled room around a green-covered table, a brilliant chandelier overhead. There were pitchers of fruit juice and mineral water on the table.

There was no formal opening ceremony. The Egyptians were taken by surprise when they learned of the Israeli intention to open the meetings of the military committee with a festive speech by Ezer Weizman. Weizman had prepared his speech beforehand and his aides had distributed it to the reporters who jostled one another outside the conference room. Gamassi had not prepared a speech. For a moment or two the situation was embarrassing; then it was decided to permit the newspapermen to look in for a moment. Weizman's speech was not delivered, but as it had already been distributed to the press, General Gamassi wanted to say a few words. He greeted the participants and wished the committee success. "I am praying for us," he said.

"*Inshallah*," said the Israeli defense minister.

Weizman hoped that the military committee would break the deadlock of Ismailia. He was enjoying the special status he had acquired in the course of the peace talks. Although it was not his job as minister of defense, he had suddenly become a central figure in the negotiations. The military meeting in Cairo was his third round of talks in Egypt. With him at the conference table were his deputy, Mordechai Zippori; the chief of staff, Motta Gur; head of intelligence, Shlomo Gazit; head of planning, Avraham Tamir; and Moshe Sassoon, representing the Foreign Ministry. Sassoon's father, before retiring from public service, had represented the state of Israel at more than one secret meeting with Arab leaders.

Across the table sat the high military officers of Egypt: the minister of war, Gamassi; the chief of staff, Ismail Fahmi; head of operations, el-Greidli; head of military operations, Shaukat; and Generals Taha Magdub, Muhammad Huweidi, and el-Kateb. Hundreds of blue-bereted guards of the republic were stationed around the wall.

Differences of opinion were immediately apparent. Gamassi suggested that the first point on the agenda be the evacuation of the IDF and the end of the occupation. Weizman objected. It was decided to conduct the talks without an agenda, a compromise that dictated the character of the military conference. Rather than negotiating, the two sides presented their positions.

Weizman: "All of us here are military men and we all bear the scars of many wars. There may be a certain advantage in that, because military men understand the gravity of war better than others; therefore they can reach a better understanding than politicians."

That was well taken. Weizman had indirectly complimented both the Egyptians and his Israeli colleagues.

Weizman: "Sadat leaped many miles ahead of everyone else and I am asking the same thing of you. The Israelis have made concessions on many security matters. The previous government of Israel spoke of Sharm al-Sheikh as if it were Jerusalem. We have given up Sharm al-Sheikh. You must understand the problems connected with our security."

The Egyptians were reminded of an old Dayan saying: "Better Sharm al-Sheikh without peace than peace without Sharm al-Sheikh."

Gamassi: "It is true that you have security problems. We shall do everything we can to understand your situation. Security is essential for you but it is important for us too. Will settlements in Sinai give you security?"

Weizman: "The settlements have implications for security. Most of the settlers are soldiers in civilian dress. They are even more important as they contribute to normalization, to coexistence. I have invited General Gamassi to see the IDF, to see our security problems in the field."

Gur: "I would also invite Fahmi, the commander in chief of the Egyptian army, to see the state of Israel, not necessarily the army."

Fahmi had been a missile commander in the October War. He had a philosophical bent and spent a great deal of his time writing history.

Fahmi: "And what about the airfields that you want to hold on to in Sinai? What is their importance?"

Weizman: "To defend Elath, for instance."

Fahmi: "From what?"

Weizman: "From Jordan or Saudi Arabia."

Fahmi: "We'll defend Elath for you."

There was confusion among the Israelis. The men did not know whether Fahmi was joking or not. Tentative smiles rose to their faces but froze at once, as the serious expression of the Egyptians' faces made it clear that Fahmi had not been joking.

Israel's security depends to a great extent on its world-famous air force, and it did not escape Weizman that the Egyptian interest in the airfields was based on their hope of diminishing the strength of the Israeli air force.

There were ten airfields in Sinai, some in full operation, others ready to be put into operation in wartime. Sinai airspace gave Israel extensive warning range against attacks on centers of population, and the broad terrain enabled the widespread distribution of planes to ward off catastrophe in the event of sudden attack.

The Israeli air force had tripled its size since the eve of the Six-Day War in 1967. Giving up the Sinai airfields would mean crowding hundreds of planes into the same small number of fields Israel had until 1967. Removing the Israeli air force from the Sinai would mean that Israel would need to launch a preemptive strike in every dangerous situation in the future, in order to give the reserve army time to mobilize. Weizman, having been an air force commander, knew what this meant.

In the course of the discussion Gamassi again raised the issue of the Israeli settlements in the Rafa salient, built on land occupied in the 1967 war. Weizman pointed out that this involved a small area, a tiny percentage of Sinai.

Gamassi: "It is easy to talk of percentages, but we cannot agree to border changes. There are other ways of ensuring security."

Weizman: "I have explained this to President Sadat. He is a wise man and and understands. Wisdom and courage go hand in hand. A bold decision must be taken in this matter and our situation must be understood."

Gamassi: "You too, Weizman, are a wise man."

It was late in the evening. The Egyptians and Israelis agreed to adjourn and reconvene in the morning. Disappointment was apparent on the faces of the Israelis. The Egyptians had taken an aggressive stand and were not ready to make even the smallest concession. They were demanding a return to the international frontier. There had not been the slightest rapprochement, despite the fact that Israel had already made the very large concession of agreeing to withdraw from Sinai and recognize Egyptian sovereignty over the peninsula. The discussion had only been a statement of views; there was no give-and-take. Weizman and his colleagues in the Israeli delegation felt that the Egyptians had opened with the highest bid, making maximal demands "to bring the price down."

The following morning, Israeli Chief of Staff Motta Gur had his first opportunity to state his position. In preparation for the conference, Gur had instructed staff headquarters to prepare a portfolio based on his original suggestion: a pullback line in the middle of Sinai, in return for no war. At the same time the planning section had prepared a portfolio ordered by Weizman containing the promise made to Sadat to withdraw from the entire peninsula and suggesting an exchange of territories between the two countries in the Rafa salient area and near Elath.

Gur had presented his plan to Begin in the presence of Weizman and his aides. Begin claimed that it was not in accord with the government's peace proposal. To him it seemed like an elaborated interim agreement of sorts, and having refused all interim agreements, he could not support it. Immediately after that the proposal for a general retreat from Sinai was submitted, as worked out by the planning section. "Accepted," was Begin's reaction.

The chief of staff's opinion is formally that of the general staff and he is considered the adviser to the government on all IDF matters. Begin had rejected Gur's proposal but accepted the proposal tabled by one of his aides; this was the second time in the IDF's history that a prime minister had decided a fundamental defense issue against the chief of staff. The first time was when Ben-Gurion decided in 1957 to withdraw from Sinai, against the recommendation of Dayan, the chief of staff.

158

Weizman took the blue portfolio prepared by the planning section to Cairo with him. Gur took the red one prepared by an aide on the general staff.

Gur chose to open on a personal note: "My father chose the career of lawyer for me. My dream was to be a teacher, but instead I became an officer in the army in 1947. Later I studied Middle East affairs at the university, thinking that some day I would be an ambassador to an Arab country. But again I found myself in the army. I was fighting the fedayeen. We operated against them, not against Egypt. We did not think then that those actions would be a turning point in your eyes."

In the mid-1950s Gur was commander of a paratroop unit. He hunted down units of fedayeen, some of them organized by men of the Egyptian army. The IDF's reprisals were ruthless, and Gur was one of the commanders of such retaliatory actions. After one of them Nasser claimed that the Israeli military action had torpedoed his readiness for peace.

Gur said: "In the 1956 war I fought in Sinai against an Egyptian force at the Mitla pass. We met an ambush. I remember that we saw a few Egyptian soldiers trying to leave their positions and retreat. I gave the order to fire. It was a mistake because the Egyptians returned to their positions and fought. I learned the lesson of that operation and I apply it both in the tactical and the strategic field: When the other side is in distress, give it a chance to save itself. If not, you must be prepared to kill and be killed. My conclusion: Both the Israelis and the Egyptians must make concessions for the sake of peace."

This personal story caught the attention of the Egyptians and they wanted to hear what would follow.

Gur went on: "So—the question is how to get out of the distress. I was the IDF attaché in Washington during the 1973 war. I remember that before war broke out I was visited by men of the Pentagon intelligence service who told me they had prepared a model for negotiations between the Egyptians and the Israelis. It was their hypothesis that the hurdles could be overcome if each side would concede on marginal issues. The question now is: What is marginal? And what does each side consider central? Let us examine that. For example, we are in great danger be-

159

cause we fight alone. We have never been allowed to finish a war. Whenever we were succeeding they confronted us with an ultimatum. That was the case in '49, '56, even '67 and '73. Even aid to Israel is made contingent: I remember that in '73 the decision to help Israel came only when the Russians began to send armaments. Until then the Americans would not listen to us and the people in the Pentagon had instructions not to talk to me. I found myself talking to the wall.

"The central question disturbing us is whether in the future Egypt will take part in a war in the event that hostilities break out between Israel and another Arab country. We must take the experience of the past into account. In 1967 you went to war because of the Syrians. As long as the Russians are in the vicinity we must be very careful. In 1973 we made our greatest mistake when we thought that after you got rid of the Russians, you had no military option."

Gur analyzed the basic elements in Israel's strategic situation: a very small country, a concentrated population crowded into a narrow strip, no strategic depth, vulnerable sources of water, easy to put under sea blockade, the army dependent in large measure on reserve forces, the need for a highly effective early warning system for which a great deal of territory is essential.

The Israeli chief of staff was guiding his hearers to his conclusion: "It is impossible to talk of a retreat to the 1967 frontier in Sinai without a significant reduction of Egyptian military forces. You must reduce your army, transfer a large part to reserves," he said. "We can help you organize your reserves. On our part we will reduce the period of compulsory service in the IDF. We must take all the Arab countries into consideration. The Iraqis have just finished building up their tenth division. Those forces will continue to exist after a peace agreement between Egypt and Israel has been signed. We must also take into account the fact that tomorrow Saudi Arabia might become a country like Libya."

Gur's speech continued for about an hour and a half and elicited an Egyptian reaction. "The speech was well delivered," said one of the Egyptian generals, "but the claims are all old ones." They had hoped to hear new suggestions from the Israelis. Never for a moment did they attempt to camouflage their own intentions. Some of the men in the Israeli delegation who had never before participated in meetings with the Egyptians were taken aback by their inflexibility.

A recess was called and after it Gamassi said: "The lecture we have heard from General Gur was constructive. I am acquainted with your security problems. We are ready to help you with some of them, but you must understand ours as well. With respect to what Gur said about other Arab countries, I must say to you: once the Palestinian problem has been solved, Iraq will have no reason to attack you. As long as the Palestinian problem exists, Israel is in danger. It will be an excuse for war. Incidentally, General Gur, do the settlements in Sinai give you depth?"

Gur: "No!"

At this point Fahmi, the Egyptian chief of staff, spoke up: "It seems to me that we are spending too much time on the past. It should be borne in mind that past enemies may become future friends. True, there will always be hooligans. I agree that you have security problems, but the solution to the problems of one side cannot be at the expense of the other. You speak of early warning, for example. Well, we too have no early warning from the direction of the sea. You object to evacuating airfields in the Sinai, but I have also heard you say on another occasion that Libyan Tripoli is within reach of the Israeli air force."

Gamassi: "General Gur, I have said that in 1967 you fought a defensive war, but in 1956 we had no dispute with you. Our dispute was with France and England in a vital sphere affecting our national interest, and you attacked us. We have not forgotten that Ben-Gurion spoke in the Knesset referring to Sinai as part of the state of Israel. We interpreted that as an expression of Israeli expansionism."

El-Arabi, the Egyptian legal adviser: "The defensive war thesis is anachronistic. Active attack is the criterion for use of force. We did not begin the shooting in 1967. Closing the Strait of Tiran was only a threat."

Gur: "It's no wonder that countries are not ruled by lawyers."

Head of the Israeli intelligence, General Gazit: "In the

161

university I learned that peace is like a 'Do not enter' sign on an unlocked door. If you're a gentleman, you do not enter."

Gur: "We should like to adopt the model of the Panama Canal, a solution that gave each side what it wanted: widening of the Canal, unrestricted traffic, and at the same time, the United States agreed to take down the American flag."

Gamassi: "The proposal you submitted in Ismailia provides that you would be ready to make revisions in the year 2001. Does that mean that until that time you will not allow Egypt into the buffer zone?"

Gazit: "The year 2001 is debatable."

Weizman had paid close attention to Gur's words. He immediately understood that what Gur said was at odds with the Israeli government's proposal to withdraw from the entire peninsula. However, Weizman made no comment. He was not disturbed by the thought that the Egyptians would see that these things were being bitterly contested inside Israel too, even in the highest echelons.

Gur: "General Gamassi, you have mentioned the Palestinian issue. I do not know how to solve the problems of the Palestinians. It would be the greatest mistake for us to permit this problem to be a stumbling block to peace."

Gamassi seemed to ignore these words. He preferred to have the Palestinian issue discussed at the political conference in Jerusalem. He was at a table surrounded by army officers who wanted to discuss military matters with other army officers.

Gur: "I accept the thesis that strategic depth need not be achieved at your expense. That can be solved: the first condition is that Sinai be empty of armies. That will be the strategic depth. Your army must sit in Cairo and along the Libyan border. In that way we will have strategic depth and Sinai will also afford us early warning. You must give us a greater feeling of security. That is why I include the matter of reduction of forces. We too will contribute to this, despite the fact that we have other border problems. For example, I would be satisfied with four hundred planes."

Gamassi laughed: "With four hundred planes fewer than you now have . . ."

This again drove home to the Israelis the Egyptian fear

of the Israeli air force. This remark remained clearly etched in the memories of the Israeli military men attending the session.

"I am a bad negotiator, as my wife can testify," General Shlomo Gazit began. Gazit, head of the intelligence branch, was known as an intellectual with a brilliant mind, one of those closest to Moshe Dayan. Although he did not say so explicitly, he seemed to support many of the chief of staff's recommendations. "We are dealing with principles, not commerce," he noted.

Gazit: "The chief of staff was right when he said it is impossible to concentrate only on a time schedule. There is no need to put the cart before the horse; thirty years of bloodshed cannot be suddenly forgotten. It is impossible for us to return to the international boundary while you deploy an army in Sinai, with no limitations on its strength. If you reject our request for the demilitarization of Sinai, in the future we will again find the two armies facing one another for battle. With a desert separating the two armies, there is no reason for either to fear."

Gazit reiterated Gur's opinion in the matter of reduction of forces. He and his superior, the chief of staff, were in complete agreement.

Gazit: "Trust is not simply a word; it is a process. I want to give you two examples of the meaning of trust: Moshe Sassoon, who is here with us, and I tried to pick up the Voice of Israel on the radio, but could not. Why? Because you interfered with Jerusalem's broadcast. Can that be called trust?"

This upset Gamassi. "That is not right," he said, "it is not so."

Gazit: "We have seen a map of Egypt and the Middle East. It was printed in Egypt. The name of Israel does not appear on it. Is that trust? Egypt exists on our maps and it is inconceivable that it could be otherwise."

The time for summing up had come. Gamassi and Fahmi expounded the Egyptian plan. It was obvious from their proposal that the Egyptians were prepared to demilitarize only a strip of 50 to 55 kilometers along the international boundary with Israel. Reduction of Egyptian forces was not mentioned. But the meeting concluded with a surprise. The Egyptians agreed to permit the Israelis to build an early warning station in the Sinai peninsula, asking to build a similar one inside the Negev, in the heart of the state of Israel.

The Israelis were astonished. Once again they parted, shaking hands but with no agreement. The gap had not narrowed.

16 BETWEEN LIFE AND DEATH

The political committee's conference in Jerusalem was preceded by a bitter controversy between Israel and Egypt in January 1978, which illustrated the sensitivities of both sides. Egypt insisted that the conference agenda include a discussion of self-determination for the Palestinians; Israel, of course, refused.

One night shortly before the conference the phone at Moshe Dayan's bedside rang. It was 3:15 a.m. when the American ambassador to Israel, Samuel Lewis, told Dayan that Vance would delay his arrival and not be in Jerusalem in time for the opening of the conference. Before Vance's decision, Sadat had convened his national security council to debate whether Egypt would attend. Notes went back and forth between Cairo and Washington, Washington and Jerusalem. The Egyptians would not agree to set out so long as they had not been assured that the Palestinian issue would be discussed. The Israelis would not hear of it. Through Vance's mediation a compromise was reached: the Palestinian issue would not appear on the agenda of the conference, but "issues concerning the West Bank and the Gaza Strip" would be included instead. Sadat gave the go-ahead, but he did not hide the fact that he was extremely pessimistic.

There was no similarity between his visit to Israel in November 1977 and the arrival of the Egyptian delegation at the political conference. The Israelis looked depressed while the Egyptians, who arrived in a special plane, were tense.

Egyptian Foreign Minister Ibrahim Kamel left no room for doubt. Even as he descended from the plane at the airport he referred to the need to restore East Jerusalem to Arab sovereignty. His address was nothing short of aggressive. Dayan was to have hosted the festive dinner for the Egyptian delegation, but Begin asked to welcome the Egyptian delegation himself to demonstrate that he was willing to continue the contacts and the negotiations.

Begin addressed Kamel as "Young friend" and then began to teach him a chapter of Jewish history. Kamel was in his fifties, and the Egyptians, with a measure of justice, were insulted. They saw it as an attempt to preach at a "younger" man who still had a lot to learn, and to show him from whom he could learn it. Begin's address was harsh. Kamel responded in kind. Discarding the text of the speech he had prepared, Kamel chose instead to respond to Begin's sharp words: "An after-dinner speech is not an occasion for political speeches," he told the Israeli prime minister.

In Cairo, War Minister Gamassi commented: "God help the negotiations with Israel." He blamed both Begin and Kamel. Other comments, from both Jerusalem and Cairo, were strained, making it more difficult to create a relaxed atmosphere at the talks. In Cairo, Sadat came out sharply against the settlements, threatening to plow them under or set them on fire.

Begin called Sadat "Nero," and threatened to take back his peace plan if Sadat rejected it. In the White House, Carter fumed. Begin had promised him he would start no new settlements, and Carter thought he had done precisely the opposite.

In Jerusalem, Kamel was in a black mood. He did not have the authority to make any concessions. Vance shuttled between floors of the Jerusalem Hilton, attempting to overcome differences between the two sides.

The outcome was almost inevitable: Sadat instructed the

Egyptian delegation to return home. As Kamel, Begin, and Dayan exchanged final words, the ringing of the phone interrupted them. Vance was asking to be updated by Begin. Begin took leave of Kamel with a handshake and asked him to tell Sadat that he would be prepared to resume the talks at any time.

Vance was deeply offended. He took the breakup of the conference as a mark of disrespect to him. He hastened to consult the White House by phone.

The move had served Sadat's purpose of forcing the Americans to intervene and throw their weight behind the effort. Even before the Egyptian plane took off for Cairo, Carter and Vance had phoned Sadat to attempt to persuade him to change his decision. Vance spoke sharply to Cairo: "You cannot conduct negotiations with surprises of this kind," he told Sadat. "Negotiations have got to be held in an atmosphere of stability. You need time and patience."

The next day, in a dramatic speech to the members of his national security council, Sadat said, "I will not allow a single Israeli settlement to remain; I shall not give up one square inch of my land, even if this means that I shall have to fight them to the end of generations." Sadat began to launch new ideas. He was not prepared to discuss the autonomy plan. The Egyptians sought a more convenient—even if only a temporary—solution, from their point of view, for the West Bank. They proposed transferring the West Bank and the Gaza Strip to United Nations control for five years and then holding a referendum to determine the future of the territories. The proposal was made to the Americans, and Israel rejected it.

A tense atmosphere prevailed at the presidential palace in Cairo. Criticism emanating from the White House reached Sadat's ears. The Egyptians expected the negotiations to continue and sought a way to get them going again. They approached the Israeli liaison delegation that had been permitted to stay in Cairo. A message was sent to Ezer Weizman through the delegation's communications station. Gamassi suggested an urgent and secret meeting with his Israeli counterpart at the Janklis estate, where their first secret meeting had taken place. Weizman suggested that instead of the secret meetings, the military committee be reconvened. His proposal was accepted.

Weizman set out again for Egypt, and Gamassi welcomed him at the airport.

The Israeli cabinet had little hope of the success of the military committee. Dayan maintained it was not right to allow the Egyptians to conduct the negotiations according to their whims, canceling one committee and continuing the other. He suggested that Israel suspend the talks of the military committee until the Egyptians agreed to resume the political committee talks.

An Israeli-American proposal that the political committee be reconvened was rejected by the Egyptians.

In the cabinet, Weizman felt the hostility of other ministers, who openly doubted the accuracy of his reports as well as those of the military delegation. Weizman maintained that the only way to save the Rafa settlements was to exchange territories with the Egyptians. Several plans were put forward; one proposed that Israel hold on the small parcels of land at the two corners of the international borders—the Etzion military airfield near Elath and the Rafa salient settlements, and the Sharm al-Sheikh area.

A second proposal was that Israel give up some of the Rafa settlements, including the village of Neot Sinai where Begin had decided he would make his home after his retirement. According to this plan, Israel would retain the small town of Yamit and the settlements near the military airfield at Eitam. A third proposal was that Israel exchange territories in order to keep the Etzion airfield near Elath.

Israel was prepared to give Egypt a modest, symbolic return for the territories it wished to hold on to: a narrow strip in the Negev along the international border. Feelers put out by the military delegation in Cairo revealed that there was a remote possibility that an exchange of territories would be acceptable. The Egyptians did not reject it outright. Even before the delegation left for Cairo, the question of an exchange of land was raised at one of the cabinet meetings. Dayan suggested that the powers of Weizman's delegation be curbed, at least on this issue, and the proposal was accepted. Weizman was not given permission to propose an exchange of territories, but was told that he should not reject it outright if the Egyptians suggested it. "All you have to do is listen and not react decisively," he was instructed.

The Egyptians were not at all interested in an exchange of territories. They believed they had good prospects of getting the entire Sinai including the airfields and the settlements.

The first subject discussed at the resumed military committee talks was, as anticipated, the Israeli settlements in the Rafa salient.

"We've got to understand that our starting point is two important principles: sovereignty and the sanctity of the land," said Gamassi "To leave the settlements where they are would mean undermining Egyptian sovereignty."

"For you it is a matter of honor," said Weizman. "For us it is a matter of security." He looked grim.

"I would like to point out," said Gamassi, sensing the gloomy mood, "that the evacuation of the settlements in the Sinai should not be taken as a precedent for what will happen in other sectors. I know that your main problem in Sinai is Yamit. We are prepared to let Israelis live with us, not in Rafa and not near the border, but in Cairo. Israelis near the border could be a spark that could kindle the flame of war in the future. We are prepared to relate to Israelis who settle in Egypt according to Egyptian law, but we will not agree to Israeli settlements."

"Why cut into the living flesh?" Weizman argued. "I suggest that for now we should decide to leave the status quo, as far as the Sinai settlements are concerned. Let's discuss the issue in the future. In fifteen years the Rafa salient will look different to all of us, Israelis and Egyptians."

"The settlements will be left for a certain period and after that will have to be removed," Gamassi answered."

"They will stay," said Weizman, "and after that we will discuss the issue anew."

"That's impossible. It would look like Israeli expansion," Gamassi said.

"Then I have no new suggestions to make," Weizman concluded.

The sessions plodded along. Weizman raised the issue of the Israeli military airfields in Sinai. He was more flexible about them than he had been: he was prepared to make do with less than three airfields. "Israel needs at least one airfield to remain at the disposal of its air force," he said.

"I would like it to be the Etzion airfield near Elath, but it could also be the airfield at Sharm al-Sheikh."

Gamassi broke in: "At a previous meeting you said you needed the Etzion airfield to protect Elath and Israeli shipping. But your air force has planes capable of providing such protection, even from the center of Israel. I suggest that the Etzion and Eitam airfields be evacuated only in the last stage, and believe me—the best protection for shipping lies in peace."

No progress was made.

The evening sessions was devoted to the early warning stations in Sinai. Over the years Israel had established sophisticated stations at a cost estimated in millions of pounds. One of these, Um Hashiba, could pick up Egyptian movements deep inside Egypt. Israel was careful to keep this station under its control even after withdrawal to the new lines under the interim agreement of 1975. "There is a direct interrelationship between the intelligence services and our readiness to take risks," said the Israeli chief of intelligence. "The more extensive our security and intelligence measures are, the greater risks we can take."

Gazit proposed that Israel hold on to three electronic warning stations in Sinai, "out of the many that we have," for a stated period beyond the withdrawal, "until we are sure that the situation is one of full peace."

"Who will operate the stations?" asked Gamassi.

"Either the present staff or civilians," Gazit said.

"And who will protect them?" Gamassi asked. "Who will provide them with supplies?"

"Special arrangements, special convoys," answered Gazit.

"For fifteen years?" asked Gamassi. "For fifteen years you will spend so much money, you will use so many satellites? Why complicate matters?"

"We have no choice," said Gazit. "If we had an alternative, we would take it. With technological progress, we can shorten the time."

"You are inventing new doctrines and complicating the situation," said Gamassi sharply.

"We are initiated into manhood at age thirteen. Perhaps thirteen years will suffice for the baby Peace," Weizman interjected.

"What do you need an early warning station for in the first place?" asked Gamassi.

"To spy on you," Gazit answered.

Silence reigned. Once again Gazit had chosen the wrong word. The Egyptian war minister was insulted and looked Gazit in the face: "Don't say 'spy,' please use the term 'reconnaissance.' When you set up your embassy in Cairo, you will be able to install devices, but I cannot accept your proposal. We shall be ready to agree on early warning stations operated by a third party, perhaps the Americans, but for a limited time only."

The results were disappointing: on the issue of the Rafa salient settlements no progress was made, and on the military airfields there were no concessions. The early warning stations proved too hard a nut to crack. A fourth subject remained for discussion: security arrangements. The Egyptians presented a map which showed that they intended to bring their army forward to 50 kilometers from the Israeli border.

"The Egyptian army," General Tamir maintained, "should stay a hundred and fifty kilometers from the Israeli border. That was agreed between President Sadat and Prime Minister Begin."

"There was a misunderstanding between Begin and Sadat in Jerusalem," Gamassi answered. "Sadat did not mean that there should be a demilitarized zone east of the mountain passes. We do not mean we will bring armies across but neither do we mean to be forbidden to bring a single soldier across. Sadat briefed me on his return from Jerusalem. I think we can safely say that there was a misunderstanding between the two leaders."

At this point in the discussion Gamassi changed the subject. "What is more important to you, the Rafa salient and the airfield, or demilitarization of all of Sinai?"

"There is no connection between the two subjects," Weizman said. "Settlements are one problem and demilitarization is another. Absolute demilitarization of Sinai would be ideal for us."

"The problem," said Gamassi, "is that you ask us to pay too high a price for Israel's security."

The sessions of the military committee in Cairo came to an inconclusive end. Weizman refused to accept the withdrawal map drafted by the Egyptians. The latter demanded the demilitarization of a narrow strip of Israel's Negev in exchange for a broader strip in Sinai and another limited forces zone and limited arms zone beyond these areas.

"OK, forget about the map," said Gamassi finally.

Bidding farewell to Weizman at Cairo Airport had become a matter of routine. The Egyptian generals who came to take leave of Weizman showed no inclination to pardon General Gazit, who, they said, had insulted their war minister. "It would be better if he stayed at home the next time," they said, "if that's how he thinks of conducting the talks with us."

Gazit had not intended to insult anyone, but the remarks of the Egyptian generals were proof enough of the difficulties in communication and lack of understanding between the two parties.

The peace talks were still wavering between life and death.

17 IN THE SHADE OF THE SYCAMORE TREE

Following the inconclusive military committee meeting in Cairo in January 1978, the focus shifted to Washington in February as Sadat and Carter held a round of meetings at Camp David. Carter had decided to devote his time to solving the Middle East conflict.

Beyond global and Western interests, Carter had a deep personal interest. His popularity had dropped to a low point; he was under attack on the domestic and foreign fronts. The Israeli embassy in Washington reported that Carter intended to admonish the Egyptian president for recalling his political representatives from Jerusalem, disrupting the methodical process of negotiating peace and undermining the prestige of Secretary of State Vance. These early reports were gratifying to government officials in Israel: it seemed that Carter had recognized the justice of Israel's posture and had gone back to serving as an "honest broker."

A few days later, everything turned upside down. The early reports were misleading; friends of Israel in the White House and the Senate warned of a sharp reversal in Carter's views. During two days of talks at Camp David, Sadat had come to a far-reaching understanding with Carter. The United States would strive to speed up the tempo of the negotiations; Egypt would receive generous backing. For the first time Sadat demanded that Carter not content himself with mediation but become a "full partner" in the negotiating process; that he intimate that American commitments could help bridge the gap between the two sides.

A meeting with Begin was next on Carter's agenda, but it was postponed as a result of a new terrorist action in Israel.

Late on a Saturday afternoon in March, Gail Rubin, a young American nature photographer who was a niece of U.S. Senator Abraham Ribicoff, was murdered in the nature reserve of Kibbutz Ma'agan Michael, just off the main Tel Aviv–Haifa highway, on the Mediterranean, by a band of Palestinian terrorists who had emerged from the sea. Moving eastward, the terrorists reached the main coastal highway linking Haifa and Tel Aviv, set up an ambush, and snared a northward-bound bus carrying a group of families returning from an outing to one of the most beautiful sites in Israel: a recently discovered cave containing stalagmites and stalactites. The terrorists boarded the vehicle and ordered the driver to turn back south and head for Tel Aviv. Not far from the entrance to the city, security forces, who had set up a roadblock, brought the hijacked vehicle to a halt. Shooting immediately broke out, and a few moments later the bus turned into a flashing death trap. When it was over, the bodies of more than thirty men, women, and children were removed from its charred remains. Israel was shocked and outraged by the tragedy and a loud outcry was raised for revenge. President Sadat denounced the slaughter.

Begin, who was about to depart for Washington, postponed his trip. A few days later Israel was to launch a major military operation into southern Lebanon—the largest military action since the Yom Kippur War—designed to strike at the terrorists entrenched there and drive them far from the Israeli border. In the light of this operation there was anxiety about the fate of the Israelis who made up the Zehava station in Cairo. It was not clear how the battle would develop or how long the IDF troops would remain on Lebanese soil, but no one doubted that the operation would aggravate the tension between Israel and the Arab states. After long deliberation the decision was made: the Israelis would remain in Zehava.

Less than five minutes after the first Israeli tank crossed the border into southern Lebanon, the telephone rang in General Avraham Tamir's hotel room in Cairo. Despite the late hour, the head of the Israeli military delegation was asked by his government to call the chief of Egyptian intelligence, General Shaukat, and pass on an important message. At first the Egyptian soldier who was asked to ring Shaukat's home at such an unusual hour was reluctant, but he gave in to the Israeli's insistent demand. The message to be transmitted had been formulated by Begin and Weizman; it stated that the IDF had initiated the action in southern Lebanon in the wake of a harrowing act of terrorism. The objective was to move against the terrorist cells and restore order to the area, not to conquer territory. The Israelis assumed that Egypt would not be able to disregard the enraged reaction of the other Arab states, and members of the Zehava station prepared to pack up and go home.

The Egyptian response was moderate, but did not approve the operation and expressed concern about its influence on the peace process. This aroused a wave of speculation among the Israeli ministers. Some regarded it as the first meaningful sign of a true change in Egypt's attitude toward the problem of the Arab world. A few ministers translated it into political terms and truly began to believe in Sadat's desire for peace.

The operation in southern Lebanon was at its height when Begin arrived for his third visit with Jimmy Carter. That day the UN Security Council had opened debate on the action, and the United States joined other nations in supporting the passage of a resolution for a cease-fire and the deployment of a UN emergency force in southern Lebanon. Carter had promised it to Sadat in a late night phone call. Israel had asked the United States to delay the passage of the resolution until Begin's arrival in Washington a few hours later. But when the Israeli prime minister reached the tarmac at Andrews Air Force Base, he was advised that the United States had refused to wait. Begin was convinced that this slap in the face had been planned for the day of his arrival at the White House.

At 10:30 a.m., March 28, 1978, the United States began dictating its ideas for achieving a Mideast solution. Carter opened the meeting by expressing his regret over the terrorist attack, which he believed had been designed to disrupt the peace process. He did not make explicit mention of the Israeli retaliation but he did drop a heavy hint in using the code words "the death of the innocent victims."

Then Carter addressed himself to the heart of the matter: "I shall do everything to preserve the Begin-Sadat momentum," he began, "and I shall do everything to maintain America's commitment to the security of the state of Israel." Then the tone and the substance of his discourse changed: "The United States is very concerned about the slowdown in the negotiations. I understand and support Israel's desire for a true, normal, substantive peace. But you must remember that Sadat once said that peace will not come in this generation, and now he is prepared for full and immediate peace. When I visited Egypt's president in Aswan, he confessed to me that he was wrong to believe that peace would not come in this generation. The unexpected enthusiastic reactions to his visit to Jerusalem convinced him that he had erred in his assessment.

"As I see it," Carter continued, "the Arab side is now willing to change and to modify its extremist position. I believe that they won't unequivocally demand the establishment of a Palestinian state."

The Israelis were astonished. Until then, they had no reason to believe that Sadat had abandoned the idea of a total Israeli withdrawal from all the occupied territories, though they had evidence that he would not insist on a Palestinian state.

Begin's answer stressed the importance of the spirit of the talks held in Jerusalem and Ismailia. He enumerated the concessions that Israel had already made: "In Jerusalem we reached an agreement on the demilitarization of Sinai from the passes up to the international border. We have given in on territorial continuity between Elath and Sharm al-Sheikh, which previous governments insisted upon." Begin's expression was somewhat melancholy when he reached the subject of the Ismailia conferences: "President Sadat refused to accept the suggestion that the Israeli settlements remain in the UN sector, but the negotiations were held in a positive spirit. At Ismailia we almost agreed upon a common declaration of principles, but because we could not reach agreement on the Palestinian issue, some of the president's advisers disrupted the process. We opposed the calls for self-determination for the Palestinians because that means a Palestinian state. We shall never agree to it."

Begin went on to refute everything Carter had said: "Since the meeting in Ismailia we have been subjected to venomous attacks and the Egyptians have demanded our complete withdrawal and a Palestinian state. We have made it clear to the Egyptians—then and now—that we cannot accept these proposals. To the best of my knowledge and understanding, these two demands do not follow from Security Council Resolution 242, and they threaten our most vital national interests." Begin knew that his next sentence would not elicit applause: "Mr. President, I ask you to make that clear to the Egyptians again and to tell them that we cannot accept their demands."

Carter replied: "Sadat told me that Egypt does not insist upon an Israeli withdrawal from all the territories captured in 1967. I don't think Sadat wants a Palestinian state in the West Bank either." The Israelis understood that they were being asked to make further concessions. Carter continued: "I suggest that Israel and Egypt accept American compromise formulas on these two subjects: the withdrawal and the Palestinian state. Each side can interpret the formulations as it sees best. The United States believes that guarantees must be found for Israel's security. The solution may be in establishing and maintaining Israeli military holdings, something to the effect of military positions, electronic installations, and UN forces, and all that for some interim period."

The moment he cited the need for an interim period, the Israelis understood that his outlook bore no resemblance to their own.

Carter went on: "On the West Bank, the military issue must be separated from the political question. Sadat refuses to continue the negotiations now because of your new settlements in Sinai, and I understand his position." The last five words made it crystal clear that Carter accepted the Egyptian president's view.

Dayan said: "Are we to understand from what has been said here that Sadat's willingness to give leeway on a full Israeli withdrawal from the occupied territories extends to Sinai as well? Is Sadat prepared to discuss secure borders in Sinai too?"

Carter looked alarmed, and the secretary of state broke in: "No, no, no, no, not in terms of Sinai."

Carter added: "Sadat did tell me he is willing to keep his forces to the west of the Sinai passes [meaning closer to the Suez Canal than the Israeli border], but he cannot guarantee the security of his country unless units are stationed east of the passes."

The Israelis were infuriated. In Jerusalem, the Egyptian president had promised not to demand the stationing of military forces to the east of the passes in the area closer to Israel. They suspected from this last statement that Carter had given in on Sadat's new position.

Dayan: "Sadat rejected the Israeli proposal to allow our settlements to exist under Egyptian sovereignty. Resolution 242 does not oblige us to pull back to the 1967 borders in Sinai, but he wants us to withdraw from the whole area. If Sadat insists on that, we will have to insist on the strict application of Resolution 242. In other words, we won't pull back to the 1967 borders in Sinai either."

Begin: "Mr. President, you say that Sadat no longer insists upon our complete withdrawal to the 1967 borders and no longer demands a Palestinian state. Then why doesn't he say so to us? Why doesn't he speak to us in operative language? If the Egyptians don't demand that, then they should employ different language. Perhaps it's worthwhile for Mr. Atherton, who is about to leave for the Middle East, to tell President Sadat that Egypt should come out and clearly state that they do not demand a withdrawal to the 1967 borders and a Palestinian state." Atherton's mediation mission had already been decided upon during the Sadat-Carter meeting at Camp David.

Carter: "What worries Sadat and me is that your statements seem to imply that Resolution 242 does not say that the withdrawal is binding on the West Bank and the Gaza Strip."

At this point the prime minister's legal adviser, Aharon Barak, entered the discussion: "Our plan for self-rule is congruent with Resolution 242. Our program does not contradict the resolution."

Dayan: "And that is because we state that we are willing to disband the military government in the West Bank and Gaza. This is not a matter of sovereignty, but there's no doubt that what we have here is a withdrawal of forces. If the Arabs object to our plan, fine: let them present a plan of their own. Resolution 242 does not say that there must be a withdrawal from the three fronts."

Carter looked at the Israelis angrily: "Well, then, we have a difference of opinion here that we did not have in the past."

The president had laid his cards on the table, and Begin tried to rescue the situation: "That is not so. The Labor party plan also held that there was to be no military withdrawal from the Jordan River." The Labor formula was that the Jordan would be Israel's "security border."

Carter: "We want to find common ground between you and the Arabs. But I believe that the only chance of reaching an agreement with Egypt is if Israel agrees to security arrangements in the West Bank. I see a difficulty arising between the United States commitment to support Israel's security and Israel's desire to administer the occupied territories politically."

Without saying so explicitly, Carter was echoing Sadat's latest public statement that he would agree to various security arrangements but not to border changes. The president's words were a clear warning.

Dayan: "I was also a member of previous Israeli governments. Even in 1967, when the government was prepared to withdraw to the June 4 borders, that plan did not relate to the West Bank. The autonomy idea is a good one because it has a chance of being acceptable to the Arabs. It is not true that this government has backed down on earlier positions, which no one was prepared to accept anyway. From my point of view as a military man, there is one vital question: Who will decide if a hostile force has crossed the Jordan, and who will prevent such a force from doing so? It will be very unfortunate if we have to go back to the era of barbed-wire fences, mines, and UN sentries. After thirty years, the time has come for us to live together with the Arabs, instead of having UN troops stationed between us."

Carter: "I have no doubt that Sadat wants peace and that he is flexible enough. The best thing for Israel is to negotiate with him. The prime minister's plan for self-rule is a good one. It can be an axis around which to construct a plan. Now I expect a little more flexibility from both sides. Let me suggest that the secretary of state and Mr. Atherton sit down with you both until dinnertime and work on the difference in wording. Of all the problems before us now, I see the problem of the Israeli settlements in Sinai as the most difficult one. By comparison, the issues of the airfields and the size of the Egyptian force in Sinai are not difficult to solve."

Suddenly Carter raised a new question: "Could you accept the option of withdrawing your army into camps within the West Bank?"

Begin: "In and of itself, no! The presence of our army in Judea and Samaria is imperative to us. It is a vital interest. But if we're talking of doing so within the framework of self-rule, the idea might be acceptable."

Vice-President Mondale began to argue with Barak about the applicability of Resolution 242 to the West Bank. All the others, from Carter down to the last of his aides, followed the exchange intently.

Brzezinski joined in: "Your proposal for self-rule on the West Bank could be interpreted as the perpetuation of Israeli domination of the area, and that would impede progress toward peace. The plan can be effective if it is anchored in Resolution 242 and in a withdrawal. But the problem is that your plan can be understood either positively or negatively. We would like to see changes introduced in the plan so that it will generate a positive interpretation."

This appeared to be more than a subtle hint that the United States had prepared a plan of its own or wished to introduce far-reaching changes into the Israeli program. But the Israelis were not sure whether appearance should be accepted as reality.

Brzezinski: "The American objective is for Israel, Egypt, Jordan, and the moderate Palestinians to find common ground for creating the basis for defense against Soviet penetration and radicalization."

Begin: "You must not distract us from the understanding between our governments. If we agreed in December that the plan is positive, why should it now be turned into a subject of contention? For us it is vital that our forces remain in Judea and Samaria."

Carter: "But what will happen after five years? Will the inhabitants be given the freedom to determine their status?"

Begin: "Considering the threats of the PLO today, the notion of a plebiscite under such conditions seems dangerous to us."

Carter: "If you don't allow the residents of the West Bank and Gaza to determine their identity in the future, there's no hope of reaching a peaceful solution. If Israel doesn't give them a voice, there's no hope for an agreement: it is vital, even if you only want to achieve a treaty with Egypt."

Dayan: "We are in favor of a pullback from control over the population, but we will oppose any wording that speaks of withdrawal from control over the territories."

Brzezinski: "Your plan might be interpreted as resembling [South Africa's] control over Basutoland."

Begin (in a sharp tone): "It is nothing of the kind!"

Dayan: "Even now any Arab can choose between Jordanian citizenship, Israeli citizenship, or registering as a local inhabitant."

Carter: "If we Americans, you Israelis, and the Egyptians believe that the establishment of a Palestinian state must be prevented, it won't come into being."

Begin appreciated the power of the United States but knew exactly what was going on in the occupied territories: the PLO had gained control over the population, and any plebiscite could easily lead to the establishment of a Palestinian state.

Begin: "A plebiscite constitutes a psychological and physical threat."

President Carter no longer concealed his anger: "The obstacle to peace is Israel's desire to perpetuate its political domination of the West Bank and Gaza. Let us hope that Israel will exchange political control for security arrangements . . ." He immediately tried to soften the negative impression: "At the same time, I want to give you credit for what you proposed in Sinai."

The meeting closed on a somber note, and it was no longer possible to conceal the breach between the two sides. "I appeal to you to be as flexible as possible," Carter concluded. "Neither Jordan, Sadat, the Saudis, we, nor you want an independent Palestinian state, and I would like to ask our experts and yours to draw up proposals that will draw a distinction between political control over the West Bank and security arrangements. That way it will be possible to achieve peace."

In presenting his peace plan to President Carter in December, Begin had assumed that he was "beginning at the end." But in his talks with Carter he suddenly discovered that he must begin from the beginning, from the worst possible starting point. As he saw it, the Carter plan for peace in the Middle East was far worse than even the Rogers plan, which did not mention a Palestinian state. Begin believed that Washington had embraced Sadat's demand that a distinction must be drawn between Israel's security needs and the issue of its borders; between control over the West Bank and vital military arrangements.

Begin's standing in the United States was at a severe disadvantage. The president of Egypt had learned the value and importance of the communications media—particularly the three major television networks—and exploited them skillfully. His statements to the American people were short and simple. He never used the word "no," repeated the word "peace" endlessly, and took pains to ensure that the atmosphere of every interview was cordial. As a result he had built up enormous esteem.

Begin was Sadat's exact opposite. To millions of viewers in the United States he came across as a shrewd and pedantic attorney who had an annoying way of pointing his finger as if making a threat. His expression was always sober and stern, and the Polish accent of his fluent English moved people to get out of their chairs and switch to another channel before they had even heard his long-winded, convoluted dissertations. By contrast, Sadat's plodding, heavy English and the hint of grandeur behind the man made him into the hero of the day.

Public opinion polls in the United States indicated, for the first time, that the American public was inclined to support Egypt. In the past there had always been a gap of dozens of points in Israel's favor; the Egyptians had lagged far behind. Now Sadat also had the upper hand in the personality contest. Even American Jewry, the primary well-spring of support for Israel, was far from content. For the first time since the establishment of Israel, American Jews—including members of the community's leadership—openly came out against Israeli government policy. Many felt that some circles in Israel were trying to torpedo the peace negotiations.

There was a concrete aspect to Egypt's successes in the United States: for the first time, Sadat managed to pry open America's weapons arsenal and purchase combat equipment. In fact, America turned over to him small quantities of their most advanced military hardware. Sadat wanted much more of it, but his main gain was that a precedent had been set. Sadat's most impressive achievement, however, was the administration's decision to link Israel, Egypt, and Saudi Arabia together in a package deal arms sale. The strident opposition of the American Jewish lobby was futile.

The next day's meeting with Carter and his aides was no less difficult for the Israelis.

"During Sadat's last visit here, I wanted to clarify his position," Carter opened. "Up to now I have been full of hope, and I have not given up hope of furthering the negotiations with the Egyptians; though as I see it, a comprehensive peace agreement is preferable." Carter pulled out a pen, tore a piece of paper off the yellow legal pad, and began to jot something down as he spoke. "This afternoon I have to report to the House International Relations Committee and to the Senate Foreign Relations Committee tomorrow. I want to present to them what I understand to be your position and what I understand to be Sadat's position."

A tense silence fell over the White House cabinet room. Point after point, Carter spelled out Israel's position, and there was no doubt that his presentation had been prepared thoroughly. He began with a negative description of Israel's policy: "You said: There is no need for a full withdrawal from the West Bank and Gaza.

"You said: The settlements in Sinai will not be abandoned.

"You said: The settlement activity will not be halted. Israel is not prepared to undertake a political withdrawal from the West Bank. Israel says that Resolution 242 is not applicable to the West Bank.

"You said: Israel is not willing to accord the inhabitants of the West Bank the right of self-determination . . ."

Carter flung a glance at Begin, whose expression was more somber than ever. After a second or two of silence, he continued dramatically: "If I have understood your positions correctly and all this is so, there's no real hope to advancing toward a peace treaty."

The Americans expected a response, and Begin rose to the challenge: "It is also possible to depict Israel's positions in a positive fashion. For example, we are resolute in our determination to engage in negotiations and arrive at a peace treaty with all our neighbors. We have not only accepted Resolution 242 as the basis for an agreement with all our neighbors, but we have offered the Egyptians far-reaching proposals regarding Sinai, Judea and Samaria—what you, Mr. President, call the West Bank . . ." Begin took the difference in terminology very seriously. His instructions to all government ministries were to use only the term "Judea and Samaria"; the West Bank no longer existed.

Begin continued to portray his policy in positive light: "One could say that the negotiations must be direct, that our proposals were far-reaching, as you yourself said to me, Mr. President, during my visit here in December. Instead of demanding border changes, we accommodated the Egyptians by proposing a full withdrawal. We also agreed that the question of sovereignty in Judea and Samaria will remain open until it is settled. We shall accord the inhabitants self-rule, and Israel will have security."

Carter took Begin's words down on the yellow sheet, and the Israelis sitting on the opposite side of the table had the impression that Carter was writing down both the substance of Begin's claims and the manner in which he was expressing them. Begin continued: "As to the settlements, I ask you, Mr. President, to adopt positive terminology toward them too: we have committed ourselves not to establish new settlements in Sinai. In regard to the Israeli settlements in Judea and Samaria, Jews have a right to settle in Judea and Samaria. The time and place will be subject to the government's decisions."

"If you are going to meet with the committees," Begin concluded with a hint of bitterness, "I ask you, Mr.

President, to present our position in a positive manner, not a negative one."

Carter: "I promise to do that."

Begin: "You have my gratitude. You must remember, Mr. President that for the sake of the peace process we have presented three important documents: the plan for Sinai; the plan for self-rule in Judea and Samaria, and Gaza; and the proposal for a declaration of principles in Ismailia. These documents can serve as the basis for discussions and negotiations, or Egypt can raise their own counterproposals. It has not done so up to date."

Carter: "I cannot agree that Resolution 242 is not applicable to the West Bank. Why don't you openly state that you don't mean that? Sadat is as sensitive on that subject as Israel is about the Wailing Wall. As far as he is concerned, Israel's desire to maintain settlements in Sinai is equivalent to an unwillingness to withdraw from Sinai. I suggested that he accept the existence of the settlements under the auspices of the UN, but he won't have it. If he agreed to Israel's plan, that would be fine . . ." Carter didn't hesitate to let his own opinion be known: "The truth is that Sadat's stand seems logical to me. I was disappointed to hear that Israel has adopted the position that Resolution 242 is not binding on the West Bank." The Israelis understood the next sentence as an explicit threat: "I don't know how to proceed from here," Carter said, "and I must ask the counsel of the Congress."

Begin: "Sadat never suggested to us that the settlements could remain in the UN sector and under UN auspices. He told us to remove them. At first he said they should be burned down. Then he corrected himself and said to dismantle them. Sadat was aware of our position and our intention to keep the settlements in Sinai even before he came to Jerusalem. I was amazed to hear that from Dayan. Sadat heard it again after he arrived in Jerusalem, and his reaction was an ultimatum: 'Dismantle them.' "

The tone of Begin's words grew steadily sharper. It was clear to him that the breach was already at its widest, and he had decided to respond aggressively by attacking both Sadat and Carter. "Now as to Sadat's other positions. According to Egypt's draft of a declaration of principles, they demand a full withdrawal and they also demand self-determination for the Palestinians in Judea and Samaria, and Gaza. As we understand it, what the Egyptians are demanding is a Palestinian state." In effect, Begin was implying to Carter that he, Carter, didn't know what he was talking about. He tried to refute Carter's statement that the Egyptians did not want a Palestinianian state.

Carter: "You're right about the settlements in Sinai. Despite my requests, Sadat refused to concede to me that the settlements could be left under the aegis of the United Nations. As for the Palestinians, his position is that the matter should be settled in discussion."

Vance: "We hoped that the Aswan formula on the right of the Palestinians to participate in the determination of their future would be acceptable on this point. As to the call for self-determination, I don't think it's a demand for an independent Palestinian state."

Carter (to Begin): "I'm not trying to criticize your position. The plans you have presented are courageous and noble, but the fact is that the talks were broken off after the [Sadat] visit to Jerusalem. We are trying to find a common language. Perhaps this can be done in the framework of an American proposal stating that Israel will not withdraw completely from the West Bank and Egypt will not demand the establishment of a Palestinian state. I want to tell you that the greatest experience I've had during my term in the White House was when you and Sadat held direct talks without me."

Begin: "When you see the members of the Congress today and tomorrow, I would like you to tell them what you said now about our proposals just now—that they are courageous."

Carter: "I certainly will say that. It is definitely a major step forward."

Toward evening, Carter met with the members of the House International Relations Committee and depicted Israel's position in a negative manner, exactly as he had portrayed it to Begin earlier that day. The Americans initiated a coordinated attack. Leaks from the White House and the State Department spoke of pointless Israeli intransigence, and Begin was depicted as an obstacle to peace.

"Imagine to yourselves what the next generation will say: 'Peace was lost because of a few words that should have been included in the declaration of principles.'" Dayan said at the end of the depressing meetings with

Carter and his advisers. "The next generation will never forgive us for that. But will future generations forgive us if we agree to give up the West Bank?"

The breach with the United States inspired many Israeli officials to try and squeeze Carter out of the picture and move back toward establishing direct negotiations with Egypt. Dayan did not think it was possible. From the start he never believed that progress could be made in the negotiations without the Americans. Weizman thought otherwise, however, and expressed his opinion on this issue publicly, sometimes even bitingly: "For thirty years we've been saying that there's no one to talk to, and now, when we finally have someone to talk to, we go chasing after the Americans!"

The chance to continue direct talks with Egypt presented itself to Weizman at the end of March 1978, shortly after Begin's return from the United States. Weizman did not expect the Egyptians to invite him to Cairo publicly, because the IDF operation was still in progress in southern Lebanon. An invitation from War Minister Gamassi surprised other ministers too. Weizman saw it as an encouraging sign: an invitation to meet with Sadat, despite the military operation in Lebanon, was nothing to sneeze at. Sadat would have to explain himself to the Arab world. What's more, the Arab League was convening in Cairo at that very time.

Weizman's standing in the Israeli government was problematic, for he was suspected of drawing fundamental political conclusions from chance conversations. "He's being taken in by the Egyptians," some of his ministerial colleagues complained in private conversations. Aware of the controversy about his judgment, Weizman decided to take the government's legal adviser, Aharon Barak, to Cairo with him. Barak had been an active participant at every stage of the negotiations, and Weizman wanted an acceptable witness at his side. It was important to Weizman that Barak's signature appear on the protocol of the talks.

The Egyptians were very cordial to Weizman when he arrived in Cairo on March 30. Television cameras awaited him, and he and his aides were flown to the president's summer retreat, Barage House, near the High Dam, in a special helicopter fitted out with upholstered seats. Weizman shook Sadat's hand and took a deep breath.

"Aramis?" he asked with a smile.

"Ahhh." The Egyptian president grinned. Weizman had recognized the scent of his after-shave lotion.

"What is most important," Sadat began, "is a clear declaration signifying that you agree to the principle of a full withdrawal. After such a declaration is made, I promise you that we shall solve everything. Things will fall into place easily, and many problems that look difficult now will be solved." The Egyptian president made the resumption of negotiations conditional on this point.

Weizman: "You ask for a full withdrawal from all the territories, but it's impossible to speak of a full withdrawal. No party in Israel, except for the Communists, would agree to it."

Sadat: "It is enough if you agree to say that you are prepared to withdraw."

Weizman: "It would never pass. But we can talk about a declaration of common intent. I suggest that the subjects be taken up with Dayan. It's worthwhile for him to be in contact with you on this question."

Sadat: "I don't think that's a good idea. Not yet. The time has not yet come for me to receive Dayan. Dayan can't keep a secret."

Weizman: "That's not so." Weizman had already asked that Dayan be brought in on the direct talks between Israel and Egypt. He believed that a visit to Cairo would change Dayan's views. But the Egyptians refused to invite the Israeli foreign minister, even when Dayan signaled them through his own channels that he wished to come.

Sadat: "You must know that there can be no talk of a separate agreement between Egypt and Israel. Such an agreement will serve neither of us."

Weizman: "We are not talking about a separate agreement but the first agreement. Afterward other agreements will come."

The discussion turned to the issue of the IDF's operation in southern Lebanon. Weizman explained the situation.

Sadat: "This operation places me in a sensitive position."

Weizman: "You were also victimized by the PLO's murderous activities. The murder of the editor of *Al Aharam* was a horrible deed."

Sadat: "I have crossed the PLO out of my lexicon."

Hearing the Egyptian president express himself so vehemently against Arafat's organization, Weizman tried to cash in on the opportunity: "Does that mean that you accept our opposition to the establishment of an independent Palestinian state?"

Sadat: "That is so, but under no circumstances are you to say that to Begin, because he will immediately announce it to the whole world. What we need is to make a good impression. We must look good through a declaration of principles and of a willingness to withdraw, and we will give you what you need."

Weizman: "What about the purchase of land by Jews in the West Bank?"

Sadat: "If an Arab wants to sell you land privately, I have no objection."

Barak: "There's also the question of refugees who want to return to their homes."

Sadat: "This will also be subject to vote, as proposed in the plan for self-rule."

Weizman told Sadat that Israel rejected the notion of a plebiscite in the West Bank, and Sadat was willing to replace a plebiscite with elections. He also agreed that for the time being Israel could maintain a military presence in the West Bank, "but the police force must be composed of Palestinian inhabitants." He was also prepared to agree that the Israeli settlements in the West Bank could remain intact.

Weizman and Barak were pleasantly surprised. Barak was trying to take down every word that issued from Sadat's lips, and from time to time he asked for clarification. Sadat, who seemed to be particularly on edge, repeated his words over and over so that the protocol would be precise.

"We must find a way that will lead us to the point where you will be the first to sign a peace treaty with us without damaging your prestige," Weizman said to Sadat. But despite his broad hints about specific concessions, Sadat left no room for doubt. He might be prepared to turn a blind eye and give in on some things, but his fundamental position had not changed: "Without a solution to the Palestinian problem, there will be no peace, even if we solve the problem of Sinai. I understand your concern, and I know that Israel has a security problem and that it is a question of life or death. But a separate agreement with us will not bring peace."

Weizman: "You must understand our insecurity. The average Israeli does not feel safe."

Sadat: "No Arab in any Arab state will offer you the kind of friendship that the Egyptians do. Do not harm me. As it is, you will have a hard enough time with the Syrians."

Weizman: "According to your proposal, who will control the West Bank?"

Sadat: "I must tell my people that I achieved the withdrawal of the Jews from the West Bank. If Jordan enters the negotiations then Jordan will be there, representatives of the residents, and you."

Weizman: "There won't be a Palestinian state?"

Sadat: "That is correct. I say no state, and a small number of military positions for Israel in the area. We must return to the situation before 1967. The West Bank will be tied to Jordan and Gaza will be tied to Egypt. The Palestinian state will wait."

It seemed that they were moving toward a breakthrough, and Weizman was encouraged. He had heard things from Sadat that had never been said before. During the meeting that same day with Mustafa Khalil, secretary of the ruling party and one of Sadat's closest friends, Weizman was subjected to a sharp attack about the IDF campaign in southern Lebanon. Weizman knew that Khalil would soon be appointed prime minister, and his words were far more biting than those of Sadat and Gamassi. At the end of the conversation the two men joined a meeting in progress between Barak and Gamassi. Gamassi told his guests that the Israeli settlements in the West Bank could remain intact. Egypt would not object to that. Nor would it object to Israel establishing additional settlements in the West Bank, but only on private land purchased by Jews at full market value. There was no chance of consenting to the expropriation of land. The question of establishing settlements on government land in the West Bank, he said, must be left to the council that would administer self-rule. As Gamassi saw it, Israel could purchase government land and develop a program of construction and settlement, just as the Arabs could.

The next morning the telephone rang in Weizman's

room. His aide, David Kollitz, took the message: "Sadat wishes to see Weizman again, immediately if possible." Weizman had intended to fly back to Israel within the hour, on the assumption that his contacts with Sadat would be resumed in the near future. Now Gamassi would escort him to another meeting within half an hour.

Weizman found Sadat restless. Vice-President Husni Mubarak had been invited to the meeting along with General Gamassi. Sadat began by telling Weizman of a meeting he had held the night before with a delegation of Palestinian representatives from the Gaza Strip. "I was deeply touched by their statement about their rights," he explained to Weizman. "They emphasized how important it is for them to be given the right of self-determination. That is essential! That is fundamental! Nothing is possible without it! So I have asked you to come here because I wish to tell you what I said yesterday is no longer valid. Now we have a problem, and not a simple problem. I think that for that we need a plebiscite."

What had looked like an achievement yesterday had now been wiped out in a single stroke.

Weizman: "Mr. President, you know that a plebiscite is not acceptable to Israel. You are a brave man! You expelled the Russians from Egypt; you went to Jerusalem; you launched an initiative that only you were able and brave enough to pursue. Why not go on now as we agreed yesterday, according to what you yourself proposed?"

Sadat: "I myself can decide and conclude things. I am not in favor of an independent Palestinian state but of a plebiscite and a tie between the territories and what will be established in them and Jordan."

Weizman: "Mr. President, you know that in the end a plebiscite will lead to the establishment of an independent Palestinian state. The solution must be sought through negotiations. We must achieve an agreement that includes the principle that the Arabs of Palestine have the right to participate in the determination of their fate." The wording that Weizman had used was very close to the Aswan formula, but Sadat was impatient and did not pay attention to it. Instead, he brought the conversation to a close. "Give my regards to President Katzir, to Begin, and to Yadin and Dayan," he said before they parted.

Earlier, Weizman and Gamassi had spoken at length

about what would happen in Sinai when the UNEF mandate ran out in October 1978. Now, at the end of his latest talk, Weizman looked Sadat in the eye and suddenly had a very unpleasant feeling. Though he believed in the man's desire for peace, Weizman was suddenly afraid that the deadline of the UN mandate might tempt Sadat into making a spectacular military move to get the negotiating process moving again. Sadat's abrupt change of heart had startled Weizman. Later on, Weizman's advisers would claim that there had not been any Palestinian delegation in Cairo that night, and Sadat had just used the claim as an excuse. The Israelis could not decide whether Sadat had second thoughts about the commitments he had made to Weizman in their first talk or whether the affair had been staged from the start. It seemed to them that Sadat's words had been some kind of signal. Or perhaps they were a flashing warning light. Weizman decided that Israel would have to be cautious.

18 STORM CLOUDS

Ezer Weizman could not bring firm Egyptian proposals to the Israeli cabinet's weekly meeting. Begin and Dayan feared that Sadat was trying to undermine Israel's relations with the U.S. rather than aspiring toward a settlement. Weizman tried to prove that Sadat's attitude had changed for the better, but only one minister, Meir Amit, supported him.

"Ezer," Begin said to him with a touch of mockery, "don't forget that after the meeting on March 30 came the meeting on March 31." Later, the discussion during which Sadat retracted the promises he had made was called "the morning after."

Relations were bad within the Israeli cabinet. The U.S. support of Egypt, the demands made by the European countries to recognize the Palestinians' rights, the Arab countries' angry opposition to the negotiations, Sadat's attitude to the peace initiative, and the internal unrest created immense tensions, which were supplemented by long-standing personal grudges and jealousies.

A bitter quarrel developed over the best way of conducting the negotiations and what Egypt's true intentions were. Dayan thought that the Egyptians could not sign a separate peace treaty with Israel. Weizman denied it. Relying on his direct contacts with the Egyptian leaders, he said: "All they want is a cover in the form of a declaration of principles." He claimed that Sadat would be prepared to sign a peace treaty with Israel even if the other Arab countries did not come to the discussion table immediately.

Sadat refused to speak directly to the Israelis. Through the Americans he made it clear to Dayan: "I will not agree to any contact as long as there is no progress." Sadat exerted pressure on Carter to influence Begin to come up with "new Israeli elements" for the negotiations.

On one occasion, after Ezer Weizman had reviewed the credibility crisis between the two countries and noted that he nevertheless believed in Sadat's and Gamassi's deep desire for peace, Chief of Staff Mordechai Gur asked for the floor. His opinion, diametrically opposed to Weizman's, was that the Egyptians might not really intend to make peace, and that peace with them could never be achieved. The negotiations were merely another stage in the Arab struggle against Israel. "The Egyptians don't regard us as equal partners," he said.

In April, Gur was replaced by a new chief of staff, Raphael "Raful" Eitan, a professional soldier who had never been involved in political moves or negotiations. Eitan's wars had been fought against the Egyptians. Soon after his appointment he declared that it would be impossible to defend Israel without controlling the West Bank. He also opposed the autonomy plan.

Concern that the historic opportunity for peace was being lost was felt by many Israelis. The left, as well as other sections of the public, made serious accusations against Begin and his colleagues. Many people who had never supported Begin had begun singing his praises when the peace initiative got underway. The political stalemate returned them to their former positions. They attacked Begin unceasingly.

The Labor party did not conceal its criticism of Begin's approach. Its leaders resented the fact that the government did not keep them informed about the details of the negotiations. Although at the time of Sadat's visit to Jerusalem, Boutros Ghali had spoken about establishing a link between Egypt and the Labor party, until February no such

194

contact had been established. Now Sadat was about to visit Vienna and the leader of the Labor party, Shimon Peres, was also due to travel to Europe. Through Austrian Chancellor Bruno Kreisky, Sadat and Peres met in a palace on the Bavarian border where Hitler used to spend his free time. The two men reviewed the stand of each side. Peres believed that the question of the Israeli settlements had become an important matter of prestige. Peres was convinced that Israel had to display "flexibility regarding formulas." The discussion was colored by Sadat's political impatience. Why could not the Israelis be generous? he asked.

Although Begin had agreed to the meeting between Peres and Sadat, he did not approve of it. He feared that Sadat was trying to appeal to the opposition and the Israeli public over his head. The meeting enhanced the prestige of Peres and his party. For the first time the Labor party had received a full report at first hand about Sadat's stand and could use it as a basis for forming policy.

The widespread attention the Peres meeting got sharpened the opposition's tone in the Knesset. Peres and his party were regarded as being more moderate and as having greater experience; Begin's popularity was on the decline. Bitter criticism of the government's activities in the social and economic spheres, as well regarding the peace negotiations, disturbed Begin's calm.

Begin's somber mood was heightened by the authors of an "officers' letter" which arrived on his desk in May. The signatories, 348 reserve officers, many of whom had fought at the front, expressed their concern at the stalemate. Some of them were part of a group of dovish intellectuals. After the failure of the Ismailia conference this group came up with the idea of becoming a mass movement, abandoning some of its ideology, and reaching the wider public. The original approach of the writers of the "officers' letter" had been to inform the public that they had done all that had been required of them in the service of their country. They noted their military rank in order to stress that they were the ones who would be the first to be called in the case of another war and were therefore entitled to demand explanations. The letter aroused a much stronger reaction than had been expected. These young men, all of them in their twenties, complete greenhorns in politics, suddenly found themselves without any preparation at the center of a wide popular movement. They found they could mobilize vast numbers of people at the drop of a hat. The Peace Now movement attracted younger people. There were hints that Weizman was secretly encouraging the movement.

The principal government discussions on the peace negotiations were held in Begin's office, and Dayan was the only other participant. Only rarely was Weizman invited. Foreign Ministry officials complained that they had no idea what was going on and were scarcely able to fulfill their tasks throughout the world. Many ordinary Israelis felt that the chance for real peace had been lost. Enthusiasm had died down. "For thirty years we have been living in a ghetto, closed in and armed!" Weizman roared during one of his arguments with other members of the cabinet. "Now, when the door is open, we're alarmed, frightened of peace."

There was controversy in Egypt too. In March a debate had begun in the press over the character and course of the country. It had opened with an article by the elderly writer Taufiq el-Hakim, who called for Egypt to be neutral, "like Switzerland or Austria." Other writers criticized this "treason." The argument raged for a month, reflecting profound uncertainty about the dangers involved in peace with Israel. Fears were expressed that peace would endanger Egypt's Arab character. Open criticism of Hakim implied a more cautious criticism of Sadat.

The Cairo press argued that Begin should be replaced so that it would be possible to continue the negotiations and achieve success. The Egyptians expected that a concerted attack on Begin would cause him to lose his self-control and his public support.

The Egyptians believed that Begin was a very sick man. They hoped that the Americans would get rid of him, thereby enabling Weizman, who was dissatisfied with the prime minister, and the Labor party to engineer a parliamentary insurrection. Gradually, however, it became clear that Begin could withstand the pressure.

Sadat's position was increasingly bad. An Arab rejectionist conference in Algiers failed to agree on how to proceed, but this did not encourage him. He had to contend with a growing economic crisis. He quietly reduced the military budget; he attempted to curtail food subsidies too, but had to abandon the project for fear of a wave of protests and riots. The finance minister, Dr. Kasoni, resigned in protest.

The Americans were afraid that the peace process would collapse. They spared no effort to get the ball rolling again but came up against two stubborn and determined men who were facing heavy pressure within their own countries. Begin was again admitted to the hospital because of an infection in the lining of his heart.

Sadat shut himself up in the Barage House. His closest aides managed to see him only rarely. For six months he did not speak to his minister of war, Gamassi. Every now and again he undertook periods of fasting.

The main bone of contention, the future of the West Bank, had not been removed: it was impossible to advance without breaking through that barrier. Consequently, Carter and his aides tackled the problem from a new angle. Assuming that Begin could not at present reach an understanding with Sadat about the fate of the Palestinians, the White House decided to try to get a commitment from Begin to decide on the problem at some distant point in time. Carter was guided by the view that by agreeing to defer making a decision about the Palestinians it would be possible to proceed to an Israeli-Egyptian settlement.

Carter's initiative was contained in two drafts which were handed to the Israeli government in July with a request for a quick reply.

First, Begin and his cabinet were asked to state whether they would be prepared to define the ultimate status of the West Bank and the Gaza Strip within five years. The American "questionnaire" mentioned ultimate sovereignty, but at Dayan's instigation, the term was modified to "final status."

Second, if so, what mechanism did Israel think appropriate for achieving this status?

The Americans provided their own proposals for Israel's reply to their questions: Israel would be prepared to determine the permanent status of the West Bank and the Gaza Strip after five years through negotiations among representatives of Israel, Egypt, Jordan, and the Palestinians living in the region. The results of the negotiations should be approved by the inhabitants of the area. In other words, the

197

American formula was intended to commit Israel to solving the fate of these areas, leaving the last word with the local population. The Americans dropped broad hints that by this they meant a referendum among the Palestinians. Later, as a result of the firm opposition of the Israeli cabinet, they backed down from the idea of giving the local Palestinians the right to veto the agreement. However, many groups in Israel interpreted the American reply as a command.

In fact it had been Dayan who indirectly encouraged the Americans to adopt this approach. He had convinced Vance that there was no longer any point in continuing the barren search for an agreed declaration of principles. Dayan claimed that it was better to take a more practical tack, examining whether Israel and Egypt could agree about the components of the agreement about the territories. In this way it would be possible to disregard the principle and deal with the actual conditions.

In addition, Dayan managed with difficulty to persuade Begin and the cabinet to agree that Resolution 242 also applied to the West Bank and the Gaza Strip, though the new Israeli interpretation regarded autonomy as the application of the resolution to these areas. This was based on the legal claim that in passing this resolution the Security Council did not necessarily mean that Israel would withdraw on every front. The withdrawal of the military occupation, the Israelis claimed, was the only thing meant by Resolution 242. Despite this talmudic interpretation, it was a small step forward.

Weizman declared that he was prepared to answer the first question in the affirmative. Israel was prepared to determine the final status of the West Bank in five years. Nevertheless, Weizman stressed that this status, whatever it was, would be determined by all the elements participating in the peace process and all of them, including Israel, would have the right to use a veto.

For a long time Begin did not express his views, listening patiently to what the cabinet ministers had to say. Weizman complained that Begin and Dayan were meeting too often.

The argument inside the cabinet was bitter, protracted, and on a personal level. The poor relations between the senior ministers were almost at crisis point. Begin was tired and sick and hinted several times that he wanted to resign. His associates have said that those were his worst days during the peace process.

During the discussion Weizman also visited Begin, and for some reason he gained the impression one day that Begin supported his version.

The answers approved by the cabinet that day did not, however, please Weizman. He felt that he had been cheated at the last moment by Begin and Dayan. As he left the meeting he shouted at the top of his voice that this government did not want peace and that he was going to prepare the army for war. The reply to the U.S., as formulated by Dayan, did not answer Washington's requirements, but left the door a tiny crack open, as would be proved later. At this stage all that had been achieved was the possibility of embarking on a discussion about the nature of the settlement in the West Bank and the Gaza Strip, without there being as yet any common ground joining Sadat and Carter on the one hand to Begin and Dayan on the other. Sadat concurred that he would not demand the immediate establishment of a Palestinian state or an Israeli commitment for a full withdrawal, but did not accept "future relations" which would be determined in another five years under an Israeli veto.

"You have left the Palestinians without hope," the head of Egyptian intelligence wrote to Weizman at the end of June. "We are very disappointed by Israel's replies to the U.S."

Weizman prowled the corridors of his office, angry and annoyed. "Sadat's visit to Jerusalem should be compared with the first man landing on the moon," he said to his associates. "But even the first man to step on the moon returned to earth afterward. The problem now is how to get everyone back to earth and to stop them from orbiting it."

At the end of the cabinet discussion of the American "questionnaire," Begin revealed to his friends with a sigh that had it not been for his illness he would have had the courage to suggest replying in the affirmative about the "final status," as Weizman had proposed.

Sadat followed the lengthy deliberations in the Israeli cabinet with amazement. This type of politics was alien to him. Occasionally he believed that these were nothing but

199

well-staged performances. But in one respect he no longer had any doubts. It was neither Weizman nor the Peace Now group which made the decisions. If he wanted to continue, he had to return to Begin and Dayan.

19 CASTLE DIPLOMACY

The beginning of the summer of 1978 did not presage any shift in the peace talks between Israel and Egypt. The negotiations were deadlocked. By this time the United States was more deeply involved in the peace process than ever. Interminable interchanges and innumerable clarifications were exchanged between Washington and Jerusalem. They all had the same object—to give birth to a declaration of principles which would pave the way for more intensive negotiations. But these communications did not bear fruit. A mutually agreeable formula for a declaration of principles could not be found. Israeli Foreign Minister Moshe Dayan suggested dropping the idea. Since he, like the other members of the cabinet, knew that the West Bank and Gaza were the main obstacles to peace, he proposed seeing if Israel and Egypt could reach agreement about the settlements there.

In early July 1978 the Egyptians came up with a surprise: they published their own plan for an Israeli withdrawal. They had rejected Prime Minister Begin's plan and he had asked the Egyptians on several occasions to offer a plan of their own. Finally, Sadat took up Begin's challenge. The Egyptian plan was based on the return of the

Gaza Strip to Egypt and the West Bank to Jordan. Naturally, Begin rejected the proposal. The Egyptian plan could not breathe new life into the dying peace initiative.

President Sadat of Egypt wanted to take a vacation and chose, as he had several times, Foschelle Castle near Salzburg, Austria. Weizman had requested a meeting with Sadat. Sadat's reply was delayed until mid-July, when he decided to invite Weizman to come to Austria. Gamassi was also to come.

The meeting between Sadat and Weizman took place July 13, 1978, at Foschelle Castle. Gamassi led Weizman to Sadat's room. After a while Sadat gestured to Gamassi to leave. Sadat began by referring to Israeli-Egyptian-U.S. talks scheduled for Leeds Castle in England.

Sadat said: "I wanted to meet you before our delegations leave for the talks in England. I very much fear that their discussions will not be successful. Therefore, it is important to create beforehand conditions that will allow the peace process to continue. However, that is not what I have to say to you. I have several points to make and I want you to be the one to hear them and convey them to your government. Only in this way can I clear my conscience."

The Egyptian president's face grew tense. He explained to Weizman that the negotiations had gone on for too long. Almost a year had passed since his visit to Jerusalem, and in October the mandate of the UN forces would end. He would have to decide whether to extend it or not.

All of a sudden he said, "If there is no change by October, I shall resign from my position."

Weizman was taken aback. "You will be making a mistake if you resign. The Egyptian nation needs you. The entire region needs you. You must not do it, because it will harm the peace process."

Sadat: "I know the Egyptian people will not agree to my resigning. But you must do something for me too, to keep the negotiations going. When I came to you in 1977 I was convinced that you would make some gesture in honor of my visit to Jerusalem. I was sure that you would say in the Knesset that you were ready to withdraw to the Al-'Arish—Ras Muhammad line immediately. What did you do? Nothing. I thought you were clever and brave. Where is the Israeli wisdom?"

Weizman: "Mr. President, I do not believe that a one-sided gesture is possible today, but I will convey what you have said to my prime minister."

Sadat: "I suggest that Israel announces it is handling Al-'Arish and Jabal Musa [Mount Sinai] to the Egyptians today. They should become Egyptian enclaves administered by us, even before the peace treaty is signed. We do not need a road. We will fly there. I wish to turn Al-'Arish into the town of peace. We will hold all the discussions there. We will invite other Arab leaders there. We'll ask King Haled, Assad, and King Hussein to come. They'll attend peace talks."

Weizman: "And what will you do with Jabal Musa?"

Sadat: "On Jabal Musa I want to build a mosque, a synagogue, and a church, immediately after receiving it from you. I want to go and pray at St. Catharine's at the end of the coming month of Ramadan . . ."

Sadat smiled and said, "I hope you won't shoot me."

Weizman said, "It's a good idea. But rather than my putting it to Begin, it would be better if you and he met. He is the man who should receive your request."

At this point Weizman decided to convey Begin's anger about the Peres meeting, which Weizman shared, although before leaving for Salzburg he too had spoken to Peres and Abba Eban. He said, "Mr. President, you have to understand the Israeli political system. Begin is the prime minister, Dayan is foreign minister, and Peres is leader of the opposition. A while ago he was minister of defense but today he is not in the government. You should know that people in Israel believe you want to cause disputes within Israel's leadership—that you mean to create a rift between the government and the people."

Sadat: "I have no such intention. I will be willing to meet Begin only when we sign the peace treaty. I am very sorry to hear that the prime minister feels bitterness toward me. I do not feel that way about him."

Weizman: "You should meet other Israeli leaders. You should get to know them and find out what's bothering them. I'll bring along our minister of agriculture, General Sharon, to our next meeting."

Sadat: "I'll put him in prison."

Weizman: "This is not just a matter of documents, but of faith between people."

The conversation continued for a long time. A trolley was wheeled in bearing a cup of tea for the Egyptian president and an enormous portion of strawberry ice cream for the Israeli minister of defense. Sadat sipped his tea. Weizman ate the pink ice cream with evident enjoyment.

Sadat kept repeating that the peace treaty had to be signed as soon as possible: "The agreement must include an obligation on your part to withdraw from the whole of Sinai, the West Bank, and Gaza," he said. "If you abolish military rule in the West Bank and Gaza I will agree that the withdrawal need not take place until security arrangements have been made."

Weizman: "And how can we resolve our argument on this delicate point? The security problem does not involve only Jordan, it applies to our entire eastern front. We also have to consider our internal security."

Sadat: "I accept that. We can establish a joint police force."

Weizman: "Will Hussein agree to that proposal?"

Sadat: "Undoubtedly. We will contribute policemen to a joint force; I think that Hussein will agree to that. He needs the help of the Saudis. My vice-president, Mubarak, went to talk to him about the plan. I am optimistic. He will come. I think that Assad will refuse. He is inextricably stuck in Lebanon. When he moved his forces into Lebanon I told him that would be the end of him."

Weizman: "And what happens if Hussein does not come?"

Sadat: "I will bear the responsibility for the West Bank and Gaza myself, but we will have to hold elections there. I will ask you to relinquish your right to a veto on a referendum. The PLO will also change. Arafat will be replaced, probably by Abu-Jihad."

Weizman: "You show too much concern for Hussein. In my opinion he has made three major mistakes. The first was when he attacked us in 1967, after we had warned him not to. The second was when he did not join the war in 1973. And the third was when he did not come to meet you in Jerusalem."

Sadat: "We will have to discuss your settlements in the

West Bank separately. The question of Jerusalem can be dealt with in that framework."

Weizman: "What is the connection between Jerusalem and the settlements?"

Sadat: "I agree with you that Jerusalem should not be divided again, but it will have to be run differently. It will be necessary to set up two municipalities, one Arab and one Jewish, over which there will be a joint council of the two nations. Our holy places will need a special arrangement. There we need Muslim Arab control, expressed clearly by a flag, for instance."

During the discussion the Israeli settlements in Sinai were mentioned. Weizman tried to dissuade Sadat from insisting that the settlements be completely uprooted. He suggested that arrangements about population and autonomy be made first in Gaza, before an agreement was signed about the West Bank. He proposed that the Gaza Strip be widened toward the Israeli town of Yamit, including it in the arrangement. He said that Israel would have to maintain at least one of its three military air bases in Sinai because of the military threat to Israel from the east.

Sadat: "You are an experienced soldier. Are you seriously afraid of the Saudis? They do not represent a threat to you."

Weizman noticed that Sadat had not reacted to his proposal about the Gaza Strip, preferring not to discuss it at the meeting.

Sadat: "As for the military airfields, I will let you hold on to them for two years. After that we will make them civilian airfields. I will not put a division in Sinai, perhaps only a brigade."

The two men talked about permitting a UN emergency force in Sinai. Sadat said he was prepared to discuss any presence, but he did not conceal his preference for the Americans. "Carter has not disappointed me yet," he said. "We need the Americans." He leaned toward Weizman. "Without America we will not be able to rehabilitate Egypt. We both need them. They will finance the peace."

Sadat switched to describing the dangers from the USSR. He warned the Israeli defense minister against Moscow's subversiveness. The Russians had managed to gain influence in the horn of Africa, South Yemen, and Afghanistan. Sadat mentioned the aid the Russians had given Colonel Qaddafi if Libya so that he could work for a coup d'etat in Egypt. "We know of all their moves," he said. "We will foil them, as we recently foiled a plot by officers who had received financial help from Libya."

Sadat grew more and more enthusiastic. Toward the end he was already talking about the rosy future and the good relations which would exist between Egypt and Israel.

"Together with you," he said, "we will lay a large pipeline from the Nile which will irrigate the Sinai and the Negev. Egypt will sell oil to Israel and will receive scientific advice from it."

It was clear that his country's economic situation grieved Sadat more than anything else. He explained to Weizman how sorely Egypt needed peace, if only for financial reasons. "Look what has happened to Egypt, compared to the other Arab countries," he said. "Until oil became central in the world economy Egypt was the richest Arab land, but today it is the poorest."

The dialogue continued for three hours. Soon after Weizman returned to his hotel room a bellboy delivered a huge ice-cream cake, which had been sent by Jihan, Sadat's wife, who had noticed Weizman's love of ice cream. Weizman phoned her room and thanked her.

On returning to Israel, Weizman called his aides to a meeting. He instructed them to let nothing leak out about Sadat's requests, particularly about Al-'Arish and St. Catherine's. He reported Sadat's requests to Begin and recommended responding positively, possibly in return for a similar gesture by Egypt such as allowing equipment to be brought to Israel in Israeli ships through the Suez Canal. "It is better to hold the talks at Al-'Arish than in Washington or Europe," Weizman told Begin. Weizman maintained there was no need for an intermediary; Israel and Egypt could negotiate directly.

Two or three days later the information about Sadat's requests for a gesture was leaked to the press. Weizman was enraged. Almost nothing of his previous conversations with Sadat had leaked out and Sadat had noted this several times. Weizman assumed the information had been deliberately leaked in order to harm him and reduce Sadat's esteem for him.

Egypt expressed its outrage at the leak through the Israeli military mission: "President Sadat is disappointed that you did not keep your promise about maintaining the secrecy of the talks." Weizman cabled his apologies to Sadat.

The leak also made it necessary for Israel to respond officially. Begin was asked to comment on Sadat's request for a gesture involving Al-'Arish and St. Catherine's. "One doesn't get something for nothing!" he said angrily. "When the talks start again we'll hear the proposals and then we'll react." This meant only one thing—a public rejection of Sadat's proposal.

Begin did not stop at that. He sent a message to the Presidential Palace in Cairo, making it clear that he had been obliged to reject as one-sided the proposal that he make a gesture, but suggesting that talks be resumed and that direct negotiations get going again. He also suggested two places for them to meet, Haifa and Alexandria, leaving it to Sadat to name any other place for a meeting.

Sadat thought that the Israelis had intentionally leaked his request for a gesture in order to be able to publish Begin's refusal. Somehow the content of Begin's message reached him via the American embassy before the head of the Israeli military mission in Cairo could deliver it. Sadat assumed that the Israelis wanted to embarrass him.

Begin's message was handed to head of Egyptian intelligence General Shaukat and returned on the same day. Shaukat said to the head of the mission, Colonel Jacob Heikal, "The message involves political matters, with which I am not empowered to deal." Shaukat suggested that the message be transmitted to Sadat through the American embassy.

Jerusalem saw that President Sadat had been insulted, but the proposal to transmit the message by means of the Americans took even Begin by surprise. For the first time, Cairo had made it clear that it was no longer interested in direct contact with Israel. Egypt was leaving it to the Americans to act as intermediaries. It was surmised that by returning the message the Egyptians wanted to hint to Israel that the role of the Israeli military mission in Cairo was coming to an end.

The atmosphere in Jerusalem, as in Cairo, was grim. Israeli voices were heard calling for Begin to resign or conduct the peace negotiations more vigorously. Serious criticisms were leveled by members of his cabinet. The opposition Labor party was in good spirits after the publication of the Vienna document and the meeting of opposition leader Shimon Peres with Sadat. The party's tone became sharper, unsettling Begin. In the Knesset cafeteria Begin used coarse language in referring to Peres. He publicly revealed information Peres had disclosed to him in confidence. Begin was irate about the conversation between Sadat and Peres and declared that he would not allow it to happen again. But the prime minister's popularity was dropping. His almost 80 percent support immediately after Sadat's visit to Israel had fallen by the summer of 1978 to a bare 50 percent.

In this heavy atmosphere Foreign Minister Moshe Dayan went to the Leeds Castle conference in England in July 1978. Also participating were Egyptian Foreign Minister Muhammad Ibrahim Kamel and U.S. Secretary of State Cyrus Vance, who repeatedly declared that he was there solely to chair the meetings. Peres and Weizman, who had met Sadat in Salzburg, made it clear to Dayan that the conference had little chance to succeed and that Sadat had agreed to it solely to be polite to President Carter.

Dayan sought some way to save the day, to avoid a deadlock and keep Israel from being blamed for any failure. At a cocktail party for the three delegations, Dayan, Kamel, and Vance were huddled together in a corner. Later Dayan was obviously encouraged. He summoned his aides and said, "In spite of everything, maybe things will work out!"

Dayan spent the night at Leeds Castle trying to work out a formula with his aides. The principal points were rejection of a withdrawal to the 1967 borders and of Arab sovereignty over the West Bank and Gaza; readiness to discuss concrete proposals for a peace treaty based on a territorial compromise; and readiness to discuss the question of sovereignty over the West Bank and Gaza in another five years, if the administrative autonomy proposal by Israel was accepted. Dayan thought this formula would be acceptable to the American and Egyptian delegations to the conference, since the West Bank was the main obstacle on the road to peace.

Late at night Vance knocked at the door of Dayan's room. Dayan debated with himself for a moment whether to reveal his new formula to Vance. In the end he decided to describe it in general terms. At midnight, Dayan phoned Yehiel Kadishai, the prime minister's bureau chief. Kadishai asked for Begin's approval of the formula and got it.

The plenary session of the Leeds Castle conference began next morning, with Vance in the chair. Dayan outlined how the parties' attitudes had developed, detailing the problems still to be solved. Israeli Attorney General Barak spoke for forty minutes. Kamel did not say much. Osama al-Baz spoke at length, bitingly. When he demanded that autonomy begin in Gaza if there were difficulties about the West Bank, he said, "Don't worry! They'll manage! They're like the Jews!"

The Egyptian proposal resembled the withdrawal plan published by the Egyptian Foreign Ministry at the beginning of that month (July 1978). It maintained that an overall agreement had to be reached, the central problem being that of the Palestinians. Israel had to agree to the principle of a general withdrawal from the West Bank; if it declared readiness to withdraw, Jordan would join the negotiations later. After Jordan the Palestinians (the Egyptians did not mention the PLO) would join too, and eventually Syria. The Egyptian plan demanded that, one month after negotiations among Egypt, Jordan, and Israel began, Israel cancel the military administration and begin preparations to withdraw. Then elections for autonomy would be held, supervised by a UN representative.

"But does Egypt accept in principle that there will be no independent Palestinian state?" Dayan asked.

Ibrahim Kamel replied, "The Palestinians have the right to an independent state, but in view of the circumstances Egypt is prepared to relinquish this idea. Instead we insist that a Palestinian entity be established, connected with Jordan." The Egyptian representative also insisted that the Palestinians be represented not only by present residents of the West Bank and the Gaza Strip but also by people who might move there in the future.

Cyrus Vance asked, "Would Israel be prepared to commit itself to a withdrawal if it received all the security guarantees, including a defense pact?"

"Israel is not prepared to commit itself to withdrawing from the West Bank and the Gaza Strip," Dayan replied.

"Is there any chance of considering the possibility of establishing a federation or confederation of Jordan, the West Bank, and Gaza?" Vance persisted.

"Egypt does not reject that possibility," Ibrahim Kamel said.

"We reject that proposal," Dayan stated.

Those attending the plenary session of the Leeds Castle conference realized that the hands of the clock had been put back. The negotiations were at square one, where they had been before Sadat's visit to Jerusalem. The Egyptians demanded the removal of Israeli settlements in the West Bank and the Gaza Strip. They did not agree to a single settler remaining there, let alone soldiers. These demands had not been raised by Sadat at any meeting in Jerusalem and even contradicted some of the things he had said.

Vance's question about setting up a federation or confederation of the West Bank, Gaza, and Jordan set alarm bells ringing for the Israeli delegation. The American administration had thought up this scheme and Vance's question was intended to introduce it to both sides.

Dayan wanted to know how far, if at all, the Egyptians were prepared to go toward a territorial compromise in the West Bank. Kamel's reply was unequivocal: "We completely reject the demand for a territorial compromise," he said. "Israel must withdraw to the 1949 borders. It will be a full withdrawal. We are prepared to consider only slight alterations to the frontiers. To make it clear exactly what we mean, let's say that the adjustment could be made in a village to prevent it from being split by the border or to give land back to a villager whose house is on the other side of the border."

Dayan asked, "How do you envisage the security arrangements in the West Bank and Gaza, in addition to the presence of UN forces?"

"Egypt is prepared for parts of the West Bank and the Gaza Strip to be demilitarized," Kamel said, "but we insist that similar areas in Israel be demilitarized too. Egypt is willing to limit the size of Arab forces in the West Bank."

This brought the Israeli delegation back to earth. The Egyptians wanted additional Arab forces in the West Bank and Gaza, apart from the UN forces. Obviously this meant a Palestinian army on the West Bank and in Gaza. Israel could not agree to this.

The Egyptians agreed to the establishment of a warning lapse. They knew that an Egyptian attempt to plant Arab forces on the West Bank and in Gaza would bring the conference to a halt. They decided to intervene. "The United States does not agree that forces of a Palestinian army should be in the West Bank and Gaza," Vance said, "but we would accept a Palestinian police force."

The Americans feared that the talks were about to col-station, like those in Sinai, in the West Bank and Gaza. They would be willing to accept supervision of a third party, after the withdrawal, to ensure free passage in the Tiran Strait. The third party could be a UN or American force. The American delegates did not react to this proposal for the use of American troops.

The gap between the two sides was immense. Vance realized almost immediately that the conference would fail. When the sides discussed the status of Jerusalem and the refugees the crisis reached a head.

Kamel said, "Egypt demands complete Israeli withdrawal from the eastern, Arab city, but agrees that this withdrawal need not lead to redivision of the city. The holy places will be given a special status."

"We agree only about the holy places," Vance said.

Kamel's stance about the refugees was even more rigid. "All the refugees have the right to return to their homes," he said, "including the refugees of the 1948 war. They may return to their former houses, or receive compensation if they do not wish to return. Incidentally, UN Resolution 194, on the return of refugees, was initiated by the Americans."

Dayan said, "We agreed that refugees of 1967 would be allowed to return, and that their number would be determined by a joint committee."

That was the end. Because there was no means of bridging the gap Dayan decided to stop the game in his own way. "If that is your stand on every issue," he said in acrid tones, "if your approach is so extreme and so demanding, wouldn't Israel be right to retract its previous proposal regarding a general withdrawal from Sinai?"

There was silence in the conference hall. The Egyptians and the Americans were astonished that the Israeli delegate had raised the possibility of going back to square one. At first there was no reaction. After they had recovered from the shock, the Americans and the Egyptians said, "At this conference only the West Bank and the Gaza Strip are being discussed, not Sinai."

The American Secretary of State was also astounded by the Egyptian shift. On the last day of the conference Vance tried to avoid a meeting of the full delegations, fearing that the gap would be further widened. He held separate talks with Dayan and Kamel, hoping to reach agreement on some one point at least. Toward noon he realized that Kamel was not prepared to moderate the tough stand he had taken. This being so, Vance asked both sides for permission to announce that the talks would continue. Begin agreed immediately, phoning his approval to Dayan. Kamel could not give Vance an answer: Sadat was in Khartoum and Kamel did not manage to contact him. Vance suggested that he send a message via the American embassy at Khartoum, but Kamel was evasive.

Vance called a press conference and announced that the talks would continue. Dayan's aides prepared TV crews in the corner of the garden at Leeds Castle. The moment Dayan's spokesman, Naftali Lavie, heard from the security men by radio that Vance had announced that the talks would continue, the Israeli foreign minister appeared before the cameras, stating that Israel was prepared to continue the talks, "even on an aircraft carrier." Lavie also ran to the hall, stopped the reporters who were leaving after Vance's announcement, and informed them of Dayan's readiness to accept the American suggestion to continue the talks. Kamel could not say anything. When he returned to London he said only that Egypt was prepared to continue the talks, but shortly afterward Egyptian embassy officials phoned the newsmen and amended Kamel's announcement, saying, "We're still waiting for instructions from Cairo."

The crisis was one of the most serious in the negotiations between Israel and Egypt. Egypt fumed. The U.S. seethed. Israel was depressed. Many of its leaders knew that Israel would be blamed for the failure of the Leeds Castle conference and for total collapse of the peace talks. The process which had begun in November 1977 with Sadat's visit to Jerusalem seemed to have come to an end, helped by the difficulties a rift with the Arab world had created for Sadat.

Colonel Jacob Heikal was summoned to the phone from the tennis court at the Jan-Klis estate, south of Alexandria. Dripping with sweat after spending an hour running after the white ball, the head of the Israeli military mission to Egypt listened to General Shaukat, chief of Egyptian military intelligence. There was a note of sadness in his voice. "I'm very sorry . . . I'm sorry I cannot say this to you in person . . . I will come to take my leave of you tomorrow . . ."

That night Weizman received a message from Gamassi: "I regret to inform you that the Egyptian national security council decided today that there is no further need for the Israeli military mission to remain in Egypt. We have taken steps for its return to Israel." Station Zehava in Egypt was closed down.

Before the doors of the Egyptian Boeing plane were closed on the Israeli military mission, Heikal gave Shaukat a medal coined to mark President Sadat's visit to Israel and the book *My Peace*, written and drawn by Jewish and Arab children.

"What a shame," Shaukat said, surprised by the Israeli gift. "I have not brought any souvenir for you or your children."

"Never mind," Heikal said. "You owe me one, and I'm sure one day I'll get it from you."

20 THE CAMP DAVID SPIRIT

In the U.S. as well as in Israel, there was a growing suspicion that toward October 1978, when the mandate of the UN Emergency Force would end, Egyptian President Anwar al-Sadat would be pressured into demonstrative military action. In Egypt there were voices, still weak, calling for a rethinking of Sadat's initiative.

Jimmy Carter felt that only a dramatic move would rescue the initiative. He was encouraged by reports from his Tel Aviv embassy that after the Leeds conference, Israeli Foreign Minister Moshe Dayan, who throughout the negotiations had not concealed his misgivings, had undergone a reversal. He still maintained that the Egyptians were rigid, but he believed that they honestly wished for an agreement. Following his meetings with Sadat, Israeli Defense Minister Ezer Weizman had come away with the same impression.

The idea of a summit meeting was born in the White House. On the basis of Secretary of State Cyrus Vance's reports, President Carter decided to convene the meeting "in order to examine thoroughly, without a time limit, all the possibilities for bringing peace to the Middle East."

Some people at the White House cautioned the

president against his decision. The stakes were too high. The president was placing all his prestige on a single card. His popularity in the U.S. was at a low point. Israeli public opinion indicated disappointment with Carter. Failure of a conference which he initiated could damage his chances of being elected to a second term.

The State Department was not involved in the White House decision. When news of the summit reached the desks of senior officials there, it was not cheered—quite the contrary. State Department officials contended that the chances for success were meager. They warned the White House that in such a conference a frontal clash between Israel and Egypt, and between one or both of the countries and the U.S., was inevitable. The risk of failure was greater than the chance of success.

The decision had already been made, however, and Vance left for the Middle East in early August. He touched down in Jerusalem and Cairo and delivered notes to Begin and Sadat written in Carter's own hand and sealed with red wax. The note to Israeli Prime Minister Begin urged secrecy. Begin read the note in Vance's presence and replied immediately: "I accept the invitation without regard to what President Sadat's reply will be." Begin kept his counsel for three days, saying nothing even to his most intimate associates. Vance proceeded to Cairo. Only after the Egyptian president consented was the announcement made.

Sadat's situation appeared as bad as could be. Sudan was the only Arab country to support him openly. His agreement to participate in the summit intensified the attacks on him and his isolation in the Arab world.

Begin was in a rather difficult position too. The Peace Now movement, which blamed the prime minister's inflexibility for the impasse in the peace initiative, raised its voice higher and gained adherents daily. A number of Knesset members who had supported Begin in his coalition announced their intention of moving to the opposition benches.

The summit was to take place at Camp David, the presidential retreat in the heart of the Catoctin Mountains of Maryland, some 115 kilometers from Washington, D.C. Constructed during World War II, it is surrounded by an electrified fence and electronic security devices. The camp has luxurious two- and three-room cabins named for local tree species, each cabin provided with a well-stocked refrigerator and larder. Today the camp has sports facilities, a garage and heliport, and even small electric carts for local transportation. President Franklin D. Roosevelt made frequent use of the 36-square-kilometer wooded site, which in his day was called Shangri-la after the Tibetan paradise on earth in James Hilton's novel *Lost Horizon*. During the war the mountain retreat hosted many famous leaders from abroad, among them Winston Churchill, for whom a special bathtub was installed.

Presidents Truman and Kennedy did not use Camp David, but Eisenhower and Nixon were frequent visitors. Eisenhower changed its name, calling it Camp David after his grandson. There, in 1959, Ike met with Soviet Premier Nikita Khrushchev and this conciliatory meeting inspired the "Camp David spirit" that lessened the tension between the superpowers for a time.

Jerusalem came increasingly to feel that the Egyptians would do their utmost to break up the conference and put the blame on Israel. There was well-founded suspicion that the Egyptian Foreign Ministry was designing proposals that Israel would have no choice but to reject. Failure of the talks would lead to a serious breach between the U.S. and Israel, the Israelis thought. The U.S. president would mobilize American public opinion against Israel. Preparations for a change were already discernible, even within the Jewish community. "At Camp David Egypt will supply Israel with a very long rope," said Boutros Ghali, "and with that rope she can hang herself." Ghali's statement was reported to Begin in Jerusalem.

Begin was prepared to accept the assessments of his experts that Sadat meant to break up the Camp David talks. Consequently, he felt that the primary aim of the conference should be winning over the Americans. He would direct his major efforts during the talks to persuading America of the justice of the Israeli position and the positiveness of the Israeli approach, and to averting a breach between Israel and the U.S., which could be catastrophic. He instructed his aides to prepare working papers accordingly.

Dayan disagreed with the prime minister. He believed the main subject at Camp David would be the future of the West Bank. The only solution he could foresee involved strengthening the Jordanian role. An autonomy plan had to be constructed so as to leave room for the Jordanians—whether in the near or distant future—even though Hussein had shown no signs of joining the negotiations.

Weizman disagreed with both Begin and Dayan. He was convinced that the conference could succeed only if Jordan was not involved. Based on his knowledge of Begin's opinions, he believed that Begin could never accede to Hussein's demands, and the chances of a settlement with Egypt would fall. Weizman said the Americans should be urged to exclude Hussein from the negotiations, even if only for the moment. His advice was to leave the matter of the West Bank vague and open for discussion.

The Israeli committee set up to prepare the ground for the conference was chaired by Eliahu Ben-Elissar and included Avraham Tamir. It was charged with preparing Israeli positions and maneuvering possibilities during the negotiations. Israel was aware that Washington might try to link a Sinai solution with decisions on the West Bank and Gaza, and Jordan. The committee knew that the U.S. would favor deciding the future of the West Bank and Gaza within the five-year autonomy period proposed by Israel and accepted in principle in June. Thus the West Bank had to be the major topic.

The three Israelis who were to negotiate at Camp David were in agreement on the chief item on the agenda. Begin was adamant about the settlements on the West Bank and the military airfields in Sinai. He believed that the Rafa salient settlements must never be given up. Dayan mostly agreed with Begin, but did not make his views public. Having fathered the idea of developing the city of Yamit in the Rafa salient, he had no inclination to give up the area. Weizman believed that the negotiations should aim for border changes that would leave at least some of the Rafa settlements in Israeli hands. He would insist on the continued operation of one airfield in Sinai, rather than the three previously demanded. Unlike his ministerial colleagues, Weizman was prepared to agree with the Egyptians and Americans on the number of settlers who would be allowed to join existing settlements on the West Bank during the five-year period following the signing of the treaty. He was also prepared to agree to freezing the number of Israeli settlements on the West Bank, enlarging six of them and turning them into small towns. Weizman made considerable use of think tanks and working papers provided by the general staff and the Ministry of Defense.

All three parties made very detailed preparations for the conference. Among other things, the delegations would bring to Camp David their own communications equipment and devices designed to prevent the monitoring or bugging of discussions and consultations, and small booths where their members could consult without fear of being overheard.

To prevent leaks, President Carter decided that participants would not be allowed to leave the camp. He believed that publicity during the discussions would run the peace talks aground. Even before the leaders left their countries, Carter asked Begin and Sadat not to allow their people out of Camp David—even on rest days—to avoid leaks. The parties agreed that Press Secretary Jody Powell would serve as spokesman for all three parties, who would issue a joint, coordinated statement.

Begin tried to reduce the tension that had accumulated on the eve of the talks. A believer in the rules of public drama, he made it his business to appear frequently before TV cameras, joking, warning, dispelling the trepidation about the coming meeting. He felt that the U.S. and Egypt had at least as much reason for concern as Israel. "What is Sadat's alternative—war? Will he drop the Americans and return to the Soviets? Who will save him—Assad, Brezhnev, Qaddafi?" Begin spoke of how Sadat had not achieved his goals in two wars, and in the Yom Kippur War had had to appeal to the U.S. to rescue the encircled Egyptian Third Army and persuade Israel to remove its forces from Egyptian soil. Failure of the Camp David talks, he felt, would also harm the status and national interests of the U.S.

Moshe Dayan also played his part in the psychological warfare: "What can the Egyptians do to us? If the Camp David conference fails, we will stay in Sinai and continue pumping oil." Still, the foreign minister left an opening. "We will go to Camp David," he said, "prepared to search for ways, for meeting points between us and the other party, but without losing sight of our own major points."

The Israelis were especially concerned about Sadat's inconsistency. A comparison of Sadat's position during his talks with Weizman and the position presented by Kamel at Leeds Castle justified the pessimism of the Israeli preparatory discussions. In his talks with Weizman, Sadat had expressed willingness to consider maintaining the Israeli settlements in Sinai beyond the transition period, without Israeli forces to defend them. At Leeds, however, the Egyptian stand was adamant: withdrawal had to be total; they would not countenance a single Israeli soldier on the West Bank or in Gaza. In the talks with Weizman, Sadat consented to continued Jewish settlement projects on the West Bank or on private land purchased from Arab owners. At Leeds, his foreign minister demanded that all settlements be removed. In his talks with Weizman, Sadat said that no Palestinian state was to be established, and that the PLO should be kept out of the neogtiations. At Leeds, Kamel asserted the necessity for self-determination and an independent state for the Palestinians. In the talks with Weizman, Sadat agreed to an Israeli veto on the entry of refugees from outside the country. At Leeds, there was no hint of a possible veto. Kamel, in the name of the president of Egypt, stated that all the refugees, including those of the 1948 war, were fully entitled to return to their former places of residence, including the state of Israel. In his talks with Weizman, Sadat said he was willing to discuss border adjustments on the West Bank. At Leeds the Egyptian position was unequivocal: "No territorial compromise."

Just before his helicopter left the south lawn of the White House for Camp David, Jimmy Carter said: "The chances of complete success are very small. Four wars did not lead to peace in that stormy region of the world, and there is no cause for undue optimism—but neither is there any reason for despair."

A red carpet awaited Begin and Sadat as each arrived at Andrews Air Force Base near Washington, on September 5. The Americans were careful to prepare identical ceremonies, giving no cause for complaint. As a result of Begin's predilection for ceremony, the Israelis were especially sensitive to protocol. Sadat arrived first and was received at the Camp David heliport by President Carter. Israeli diplomats watched the reception of the Egyptian president on television.

"Look, look how enthusiastically Carter is embracing Sadat," one Israeli diplomat broke out. To which Dan Patir, Begin's press consultant, retorted: "When it comes to hugging, you can count on Begin."

The Israelis monitored the greetings between the American and Egyptian presidents. They noted that the two had hugged each other more than once. They were also sensitive to the number of cannon salvos. As a president, Sadat received twenty-one, but Begin, as a prime minister, would receive only nineteen.

Begin did not disappoint his viewers. He hugged Carter once, and then again, and scattered smiles about despite the serious nature of the meeting. The Israeli diplomats noticed that the prime minister did not content himself with kissing Rosalynn Carter's cheek. In the Polish manner, he also kissed her hand.

From the first moment Carter sought to relieve the tension. "What do you say we finish everything tomorrow," the president said, flashing his famous white teeth. "Then we'll have the rest of the week to enjoy ourselves."

Begin did not smile. He introduced the team that accompanied him. Mrs. Carter expressed surprise that Begin had come alone (his wife had gone to Canada to attend a wedding).

"Aliza Begin will get here tomorrow," Ezer Weizman told her. "And then she'll be Aliza in Wonderland."

The Carters escorted the Israeli prime minister to his cabin. In a fifteen-minute talk the president told Begin of the arrangements for the meetings. He told him and the members of the delegation that life at Camp David would not be governed by protocol. He asked not to be treated like the president of a great power, and did not wish that any schedules be set. "It will be like a resort," he said.

Earlier, when Carter had escorted Sadat to his cabin, the Egyptian president had been astonished at the greenery and abundant vegetation. During his visit to Camp David in February 1978, the trees and lawns had been covered with snow. Because of the cold, Sadat had been unable to take his daily walk.

At the threshold of the cabin, Carter told Sadat: "This

evening I shall meet with Mr. Begin. He rested enough in New York before coming here, and you need rest. Go to sleep. We shall meet tomorrow morning."

The White House spared no effort to keep the guests comfortable. Waiters served sandwiches and drinks around the clock. In one of the cabins, movies were shown without a break. The guests were asked not to wear ties: dress was to be informal. The front of each cabin had a plate showing the names of its tenants, and small flags of their country. Sadat was in one cabin with a valet and cook. Begin requested that two of his aides, Kadishai and Poran, be housed nearby.

Begin turned in for a nap. He asked to be awakened at 6:30 p.m., half an hour before the first consultations of the Israeli team. The first meeting between Begin and Carter was to take place at 8:30 that evening.

Begin was still napping when Jody Powell, Dan Patir, and Osama al-Baz met. Al-Baz arrived with a bunch of papers which turned out to be Sadat's opening speech for the first session the next day.

Jody Powell spoke first. "The president's wife, Rosalynn, suggested to her husband that the heads of the delegations ask the faithful of the three religions to pray for the success of the peace conference." Al-Baz agreed immediately to the wording proposed by Rosalynn Carter.

Dan Patir would not undertake to make such a decision without the prime minister's permission. When Begin awoke from his nap, the text of Mrs. Carter's prayer was set before him. Where the text had, "The Holy Land is the cradle of the three religions," he drew a line. "With all due respect," he said, "the land of Israel is the cradle of Judaism and Christianity, but not of Islam. The cradle of Islam is Saudi Arabia."

He corrected the text to read, "The Middle East, the cradle of civilization and of the three great religions, has not enjoyed the blessings of peace."

Where the original text had "Four wars have afflicted the Middle East," he argued insistently that the region had suffered more than four. Eventually he agreed to the wording, "after four wars . . ."

Later, when Begin told the members of his delegation of the publication of Mrs. Carter's text, Dayan quipped:

"You'll have to take off your hat to the Christians, remove the Muslims' shoes, and put a skullcap on yourself."

But it was no time for jokes. It was almost time for Begin to meet Carter for the initial working session.

Carter told Begin: "Mr. Prime Minister, we must come out of this conference with an agreement. There is a risk in convening a conference like this because, in case of failure, there's not much chance of going on. I want to tell you that the achievement of a peace agreement between Israel and Egypt is more important to me even than my political chances."

Carter endeavored to flatter his guest, in order to generate a pleasant atmosphere. "I know the world has not properly appreciated your efforts and contribution to peace, Mr. Prime Minister," he said.

After outlining the meetings scheduled for the next day, among them a joint meeting at three in the afternoon, Carter addressed himself directly to the problems. He spoke cordially and genially as though there were no bitter residue between them.

"Sadat insists," Carter said, "that Israel accept the principle that no land be taken by force."

Begin responded: "Security Council Resolution 242 does not say that. It says that land is not to be taken by war. Mr. President, the difference is significant. There are defensive wars, too. It's not so simple." Begin was aware that Carter's definition could be used by the Arabs as justification for starting war for the recovery of lost territory.

"I figure that the Egyptians are now likely to agree on three subjects," Carter continued. "That Israel should withdraw to the international border in Sinai; that no independent Palestinian state should be established; and that the Israeli defense forces should remain on the West Bank in a Gaza even after the five years set for the autonomy plan."

"We shall propose to Egypt," Begin responded, "to leave open the question of sovereignty in Judea and Samaria [the West Bank], and Gaza. We will not be prepared to accept any other sovereignty."

"We should like to discuss determination of the ultimate status of these territories even before the end of the five-year period," Carter said.

"Although I believe with all my heart that that land belongs to the Jewish people—not to the Egyptians or the Jordanians—we will leave the question of sovereignty open," Begin replied.

Carter noticed that Begin made no mention of the Palestinians, but ignored it. Begin went on dramatically: "Some people ridicule the Bible. But not you, Mr. President. And not I."

Carter did not react to this opening pronouncement, which was in fact the first obstacle. He moved on to another sensitive subject that had angered him more than once in recent months. He knew the next moment would be a difficult one.

He said: "The United States expects Israel to put an end to the settlements in the occupied territories. Such operations can only disrupt the peace process and spoil the atmosphere."

Begin replied forcefully: "We cannot accept that! We agree to stop the settlements in Sinai, but Judea and Samaria is an entirely different question. It is our absolute right."

The discussion slid into a difference of opinion. When Carter touched on the Lebanese civil war, Begin told of the considerable aid Israel had supplied to the Christian forces in southern Lebanon. He noted the moral aspect of this aid to a Christian community whose sons had been slaughtered by Syrian and Palestinian forces.

At first Carter did not relate to Begin's report. He ignored the stories of aid. He told Begin he was considering appealing to Syria to end its involvement in the battles within Lebanon, and then suddenly said: "I demand that Israel should not supply the Christians with tanks, with any heavy military equipment. That could complicate the war." Begin was astonished. Until that moment he had been convinced beyond all doubt that the Israeli involvement merited praise, not remonstrance. He did not react.

From Lebanon the conversation veered to Sinai. Begin raised the possibility that one of the three Israeli airfields in Sinai should be turned over to the U.S. Air Force. He was amazed at Carter's reply, which showed for the first time that the committee of the armed forces chiefs of staff had already discussed the possibility.

"If there is an agreement between Israel and Egypt," Carter said, "and both parties consent, only then will the chiefs of staff propose that the United States set up a training base in Sinai." Carter did not sound enthusiastic about the idea. He stressed that it was not, and would not be, on the initiative of the U.S. The matter depended entirely on Israel and Egypt. The president's point accorded with Begin's conception. In the preparatory session before leaving for his talk with Carter, Begin had told the Israeli delegation that he intended to offer the United States facilities at Haifa port for the Sixth Fleet. Now, in view of Carter's statement about American bases in Sinai, Begin did not bring up the matter of port facilities for the U.S. Navy.

The conversation concluded with a survey of the Iranian situation. Carter expressed great concern about happenings in Teheran. Begin pounced on the subject as though he had discovered a treasure. He pointed out the dangers inherent in Soviet expansion in the Middle East. His exposition found an eager listener.

The darkness of the first night at Camp David enveloped the three delegations. The conference discussions had not yet begun, but the lights glowed late into the night in many of the cabins as the teams gathered for consultation before the first working day. Begin strolled among the trees of Camp David sunk in thought and enjoying the silence. "What a paradise on earth," he thought.

No one at Camp David got much sleep that night. President Carter awoke at five, as he had ever since serving in the navy. Begin awoke at about the same time, a habit he acquired in his days in the underground. Sadat arose at eight, and immediately set out for an hour-long four-kilometer walk. His doctors' advice was to walk quickly and perspire.

In the morning the U.S. secretary of state and ministers from Egypt and Israel met to determine working procedures. By ten o'clock, Sadat was settled comfortably in Carter's cabin.

"I suggest we do not confine ourselves to a meeting of heads of delegations only," Carter began. "I suggest, for instance, that you see Moshe Dayan as well. It is my experience that he has particularly distinguished himself with proposals that have contributed to extrication from complicated situations. He is a creative thinker."

Almost from the first moment of the peace initiative,

Sadat had displayed some aversion to Dayan. Despite Weizman's urging, he had refused to meet the Israeli foreign minister. But that morning in Carter's cabin he said that he had no objection to such a meeting.

"Before I came here," Sadat said, "they thought I was coming to Camp David to discuss a declaration of principles or to announce a declaration on a comprehensive solution. I told my national security council that we have passed that stage. It is not logical to meet on such a high level in order to discuss a declaration of principles, and then have everyone return to his own country. That was the point at issue when the joint committee met in Ismailia last December. We cannot avoid going into the content of the settlement, the framework of the overall settlement."

"Have you prepared a framework for the overall settlement?" Carter asked.

"Yes."

"For my part," Carter said, "I haven't prepared a thing. As I promised you, I insist on functioning as a full partner, and if there is need of American intervention, I will prepare proposals and present them."

"My program is ready," Sadat said.

The Egyptian president's reply fired Carter's imagination. Sadat had hit the bull's-eye by adapting to Carter's desire to leave the woods of Camp David with a great accomplishment—the framework of a peace treaty. The conversation was pleasant. They discussed Sadat's favorite subject: the danger of Soviet expansion in the Middle East and the need to avert it. On this subject Sadat always found willing ears among the Americans.

As noon approached, the tension at Camp David grew. The meeting between Carter, Sadat, and Begin was set for 3:00 p.m. The two leaders had not met since the conference in Ismailia in December 1977, and the president of Egypt had expressed himself in strong words about the prime minister of Israel. Furthermore, the Egyptian communications media had been attacking Begin incessantly. There was anxiety in the three delegations about the moment the two leaders would meet face to face.

Before the meeting with Begin, Sadat went out for a walk in one of the groves. He was wearing a blue sweat suit and carrying a golf club. At exactly the same time Begin set out for a stroll. Just as Sadat was about to turn off

the main path and head back to his cabin, he ran into Begin and his companions.

Begin dispelled the momentary consternation. "How are you, Mr. President?" he said, shaking hands with Sadat. "You are looking well. I hope you are feeling well, too."

"You are looking well, too, Mr. Prime Minister," Sadat replied.

The crowd on the path attracted the attention of Ezer Weizman, who was riding a bicycle nearby. He turned toward the group, calling for them to clear the way for him. Only when he was very close did he see that Sadat and Begin had met. He discarded the bicycle and hurried over. Sadat waved his hand. "Hello, friend!" he cried, and embraced Weizman. The two kissed.

While Sadat was telling Begin, "We shall meet this afternoon at three," Tuhami was telling Weizman, "I suggest you call on President Sadat at two."

Weizman reported the invitation to Begin and received permission to meet with the Egyptian president before the three-way Carter-Begin-Sadat meeting. The Israeli delegation was aware that this was the third time Sadat was meeting for preliminary discussions with Weizman before meeting the Israelis. It had happened at Ismailia and it had happened at Leeds.

At his cabin Begin found Carter's appointments secretary, Phillip J. Wise, Jr., waiting for him. "The president would like you to come to his cabin a few minutes before the three-way meeting. He would like to speak to you alone." Begin realized that something had happened during the Carter-Sadat meeting in the morning. He did not know what to expect.

In the meantime Weizman went to Sadat's cabin. Sadat was praying and Weizman waited patiently until he had finished. Then he asked whether Sadat had received the telegram sent after the last meeting in Salzburg, in which he apologized for the leak to the press in connection with Sadat's request for an Israeli "gesture" at Al-'Arish and Jabal Musa.

"Your personal attacks on Begin made things difficult," Weizman said. "You offended him."

"I had absolutely no intention of doing so," Sadat answered. "If I offended Mr. Begin, I apologize. You must know that for me respect of a person is primary and respect for my fellow man is above everything. I, for example, never smoked in my father's presence."

"I suggest that you also meet Moshe Dayan for a talk," Weizman offered.

"It's interesting that Carter also suggested that to me. I have no objection. I'll meet with him here, at Camp David."

The conversation also touched on global matters. Sadat surveyed Soviet infiltration in the Middle East and voiced his concern. "That madman Qaddafi," he said, "has Russians, Cubans, and East Germans. I'm worried about that."

The talk turned to recent events in Iran. The situation there was upsetting to Sadat. He felt that the West had not reacted properly. He praised French President Valéry Giscard d'Estaing, who had dispatched planes, soldiers, and equipment to Chad, while "the Americans did not come to their friends' aid." The conversation lasted twenty minutes and was cordial. Sadat did not conceal his affection for the Israeli defense minister.

Begin arrived at Carter's cabin ten minutes before the appointed meeting with Sadat. Carter was extremely nervous. He asked Begin to take a seat across from him.

"President Sadat brought a written proposal with him," Carter began. "He showed it to me today."

Begin sensed an approaching storm. If the proposal had been reasonable, Carter would probably not have invited him to a preliminary meeting. He concluded that Carter wanted to forestall trouble.

"I know you will not be able to accept Sadat's proposal," Carter continued. "But I would not want that to break up the conference."

Begin understood. He realized Carter was apprehensive of a tough response and drastic statements that might be made in the opening meeting. He did not intend to submit a proposal of his own: at Dayan's suggestion, Israel had decided not to do so but to examine the demands and tactics of the Egyptians first. Dayan remembered that separate proposals by the two parties generally led to American compromise proposals. He did not want that. Begin agreed.

Carter's statement did not augur well.

The meeting of the three leaders took place on the porch of Carter's cabin. From the outset the atmosphere was quite pleasant, though all three knew what to expect. Carter began, and immediately thereafter Sadat proposed that Begin should take the floor.

"We must turn over a new leaf," Begin said. "Negotiations require patience."

"It's true we need time," Sadat said. "After all, we won't sign a peace treaty here. To my mind, there's no sense in a declaration of principles or in a separate agreement. We should talk of the contents of a comprehensive settlement, and Camp David should not be turned into a television battle, as happened with the Geneva conference. All the parties there competed for the little screen as if they were amateur singers hoping to become professionals. We should settle the framework, and our assistants will handle the details later. I think we will need three months' work."

There was a moment of silence. Sadat pulled three copies of a set of papers out of a brown case. The plan was eleven pages long.

"Shall I read the Egyptian view of the framework of a comprehensive settlement?" Sadat asked.

Carter and Begin responded in the affirmative.

Sadat put on a pair of reading glasses and began to read the plan. He did so slowly, and with emphasis.

The opening was replete with flowery phrases: "Further to the historic initiative of President Sadat, the initiative that revived the hope of the entire world for a happier future for mankind, and in consideration of the desire of the Middle Eastern peoples and all peace-loving peoples to end the pain of the past and to rescue this generation and coming ones from the afflictions of war, and in order to turn over a new leaf . . . out of the resolve to turn the Middle East, the cradle of civilization and birthplace of the prophets, into an illuminating example of coexistence and cooperation among nations, and out of the desire to develop good neighborly relations in accordance with the principles of international law . . ."

Carter and Begin listened attentively. Sadat read the terms of the plan he brought with him from Cairo, paragraph by paragraph.

1. The parties declare their firm resolve to arrive at a comprehensive settlement of the Middle East problem by signing peace treaties on the basis of the full implementa-

tion of Security Council Resolutions 242 and 338 in all their parts.

2. The parties agree to establish a just and lasting peace, requiring

a. The withdrawal of Israel from the conquered territories, in accordance with the principle of prohibiting the acquisition of land in war. The withdrawal from Sinai and the Golan will be to the international borders between mandatory Palestine and Egypt and Syria. The withdrawal from the West Bank will be to the Jordan-Israel 1949 armistice line. If the parties involved agree on small changes in those lines, it is understood that such changes should not reflect the extent of the conquest. The withdrawal from the Gaza Strip will be to the 1949 Israel-Egypt armistice line. The Israeli withdrawal will begin immediately after the signing of the peace treaty and end according to a timetable agreed on in the course of the period mentioned in paragraph 6.

b. The evacuation of the Israeli settlements from the conquered territories, in accordance with the time agreed on, in the course of the period mentioned in paragraph 6.

A cool breeze was blowing on the porch of Carter's cabin, but the atmosphere quickly heated up. Begin listened carefully to every word. He burned with rage but outwardly seemed cool. From the first words, he felt that this was the most extreme Egyptian document submitted since the start of the peace process. At Ismailia and Salzburg, the Egyptians had exhibited more willingness to make concessions. Besides listening attentively, Begin was following the text of the proposal he held on his lap. From the corner of his eye he noticed that Carter kept glancing at him, trying to gauge his reactions.

c. A guarantee of the security, sovereignty, territorial integrity, and political independence of each state, by means of the following arrangements:

• The establishment of demilitarized zones on both sides of the border.

• The establishment of limited weapon zones on both sides of the border.

• The stationing of UN forces on both sides of the border.

• The installation of early-warning equipment on a mutual basis.

• The definition of the types of armament to be acquired by the countries party to the agreement, and the manner of their use.

• The participation of all parties to the treaty to prevent the distribution of nuclear arms, and the commitment of all parties not to produce or retain nuclear weapons or any nuclear explosive material.

Begin kept his face expressionless. It was clear that in this paragraph the president of Egypt meant to imply that Israel had atom bombs. The subject had preoccupied the Egyptians during negotiations, and had already been raised by them during the first meeting in Jerusalem. The Israelis had not reacted. They hadn't said yes, they hadn't said no. Begin kept quiet.

• Application of the principle of free navigation in the Strait of Tiran.

• The establishment between the two parties of relations of peace, good neighborliness, and cooperation.

d. All parties undertake not to use the threat of force or force to settle the conflicts between them, and to resolve all conflicts by peaceful means, according to paragraph 33 of the UN Charter. The parties also undertake to accept the decisions of the International Court of Justice in regard to differences of opinion deriving from the implementation or interpretation of the obligations between them.

e. With the signing of the peace treaty the military government of the West Bank and Gaza will be abolished and authority will be transferred to the Arab side by orderly, peaceful methods. There will be a transition period of no more than five years from the day the framework is signed in the course of which Jordan will undertake the supervision of the administration on the West Bank and Egypt will undertake the supervision of the administration of the Gaza Strip. Egypt and Jordan will carry out their functions in cooperation with representatives of the Palestinian people, at the time the Israeli military government is abolished, and six months before the end of the transition period, the Palestinian people will exercise its fundamental right to self-determination, and will be able to establish its national entity.

Sadat was perspiring and making frequent use of his handkerchief. Begin was fuming, but took care not to interrupt the Egyptian president's reading. Carter made notes from time to time in a notebook. He felt this was a most unhappy way to start a peace conference, but it was not in his power to avert the imminent breakdown.

Begin, too, was perspiring. The slow reading was wearing. Sadat continued without pause.

f.   Israel will withdraw from Jerusalem to the 1949 armistice line, in accordance with the principle prohibiting the acquisition of land in wars. Arab sovereignty and administration will be restored to Arab Jerusalem. A joint municipal council for the city will be established, composed of an equal number of Palestinian and Israeli members.

Sadat hit Begin hard. Many points have been or will be open for discussion between Israel and the Arab countries, but the sovereignty of Jerusalem is not a point Begin is willing to discuss. Sadat continued with a list of items to be supervised by the Jerusalem municipal council. Then he promised full recognition of Israel, the end of the Arab boycott, and a guarantee of unrestricted passage through the Suez Canal.

The next provision drove Begin wild. He quivered with exasperation and grew more agitated by the minute. Carter sensed that the peace negotiations would break down before they had really begun. "Israel," Sadat read, "undertakes to pay full compensation for the damage inflicted as a result of operations conducted by her armed forces against residents and civilian installations and for the natural resources exploited in the conquered territories."

After ninety minutes of slow reading, Sadat finished. Begin cast a glance at Carter, who was likewise surprised at the extreme Egyptian demands. Begin had also noted an expression of surprise on Carter's face when Sadat had demanded a Palestinian state. Since March 1978 Carter had been claiming that Sadat would not insist on a state.

Silence reigned on the windy porch.

Finally Carter turned to Sadat and asked, "Do you want Mr. Begin's reaction now or later?"

Sadat turned to Begin and said, "I don't expect an immediate answer. I know you have a delegation of ministers and advisers, and you must go back to them."

Carter and Begin had no doubt that Sadat wished to postpone the reaction, to avoid being subjected to Begin's sharp response.

Begin replied with composure. "I agree with you that

we have passed the stage of discussing a declaration of principles and cannot avoid dealing with an overall settlement. I merely request that you do not press me."

"I'm not in a hurry," Sadat answered. "I've presented the Egyptian point of view. I suggest that you and your aides examine it, and I will wait for an answer."

Dusk had fallen by the time Menachem Begin arrived at his cabin. Sadat turned in for a nap. Carter immediately summoned his aides and telephoned Begin. His words and voice made it obvious that he feared a caustic reply from Begin and his colleagues. He was especially concerned that Begin would want to return the document to Sadat as though it had never existed. "It is certainly an extreme document," said Carter, "but I believe it is only an opening position." He tried to calm the irate Begin, and told him he had turned the paper over to Secretary of State Cyrus Vance and National Security Assistant Zbigniew Brzezinski in order to develop an American reaction.

It was a gloomy night at Camp David. The first day of discussions might be the last. The mood of the Israeli delegation was low. The consultations began with the prime minister's declaration: "No force in the world can compel Israel to accept that document."

The members of the delegation nodded. Agreement was unanimous.

Begin continued: "The Egyptians have never before written such an extreme document. I propose demanding that they withdraw it. The Americans should be told that it is not at all reasonable. We should not touch this document at all."

Legal adviser Aharon Barak said, "The Egyptian document should be rejected because of its extreme demands."

Weizman said, "The document is not acceptable, not even superficially. Incidentally, I asked Sadat to meet with Dayan and he said he had no objection."

"I didn't ask for that," Dayan said.

All reactions were extremely sharp. The Israeli delegation assumed that the Americans were listening in to their discussion, but they didn't care. On the contrary, they wanted to demonstrate their unanimity in rejecting this unparalleled Egyptian document.

"This document is not a basis for negotiation," Dayan

said. "It must be rejected out of hand. We are willing to discuss other proposals with them. The Egyptians are behaving like landlords, as if they had occupied the West Bank and the Old City, as if nothing had happened."

Weizman added, "I told Cyrus Vance that things didn't start just in 1967, and that thirty years can't be forgotten."

There was a good deal of puzzlement among the Israelis. Why had the Egyptians submitted such a document? Where were they heading? What was their goal? Were they interested in a breakdown of the conference, and putting the blame on the Israelis? Or was it a tactical move, from which they could back down later?

Begin felt the Egyptians were eager to break up the conference right away, but that they wanted the Israelis to do the job for them. He suggested "not playing the Egyptian game" but preparing a counterdocument with positive proposals. His suggestion was generally approved. There was a question whether the Israelis should submit their document to the Americans right away or await further developments. Most of the delegates felt that the Egyptians would leak the provisions of their own document in Egypt and the U.S.

"We must consider the matter from the point of view of our information services," Dayan said. "I think we will have to tell the American public what has happened during the last thirty years."

Dayan favored preparing the Israeli proposal but not submitting it, so that it would not be interpreted as an ultimatum. His suggestion was accepted. It was decided to prepare the paper for informational purposes, especially in case the conference broke up the next day.

The job of composing the Israeli counterdocument was assigned to Avraham Tamir, Aharon Barak, Meir Rosenne, and Simcha Dinitz. They worked till late at night preparing a document that included a survey of Egyptian aggression during the past thirty years, along with the peace plan Israel had brought to Camp David.

At that same late hour Carter was with Sadat. The main topic of conversation was the Israeli settlements in Sinai. It was clear to all parties that this was a powerful mine that had to be dismantled before it exploded.

It was well past midnight. The movie theater was patronized by a few Americans and Egyptians. The Israelis were busy composing working papers. In the middle of the night Carter joined Vance and Brzezinski in their consultations.

There was a sense of urgency. When the lights went out at Camp David and the delegations retired for a few hours' sleep, the Israelis had no doubt that within twenty-four hours they would be packing their bags and leaving. They were already coming up with ideas for ways of winning the struggle for American public opinion. The Camp David conference was over, they believed: a total failure, right from the start.

21 TWO HARDENED WARRIORS

By Thursday morning, September 7, the Israeli delegation had bloodshot eyes. Some of the delegates had not slept all night, others had managed only a few hours' sleep. They looked miserable, and they all felt a heavy sense of failure.

Begin was outraged, defining Sadat's proposal of the previous day as *chutzpah* ("cheek"). More than anything else, he was furious at the Egyptian demand that Israel withdraw to the 1949 borders and pay reparations for losses incurred through war. "With a plan like that," Begin said, "Sadat will be welcomed with open arms by the Arab world."

At the Israeli delegation's meeting that morning a ten-page document prepared during the night was presented. It was studded with positive phrases reflecting Israel's desire for peace and its readiness to be forthcoming toward the Egyptians by making certain concessions. At that hour the Israeli statement of attitudes seemed perfect. Begin as well as the delegation approved it, though they agreed it would not be shown to anyone else, and certainly not to the press.

When the Israeli delegation arrived at the American delegation's cabin they found a mood of dejection there too. Carter, Vance, and Brzezinski were grim.

"It's a very tough document," Carter began. This encouraged the Israelis a little. They expected him to take some kind of action to induce Sadat to make far-reaching changes in the Egyptian paper.

Carter turned to Begin, Dayan, and Weizman, and asked for some positive gesture on Israel's part to create an improved atmosphere for the forthcoming days of discussions. The American president also feared that the Camp David conference might end in failure very soon.

Begin seemed not to have heard Carter's request. He spoke about the Egyptian document excitedly: "Israel cannot live with a paper of this kind," he declared. Begin added that acceptance of the Egyptian demands would constitute a danger to his country's security.

The meeting continued in a different spirit. Carter, Vance, and Brzezinski laid demands before the Israeli team. Vance asked the Israelis to stop Jewish settlement of the West Bank and the Gaza Strip. He demanded that the number of settlers be limited, as well as the number of settlements, and added: "I propose that this freeze come into force immediately."

Dayan rejected Vance's proposal completely. Begin argued with Carter, the discussion extending to the subject of Israel's settlements in the Sinai. "You promised me that you would persuade Sadat to allow the Israeli settlements to be in a UN-controlled area," Begin said.

"I tried, but did not succeed," Carter said.

"Whatever happens," Begin replied, "you should be aware of the fact that settlement of Judea and Samaria, and Gaza, have nothing to do with the Egyptians in Sinai."

The meeting ended without anything having been achieved. Carter and Begin left for Carter's cabin to meet with Sadat. Carter sat behind his desk facing Begin. Sadat was ten minutes late.

Both Carter and Begin were surprised at the topic with which Sadat chose to open the discussions. Sadat complained of Israel's unnecessary involvement in the civil war in Lebanon. "Israel must stop its interference," he said.

"We have saved many thousands of Christians," Begin

replied. "We are protecting them from being killed. Could you guarantee the welfare of the Christians?"

"Yes! Provided Israel does not intervene in Lebanon," Sadat said.

The atmosphere grew heated.

"Were it not for Israel, no one would help them," Begin claimed.

Sadat countered: "King Haled could end the war in Lebanon by stopping aid to the Syrians."

"It would be desirable that King Haled write in that vein to Assad," Carter agreed, "but it would be better if Sadat wrote to him too. I may send a message of my own to President Assad."

"The main thing is that the Israelis should not interfere in Lebanon," Sadat insisted.

"We gave the Christians arms so that they could defend themselves," Begin said, "otherwise they would have been slaughtered. We do not give them orders, just as the United States government does not give orders to Elias Sarkis's government in Lebanon. It is only our firm stand which prevents the Syrians and the Palestinians from killing the Christians in Lebanon."

It was Carter who brought the discussion back to its main subject: Israel's reply to the Egyptian proposals of the previous day. Carter asked Begin if he could make some far-reaching gesture, paralleling Sadat's gesture in making his historical visit to Jerusalem.

"We are prepared to return the Sinai to Egyptian sovereignty, even though it was used as a base from which to attack us," Begin said. "The warm reception accorded to Sadat in Israel was the result of his initiative. It should not be forgotten that we welcomed a leader who, only four years before, had suddenly and maliciously attacked us, knowing we would all be in the synagogues."

"It was strategic deception," Sadat said.

"Deception is deception," Begin countered.

Begin addressed Sadat directly. He analyzed Sadat's document and explained, at great length, why Israel could not accept it. Carter listened, writing brief notes and barely reacting.

Begin reached the heart of the matter almost immediately, referring to paragraph 6 of the Egyptian document and stating that the Egyptians were working toward the establishment of a Palestinian state. "President Carter has told me that the U.S. does not want a state of that kind; you, too, Mr. President, have told me that you do not want an independent Palestinian state," Begin said.

Sadat replied: "I do want a Palestinian state, but one that is linked with Jordan. I want the inhabitants to decide for themselves about having a link of that kind."

"We will not allow the establishment of a base for Yasir Arafat's murderers within our borders," Begin persisted. "The Egyptian paper means that Israel will return to the 1949 borders, including the redivision of Jerusalem. There can be no agreement on the basis of these demands."

"No! I said already yesterday that there is no need to divide Jerusalem," Sadat exclaimed.

"In the paper you submitted to us you address us as if we were the defeated nation," Begin said. Sadat may not have heard quite what Begin said. At any rate, the Egyptian president took Begin's mention of a defeated nation to refer to him and his country. He was livid.

Sadat declared: "Are we a defeated nation? We used to be! But after October 1973 we are no longer a defeated nation."

The misunderstanding was cleared up within a few seconds; nevertheless Sadat continued to mutter: "We are not defeated! We are not defeated!"

"You demand that we pay compensation for damages incurred by Egyptian civilians," Begin said. "I would like to remind you, Mr. President, that our nation overcame aggression and defended its existence."

"For what do you request compensation?" Carter asked Sadat.

Begin said: "If you request compensation, I would like you to know that we also claim damages from you. I can bring you a very long list of damages incurred by us because of you."

The argument became heated. Both Begin and Sadat raised their voices, though they adhered to formal politeness. Sadat tried to justify the Egyptian claim for damages by giving an emotional description of the suffering of the Egyptian people because of the wars. Carter, who wanted to interrupt the discussion, was stopped by a wave of Sadat's hand. "Mr. President, please let me finish," Sadat said in an angry tone.

President Carter asked for both men to calm down.

"I thought that after my initiative there would be a period of goodwill," Sadat said. "We are giving you peace and you want territories. You do not want peace!"

"How can you say that?" Begin replied. "We want a situation in which we can defend ourselves, without the UN having to do so!"

Sadat said: "I am also sovereign. I also want to defend Egypt! I said that I would be prepared to accept demilitarized zones."

"But in Jerusalem we agreed that your forces would not go beyond the passes in Sinai," Begin argued, "and now you are demanding something else."

"What I meant was that strike forces should not cross the passes," Sadat answered. "All we are asking is that one battalion should cross the passes, as well as border guards and police."

Begin said: "I suggest that Weizman and Gamassi discuss those topics and bring them to a conclusion."

The discussion was back to square one. Begin returned to the Egyptian demand which meant the establishment of a Palestinian state. He made it clear to Sadat in no uncertain terms that this was unacceptable to Israel.

Sadat said: "But it is a Palestinian state which is linked to Jordan."

Begin replied: "Even our opposition in Israel, the Labor party and its leaders, Shimon Peres, whom you met in Vienna, oppose an independent Palestinian state. They are prepared to make a territorial compromise."

"Never! Never! Never!" Sadat said.

"I wish Shimon Peres were here to hear that for himself," Begin said. "Apart from that, Mr. President, your paper does not include another matter we discussed in Jerusalem, free passage in the Strait of Tiran."

"Correct, I will add it to the paper," Sadat conceded.

President Carter wrote down the topics on which agreement had not been reached and which required further discussion. He read them out to Sadat and Begin. Begin asked to add another subject which Carter had not recorded: "The presence of Israeli forces in Judea and Samaria, and Gaza." Carter did not write down Begin's request, possibly because he had not been paying attention.

"Sir, I would like to add the question of the presence of

Israeli forces in Judea and Samaria, and Gaza," Begin repeated.

With evident reluctance, Carter wrote this down on the piece of paper before him. Sadat did not say a word.

Carter said: "The U.S. would prefer it if at this conference there was at least partial success and discussions were to continue."

"No! No! No partial agreement!" Sadat said.

Once again Sadat had misunderstood what Carter had said. Carter soothed the excited president.

Carter said: "I do not wish to impose my suggestions on you, but since the situation is as it is, my people will submit an American proposal and both sides will discuss it. The world ardently wants the conference to succeed, and so I will put down on paper some ideas of my own. Some of them will seem acceptable to you, others not."

Before parting, while still in Carter's study, Sadat feared that Begin had misunderstood him on the subject of the Israeli settlements in Sinai. Sadat agreed to defer discussing Sinai until Weizman had met with Gamassi, who was not participating in the Camp David conference, but Sadat immediately made it clear that he had made up his mind to conclude the subject during the conference.

Sadat said: "The question of the Israeli settlements in Sinai is a matter of principle! I will be unable to appear before my people without an agreement to evacuate the Israeli settlements. The Egyptian nation will be under the influence of the extremists."

Sadat added that he could accept "Israeli settlements even in the Nile delta," but on no account near the border, in Egyptian territory which had been conquered in war. When Begin suggested transferring some of the Israeli air bases in Sinai to the Americans, Sadat flew into a rage: "No one in Egypt will accept that. The air bases must be under Egyptian sovereignty!"

The three men parted under a cloud. Begin went back to his colleagues and told them of Sadat's demands that the settlements in Sinai be evacuated. "I'm afraid that the Egyptians will try to break up the conference over the settlements issue," he said.

They were all disappointed. "The talks are about to end," Weizman remarked.

The afternoon meeting of Carter, Sadat, and Begin

opened in the shadow of the failure of the previous meeting. Sadat commented angrily that he had nothing to add to what he had said a few hours earlier. Begin suggested discussing security problems in Sinai. Within a few moments the discussion had shifted to the Israeli settlements in Sinai.

"I am not prepared to accept your request for the Israeli settlements to remain as they are," Sadat said. "I could have signed a friendship pact with the USSR but my people opposed it. I expelled the Russians from Egypt and my people wholeheartedly supported me. I know the Egyptian people. They are good. Now there are Israeli settlements on their land. Neither I nor my people will accept this. I will never agree to having those settlements on my land. Never! If you do not agree to evacuate the settlements there will be no peace!"

"We will not agree to dismantle the settlements," Begin answered. "The opposition in Israel will not agree to it either."

Carter intervened: "If it transpires that peace will not be attained only because of the settlements and you, Mr. Begin, go to the Knesset to ask that they be dismantled, I'm sure you will obtain an overwhelming majority."

The spark of the idea, as was to become clear later, fell on fertile soil. Begin engraved the proposal in his mind.

"The question of the settlements is no mere caprice," Begin said. "Not is it a desire to conquer territory. For nineteen years our settlements were exposed to terrorist attacks. We need a security belt. It is a question of security."

Carter reminded Sadat that he had also tried to persuade him (Sadat) to leave the Israeli settlements where they were, apparently in order to prove to Begin that he really had talked about this problem with the Egyptian president. "A great responsibility is placed on all of us," he said. "If we fail and the situation deteriorates I will not be able to call another such conference in the near future. Give me credit and try to give your most serious attention to my proposals."

Toward the end of the meeting tempers flared again. Begin concluded with fiery words directed at Sadat: "There is no doubt that the step you took required courage, but our response was also courageous," he said. "You came to us after having made war against us, causing us heavy losses. You deceived us and attacked us, and you know how sensitive we are about casualties. Despite this, we welcomed you warmly in Jerusalem."

This meeting also ended without any results.

During the conversation the American and Israeli ministers were also meeting. Vance had met with Kamel shortly before and looked tense. He now asked the Israelis for a freeze on Jewish settlements on the West Bank. Dayan reacted immediately: "If Jewish settlement is stopped, Arab refugees will not be accepted back there either." Dayan had linked the two subjects for the first time. He asked the Americans whether the Egyptians would agree to a comprehensive plan regarding settling the West Bank, including settling refugees there. According to Dayan's suggestion, Israel would establish a certain number of settlements and in return would absorb 50,000 refugees. The American team did not have an answer.

"What does Israel think about the idea of a federation or confederation?" Vance asked.

Attorney General Barak replied: "If those ideas involve foreign sovereignty in the West Bank and Gaza, then our answer is negative."

The Americans made it clear that they were not prepared to consider a military presence of their own forces on the West Bank and in Gaza.

The Israeli delegation once again took counsel under the shadow of crisis and failure. "On no account can we accept the conditions of stopping settlement," Begin said. "From the public's point of view this kind of stopping would not hold water for very long. What will we say to the youngsters? It's madness! Particularly for a government which claims the right to sovereignty over the whole of the land of Israel. What kind of stopping can one undertake in the land of Israel? We must inform them that if they demand Arab sovereignty over the areas, we will demand Israeli sovereignty."

"I propose that we speak frankly to the Americans about our settlement plans, so that they don't get a shock," Dayan said. "We have to tell them how many settlements we can establish. We should mention about twenty settlements. We have to try and reach a full understanding with them. As for Sinai, maybe the area of the 'Otem' airfield will become an enclave enclosing an American training base, with Israeli settlements nearby."

Weizman was prepared to make more concessions than Dayan: "There's a difference between settlements in Sinai and those on the West Bank and in Gaza," he said. "I'm prepared to stop the settlement process if we are allowed to strengthen the existing settlements. If we tell the Americans that we will establish only another ten to fifteen Israeli settlements, this will not harm our principle or our right to settle in the West Bank and Gaza. Nothing will happen if we do not set up a new settlement in the Jordan Valley, but a lot might happen if we leave Camp David with nothing."

Begin left no room for doubt. He was not prepared to stop settling the West Bank and Gaza, even if this meant clashing with the U.S. "There might be difficult times ahead," he said, "but we will have to weather the storm."

No one came into or left Camp David. In the nearby town of Thurmont, once known as "the goldfish capital of the world," hundreds of journalists milled about, knowing nothing about what was going on at the camp. The White House spokesman limited himself to briefings that provided no information. The newsmen had to make do with guesses and with interviewing one another. The Middle East summit was the twenty-first international conference to be held at Camp David. It was the first, however, from which the media had been entirely excluded.

In the evening the reporters were given a glimpse of what was happening inside the camp as they were invited to watch an impressive demonstration of marines on parade. Carter, Sadat, and Begin were on the VIPs' platform and the journalists noticed that Begin and Sadat did not say a single word to one another. Carter's face was grim.

Marines separated the newsmen from the delegations and the leaders, but that did not prevent the Egyptian spokesmen from assembling the Egyptian reporters to tell them, if only in a few words, that "nothing was moving." That was enough for the reporters to gain some idea of what was happening inside the camp. They hastened to report in thousands of words on events that had never occurred.

Late that night Carter met Sadat again. The following

day was to be one of rest and prayer for the Egyptian delegation and Carter did not want to waste time. The members of the other delegations had a chance to relax a little from the pressure of events and the tension. Many of them went to the movies, where they soon fell asleep on the comfortable seats.

On Friday the tension relaxed somewhat. The Americans, Israelis, and Egyptians held internal consultations, and late in the afternoon Begin and Carter met for another session.

Carter wanted to prove that he had spared no effort on the Israeli settlements in Sinai. He told Begin that he had discussed the matter again with Sadat, but to no avail. He had no good tidings for Begin. He mentioned that he had told Sadat of Begin's proposal about the "Otem" air base.

"And how did Sadat react to that?" Begin asked.

"He rejected the idea completely," Carter replied.

Carter added that he had told Sadat that unless Israel's security interests in the West Bank were protected, he did not think that Israel would sign an agreement.

The conversation between Carter and Begin ended on another subject altogether—Iran. Begin told Carter that his experts had given him a very grave appraisal of the situation. For several months they had been telling him that the shah's chances of continuing to rule his country were very slim. Carter expressed concern about the situation in Iran, but unlike Begin he did not think the shah would lose his crown. "He will rule, though not as absolutely as in the past," he said.

In the evening Carter met Sadat, who assumed that Carter would bring the American proposals to this meeting. He was disappointed: "Without an American document I do not see how we can move on," he said. Sadat assumed that the American proposals would be nearer his own views than the Israelis'. He waited for them impatiently.

Friday evening, the beginning of the sabbath in Camp David was a festive occasion for the Israelis. Even so, Egypt's ultimatums and the American document, which no one had seen yet, cast a shadow over the celebrations. The sabbath meal, graced by Jimmy and Rosalynn Carter, was accompanied by singing, but even at the long table the Israelis did not stop consulting with one another. The feeling of failure was there.

On Saturday there was little activity. Begin observed the sabbath, but other members of the delegation met with Americans and Egyptians. Dayan met Vance; Weizman met Boutros Ghali and, later that day, Vance. "We want to learn more about the Sinai affair," Vance said to Weizman. "We are not fully informed about that matter, since it was more an issue between Israel and Egypt." Weizman promised to bring Vance and his associates up to date on all the details.

The same day Harold Saunders presented himself to Carter and Vance. The American undersecretary of state submitted the first draft of the American document, which had been written during the previous twenty-four hours. Carter was pleased. He considered the document a good basis for continuing the talks.

Sadat rose early Saturday morning. As was his custom, he went for a walk near his cabin. He spent a lot of time alone, shaking off the members of the Egyptian delegation. The Israelis noticed the absence of contact between the Egyptian president and his foreign minister, Ibrahim Kamel. Sadat hardly consulted him and barely allowed him to open his mouth at meetings. The Israelis noticed that within the Egyptian delegation Hassan Tuhami and Boutros Ghali tended toward a more flexible line and separate negotiations on Sinai and the West Bank. Osama al-Baz and Ibrahim Kamel held to a more rigid approach, were less prepared to compromise, and refused to separate the discussions on the West Bank from those on Sinai.

Weizman also met Sadat, and returned from the Egyptian president's cabin crestfallen. "He is not prepared to make any compromise," he said. "I think we'll have to dismantle the settlements in Sinai."

The members of the Israeli delegation spent much of the day engaged in sport, particularly ping-pong. Dayan spent a large part of the day on his own, in the woods; he asked not to be disturbed. Begin played chess with Brzezinski. In his youth Begin had been a talented chess player, but he had not played for thirty-five years. When the result was 2 to 1 in Begin's favor, the Israeli team met the president's adviser Hamilton Jordan.

"I heard that Begin's playing chess with Zbig," Jordan said.

"Yes, he's leading two to one," answered the military adviser, Poran.

"Do me a favor," Jordan said, "and make sure that Begin wins. Otherwise Zbig will be unbearable."

Begin won, even though in the fourth game Brzezinski had an extra pawn. The Israelis hastened to phone Jordan to tell him of Begin's victory. Jordan did not tarry and went over to Begin to congratulate him on his victory.

The political moves began again in the evening. Begin met Vance and heard about the preliminary ideas for the American working paper. Dayan did not like what he heard. During the day and the night the Americans worked on the final draft of the document, but had not yet submitted it to the Israelis or the Egyptians.

The meals in the communal dining room created social relationships among the members of the two delegations, which had not been so in the discussion rooms. Despite the tension between Begin and Sadat, increasingly warm relations were established between the lower echelons of both delegations. Begin preferred to eat in his cabin.

Saturday had not brought peace between Israel and Egypt any closer.

22 PACKING UP

Menachem Begin, upon going to bed, reflected on the new situation that might be created Sunday. The Egyptians had submitted their proposals. The Americans might submit in the morning a paper in which they would list their recommendations. Israel had not prepared even one proposal paper of its own. Begin feared a trap: if the conferences reached a stalemate the Egyptians and Americans would claim that Israel had not submitted suggestions of its own, that its only action had been to decline the Egyptian and American proposals. When he woke up at 5:00 a.m. Sunday, Begin made up his mind: he would prepare an Israeli proposal paper with a positive stance.

Begin woke Kadishai, his bureau chief, and dictated a draft of a proposal for an Israeli working paper. The emphasis was put on positive attitudes, but from the "yes" side the strong Israeli "no" could also be heard. Israel would not agree to withdrawal from the settlements, from the airfields in Sinai, and of the IDF from the West Bank, and would oppose any attempt to interfere with the unity of Jerusalem or the right of Israeli citizens to settle in the West Bank and Gaza.

At 7:30 a.m. Dayan, Weizman, and Barak had already

reported for duty at Begin's study. Time was running short. Begin ordered sandwiches from the camp kitchen rather than take a break for a meal. Begin read aloud the draft he had prepared in the two previous hours.

Dayan said: "The American paper hasn't been submitted yet and we don't know what it's going to include. So I propose we don't submit our own paper yet. Let's withhold it; after we get the American paper, we can bring ours up to date."

Begin felt the Israeli paper should at least be read by the Americans before they met with the Israeli team to present their own proposals. He thought that in this way he could influence the Americans and prevent their compromising between the extreme Egyptian proposals and the American ideas. The question was furiously discussed and eventually it was decided that four members of the Israeli team would stay at Camp David and not leave for a scheduled morning tour of the Gettysburg battlefield. The team of four—Barak, Rosenne, Tamir, and Dinitz—were assigned to write a final draft of an Israeli proposal, mainly based on the Israeli peace plan and putting a strong emphasis on its positive elements. To avoid a conflict with the Americans, the Israelis decided to call their proposal a reply to the Egyptians rather than to the Americans.

The Israeli government was scheduled to convene a few hours later for its weekly meeting and Begin felt the need to call Deputy Prime Minister Yigael Yadin and to instruct him what and how to tell the government. His report on the conference to Yadin was sparse; he was cautious about what he said, since he suspected his telephone was bugged. Begin instructed Yadin to inform the government that the Egyptian paper was very extreme, that the Americans were to submit a paper, and that the Israelis too had prepared a paper. On a domestic subject, Begin implored Yadin not to give in to the wage demands of schoolteachers who had proclaimed a general school strike in Israel.

The morning was cool. At about 10:00 a.m. the members of the delegations and hundreds of newspaper reporters gathered to visit the battlefield of Gettysburg, where the forces of the Confederacy were beaten by the Union forcs during the American Civil War. The idea of visiting the battlefield, which is not far from Camp David, was Begin's. He suggested that Carter and Sadat join him in this trip into the past. They enthusiastically consented.

Efraim Poran suggested that the members of the various delegations go together in one another's cars. Jody Powell liked the idea; so when the limousines started on their way to Gettysburg, the Egyptian, American, and Israeli delegates sat crowded next to one another.

Carter, Sadat, and Begin drove in the presidential limousine. At the beginning the tension between Begin and Sadat was high, and not a word was said. Begin eventually broke the ice. In high spirits, he told Carter and Sadat anecdotes about his experiences in a Soviet concentration camp, where he had been imprisoned at the beginning of the 1940s. Begin used very sharp language while he talked about the Soviets, and Carter and Sadat did not hide their satisfaction at the derision Begin hurled at their mutual enemy.

"Moshe, you've been avoiding me," Tuhami said. "Are you angry with me?"

Dayan answered, "I certainly am."

There was a substantial reason for Dayan's coolness. In Salzburg, in a newspaper interview, Tuhami had hurled grave accusations at Dayan, alleging that he had violated promises about Jerusalem and Sinai. These accusations were untrue, and made Dayan angry at Tuhami. The conversation between the two on the Gettysburg battlefield was conciliatory. Dayan had forgiven him.

Sadat, Begin, and Carter looked at the battlefield. They were listening to the guides when Sadat turned suddenly to Carter and Begin and said, voicing an old ambition: "I would like to visit Mount Sinai and pray there."

"I'd love to join you," Begin said. "The sunrise as seen from Mount Sinai is out of this world."

"So I've heard," Carter chimed in.

"You're also invited to pray on Mount Sinai." Begin smiled.

The visit to Gettysburg lasted longer than was planned. Begin asked for a postponement of the meeting with the American team until 4:00 p.m. He wanted some rest. Carter consented, but at the same time suggested limiting the teams: each side would be represented by the head of the delegation and three others.

The American-Israeli day at Camp David started at 4:00 p.m., Sunday, September 10. Begin, Dayan, Weizman, and Barak met with Carter, Mondale, Vance, and Brzezinski.

Carter presented his proposals to the Israeli team on seventeen typewritten pages. The American proposal was designed to be the framework for a general agreement. The major part of the proposals dealt with various questions on the West Bank, Gaza, and the Palestinians. A special section dealt with the Jerusalem problem.

The immediate Israeli impression was that the American proposal had been prepared hastily. Dayan said this to their faces. He noticed, almost at first glance, that nothing had been said in the proposal about the settlements on the West Bank or about Israeli sovereignty; also, there was very little about Sinai.

The meeting lasted for an hour. Carter again stressed that Israel should show flexibility and make far-reaching concessions. "Sadat cannot yield anything," he explained. "If the conference fails, the Egyptian will turn to the radicals and we, like you, do not want this to happen."

The meeting was adjourned when Begin said that the Israeli delegation had to "study the American proposals in greater depth." "We," he added, "work and consult in a collective way." The break in the negotiations confused the American timetable. Carter and his team had originally thought that they would be able to meet Sadat by afternoon and submit the Israeli comments on the American paper to him. Under the circumstances, Carter was forced to postpone his scheduled meeting with Sadat. He asked the Israelis to give him their comments that evening as soon as they had finished.

The Israeli consultation, which took place after dinner, was relatively brief. The American proposal had many sections which Begin and his ministers could not accept. "I turned the Rogers plan down," Begin said. "If we find anything unacceptable here, we will turn it down too."

When the Israeli consultation was finished it was already evening. The Americans and Israelis gathered to discuss the proposals submitted by Carter. The delegates read item after item and made their comments.

The meeting, which began calmly, soon grew heated. Carter said that during the negotiations the question of the national rights of the Palestinians, including their right for self-determination, would also be discussed.

The Israeli delegation's reaction was: "This is out of the question." They regarded it as a loophole which might in the future bring about the creation of a Palestinian state. Carter suggested imposing a freeze on settlements, and the Israelis turned this down too. He proposed that the IDF remain in the West Bank for more than five years and here the Israeli team found a proposal with which they could agree.

Carter also touched on questions connected with the Sinai. He expressed the opinion that Sadat would not yield on the questions of the Israeli settlements and the air bases. Carter proposed that Israel withdraw from the settlements and airfields.

"We do not dismantle settlements, nor do we ruin them or plow them under," Begin said.

The long journey into the night continued. From time to time the White House staff sent in coffee and sandwiches. The atmosphere became more somber. The conflict between the Israeli and American teams caused voices to be raised, but Carter presided at the meeting with an iron hand. He would not let the participants interrupt each other.

When the two teams arrived at the article which dealt with the "Principle of Acquiring Occupied Territories," Begin's reaction was very sharp: "Such a principle does not apply in our case. The areas we occupy were taken in a defensive war . . . You must realize, Mr. President," Begin continued in an aggressive tone, pointing his finger at Carter, "that in all our wars we have been the victims of Arab aggression."

The Israelis opposed vigorously the preamble sentence to the proposal, which stressed that "the acquisition of territories by force cannot be accepted." Begin and his team were wary of the trap that this seemingly naive sentence had in store for them. It could in the future be interpreted in a way which could cause an Israeli withdrawal from the Golan Heights.

"This we will never accept," said Begin.

The discussion went on and every word was weighed. Even though the debate was centered in principle on the West Bank, it touched on Sinai as well. The idea that the

Americans would offer a contribution toward the resettling of the air bases was raised. The air bases could become American training bases, and the Americans might extend financial help for building alternative airfields. The Americans did not rule out the possibility that the Israeli air force could use the Sinai airfields until alternative airfields were built.

The Egyptians followed the lengthy discussion with apprehension. They feared that Begin, Dayan, Weizman, and Barak would cause a turnabout in the American attitude, which had until then leaned toward the Egyptian side.

Begin's uncompromising attitude was supported by Dayan. Carter had noticed almost immediately that Dayan had an influence on Begin. He decided to isolate Dayan from the Israeli group and try to influence him separately. When all the others turned to go, tired and exhausted from the lengthy discussion, Carter asked Dayan to remain for further discussion. Carter complimented Dayan, promising him to introduce some changes in the American proposals. He also promised to pay more attention to the comments made by Begin and his colleagues.

"Please," the president asked Dayan, "please make an effort to placate Sadat."

When the American and Israeli teams returned to their respective cabins it was 3:00 a.m. Monday. It had been a hard day's night.

Less than four hours later, the Israeli delegation had already gathered for work. They had promised the Americans a response to each of their proposals by 10:00 a.m., when President Carter was scheduled to meet Sadat.

The two legal counselors, Barak and Rosenne, recorded the Israeli comments by hand on a copy of the American document. To save time, an Israeli courier delivered the Israeli comments to the American delegation's cabin by bicycle as soon as they had begun to accumulate.

As he read the Israeli response to the American proposals Carter realized that it was far from satisfying. Israel remained adamant about not withdrawing from the West Bank or from the settlements in Sinai. The Israelis showed a determined opposition to the sentence "The acquisition of territories by force canont be accepted." At the suggesttion of Barak, Israel requested a letter of understanding from Carter, in which he was asked to affirm that his interpretation of Resolution 242 of the Security Council (adopted after the 1967 war) was not in the spirit of the interpretation adopted by Egypt, that is, withdrawal from *all* the territories rather than withdrawal from territories. The latter had always been the Israeli interpretation.

The meeting between Carter and Sadat, at 10:30 a.m., was doomed to failure. Carter knew Sadat would not accept the Israeli attitudes.

"If these are Israel's final words," said Sadat gravely, "we have nothing to wait for here."

Sadat also attacked the American stand. He did not agree with some of the proposals put forward in the American paper. He spoke impatiently: "If Israel is not going to withdraw from the settlements and air bases," he said angrily, "I see no place to continue with the negotiations."

Carter tried to pacify Sadat. "The Israelis have not yet spoken their last words," he told Sadat, attempting a guess. He hoped to wring more concessions from Begin throughout the day. The meeting terminated with something of a concession on Sadat's part; he agreed to separate the discussion on the West Bank from the negotiations on Sinai. Carter regarded this as a consolation of sorts.

When Sadat returned to his cabin there was a message from King Hussein, who was in London, asking Sadat to phone him. Sadat did so, imploring the monarch to join the conference. Hussein repeated what he had already said to Sadat, that he could do nothing as long as Israel had not guaranteed a complete withdrawal from the West Bank. Before hanging up, Hussein wished Sadat good luck.

Carter decided to follow the course he had taken the night before. He summoned Weizman, who came accompanied by Avraham Tamir. Carter told Weizman that Sadat could not accept the Israeli demands for maintaining the settlements in the Sinai. According to Carter, Sadat also refused to consider leaving the settlements under the auspices of the UN, or to operate the Ophira airfield under a similar arrangement.

"Sadat didn't say that the Israeli settlements should be burned down," Carter said, "but he said that the settlers would have to leave, and if they were so keen to live on Egyptian soil, they could come and settle near the Nile."

It became apparent to Weizman that Carter's aim was

to divide the Israeli ministers and in this way to shake Begin's confidence. As Carter left, Weizman went directly to Begin's cabin. "Carter is drawing closer to Sadat's ideas on the settlements in Sinai," he reported.

Dayan and Barak were the next Israeli guests to be invited to Carter's cabin. Dayan's impression was similar to Weizman's—Carter showed greater consideration for Sadat's difficulties, less for Begin's; he would exert no additional pressure on Sadat.

Dayan tried to guess the tactics Sadat would adopt: if a peace treaty could not be reached the way he wanted it, his primary objective at Camp David would be to reach a memorandum of understanding with the Americans. For the Israelis, who had had a special relationship with the U.S. since 1948, this was very grave.

In his meeting with Carter, Dayan learned that Sadat had submitted a new proposal for the West Bank and the Gaza Strip. He intended to deploy Egyptian army units in Gaza and the West Bank, pending a final decision on the status of these areas. Dayan turned it down flat. "It is out of the question," he told Carter.

Carter suggested building a highway between Egypt and Jordan which would pass not far from the Israeli town of Elath, and proposed that Israel stay in the Etzion air base, near Elath, for three years. The road between Egypt and Jordan would serve as a trade link and be used for tourism.

The report of the meeting did not encourage Begin.

At Tuesday morning's meeting of the Israeli delegation, the feeling was that negotiations could not continue indefinitely, that they would have to be more or less done by Friday. Begin proposed preparing a paper that would include possible courses of action if the conference failed: what had been agreed in the conference, and what had not. At his request a declaration was prepared which stated, "We are ready to continue with the negotiations anytime, anyplace." However, Begin felt that such a statement might intensify Carter's anger. Carter had hoped to finish the entire negotiating process during the conference and had gambled his prestige on success. Dayan was more restrained. He advocated neither publishing a statement nor preparing a new paper, pending receipt of amendments to the American paper.

The morning meeting was adjourned on a pessimistic note: "I shall ask for a meeting with Carter today," said Begin to his fellow ministers. "I'll present our views to him and tell him what we intend to tell the Israeli people and world public opinion."

Coming out of the meeting, Dayan bumped into Samuel Lewis. Dayan's face betrayed his disappointed feelings. He gave the U.S. ambassador to Israel a weak handshake: "There is no sense to these meetings and negotiations," he said. "Things got stuck and I would like to leave for Israel tomorrow."

Lewis hurried to the American delegation's cabin and reported Dayan's pessimistic remark. Lewis knew Dayan to be an impatient, sometimes even discourteous person, and he believed that whatever Dayan had said was in dead seriousness. Lewis's brief report caused an uproar in the American cabin.

When the Israeli delegation gathered for coffee in the afternoon, Begin was still in a militant mood. He said angrily and resolutely to the Israelis who surrounded him: "If I ever sign the preamble the way it is phrased in the American document, let my right hand wither! I shall not sign." He was referring to the principle that territories could not be obtained by force.

Begin looked around him: "Are there any misgivings among any members of the delegation?" he asked.

Silence.

A few moments later Carter's secretary arrived. Begin's appointment with Carter had been set for 8:00 p.m.

Suddenly the American secretary of state entered the Israeli cabin. Vance, dressed in a sweat suit, turned to the Israelis: "The American delegation will submit a new paper, following a meeting between the president and Sadat. There is no need to hurry," added Vance, thus hinting that he was aware of Dayan's plans to start packing. "Patience is a virtue."

It began to rain as evening fell. The Israeli delegation were still in their cabin when Carter arrived unexpectedly, accompanied by Atherton and Lewis. Carter shook the hands of each member of the delegation. "Tomorrow you will receive an updated paper from us," he said. "Let me suggest that one Israeli and one Egyptian delegate sit down with me for the drafting."

Carter turned to Begin: "Under the circumstances, let me suggest that we hold our meeting tomorrow after this scheduled meeting between the Egyptian and Israeli delegates and me."

"I beg your pardon, Mr. President," Begin said, "I have asked to meet you tonight for a very important discussion, maybe the most important I have ever had in my life."

"All right, then," Carter said.

The president stayed to dine with the Israeli team. Begin gave up his original plan to attend a concert of the Israel Philharmonic Orchestra in Washington.

Shortly before eight, Begin stood up: "I am going to shave for my meeting with the president. The others can go and watch a movie."

"In that case," Carter quipped, "I must also go and shave for the meeting with you."

At eight o'clock sharp, Begin called on Carter at his cabin. Carter, who had in the meantime conducted a brief conference with his team in another cabin, arrived at the last moment riding a bike. He was well aware of the somber mood of the Israeli delegation. He decided to avoid a frontal collision with Begin in the sensitive areas.

The conversation turned to the subject which threatened to cause the failure of the Camp David conference: the principle of not obtaining areas by force. Carter returned to deal with the subject and Begin did not budge an inch.

"From public opinion polls in Israel," Carter said, "I learn that the majority in Israel is ready for a territorial compromise."

"In such matters," Begin responded, "it is better not to pay too much attention to public opinion polls. I am positive that a decisive majority in Israel supports the government."

Begin had prepared himself well for the meeting with the president. Even though Carter tried to ease the atmosphere, Begin decided to be more firm than ever. He looked Carter in the eye.

"I am confident that the decisive majority of Israel supports the government," Begin said. "But even if this was not the case, I would never agree to the sentence which bans obtaining territories by war—and if I ever sign such an agreement, let my right hand wither!"

The president, who is well versed in the Bible, interpreted Begin's last words to be a vow. That was exactly the meaning of his words.

"I also will not withdraw from the settlements," Begin continued, "and may I tell you, Mr. President, that if the Knesset does not back me in those matters, I will submit my resignation. You told us at the beginning of the conference that the peace agreement is more important to you than your reelection. This is also my feeling. I will not surrender to Sadat's ultimatums or threats."

Begin proposed to publish a statement on what had and what had not been achieved at the Camp David conference. The prime minister also said that the Israeli statement would confirm that "Israel is ready to continue negotiating anytime, anyplace." Nothing had been achieved so far.

Carter recoiled. This would have meant the failure of the conference. The words may have had an effect. As the conversation continued, Begin grew calmer and Carter expressed his readiness to delete the phrase which referred to "areas obtained by force." He also accepted in principle the continued presence of the IDF in the West Bank. Begin, for his part, gave in to the president on one principal phrase: he was ready to "decide" on the subject of the future of the West Bank after five years, rather than "consider" it, as he had formerly demanded.

Begin's mood improved, but before he turned to go he still had a complaint: "Yesterday Brzezinski accused us of not being sensitive enough to Egypt's difficulties on the subject of Gaza, and Judea and Samaria."

Carter confirmed this.

"The only thing I can say on this to all of you," Begin continued, "is that there's only one thing to which I'm sensitive: I am sensitive to Jewish blood . . ."

Carter decided to conduct the negotiations on Sinai personally, so as to draw Begin and Sadat closer to each other. The way the negotiations were going struck him as too elaborate and difficult and he had therefore decided to propose an alternative way: each side would be represented by one delegate, preferably a jurist, and the two, together with Carter, would eventually find a solution. The other members of the delegations would take part in internal consultations only. The proposal was put to the two sides and Begin and Sadat agreed. Begin chose Aharon

Barak as his personal representative; Sadat's choice was Osama al-Baz.

It rained on Wednesday, September 13. Barak requested last-minute instructions from Begin before the first meeting with Carter and Osama al-Baz.

"Be strong and keep your courage!" Begin said.

The delegates heaved a sigh of relief. The toll of the negotiations was lifted off their shoulders. They went to see a movie in the projection room. It was called *The Touch of the Medusa*.

At age 42, Barak had already made a name for himself in Israel as an authority on law. He had received his Ph.D. when he was 24, not long after finishing his military service. Soon after, he became an associate professor at the faculty of law of the Hebrew University in Jerusalem. Many regarded him as a genius. He was the youngest professor on the faculty. His work was cited by the members of the Supreme Court. At the beginning of the 1970s he was invited by the UN to draft an international agreement on bills of exchange. He was only 38 when he was awarded the Israel prize for legal studies. In the mid-1970s Barak, whose special field was commercial law, was appointed Israel's attorney general. During his term, he made the office of the attorney general one of the most powerful in the government. Following his legal opinion, former prime minister Yitzhak Rabin was forced to resign because of a minor offense against foreign currency regulations (which had been committed by Rabin's wife).

At 44, Osama al-Baz was one of the prominent figures in Egypt's political and legal life. He had earned his doctorate from Harvard. Until the beginning of the 1970s he was an adviser at the Institute of Palestine and Israel Studies. Among other things, he used to conduct lengthy discussions with Arabs who had left Israel; he was well versed in Israel's internal problems. In 1974 he joined the team headed by Foreign Minister Ismail Fahmi. In 1977 he became director general of the Foreign Ministry and head of the political bureau of Vice-President Hosni Mubarak.

The two jurists met at 8:00 a.m. at President Carter's cabin for a discussion which was one of the most exhaustive held at Camp David. For many hours, Barak, al-Baz, Carter, and Vance analyzed the American document.

Al-Baz was not pleased. He demanded the return to the American document of the clause which dealt with the principle of banning acquiring territories by force—the clause Carter had agreed, after strenuous persuasion, to delete from the document. Carter did not accept al-Baz's demand. He only consented to refer again in the text to Resolution 242, which called for withdrawal from occupied territories.

After ten years of debate, proposals, resolutions, and renunciations at the Security Council, it became clear to Barak that the U.S. had a completely amorphous conception of Israel's attitude on Resolution 242 and its application to the West Bank. American opinion had been for many years that Israel had not accepted the resolution as binding for the West Bank. Barak had to explain that Israel was ready to apply Resolution 242 to the West Bank too, but once the territory ceased to be occupied by virtue of becoming something else, the principle of withdrawal could not remain applicable. Autonomy for the area, as proposed by Begin, overrode the principle of withdrawal.

Carter enjoyed this explanation. He did not hide his appreciation of Barak's capabilities. "You could become a justice on the U.S. Supreme Court," he told him. To his close associates he confided later: "This Barak exhausted me completely . . ."

Carter was pleased with his decision to sit with the legal experts. He had created the impression that the discussion was technical rather than political. This, he hoped, would bring him closer to a successful end.

Mrs. Carter used the afternoon to pay Mrs. Begin a visit. She presented Mrs. Begin with a silver platter with the presidential seal inscribed with the name of Camp David and the date of the conference. Aliza Begin had prepared herself well for such a visit: she responded with twenty lithographs on the subject of war and peace by ten well-known Israeli artists.

In the presidential cabin the meeting with the legal advisers continued into the afternoon. The Egyptian representative brought forward the question of Jerusalem, the birthplace of the three religions: "An Arab flag must fly on the Temple mount," he said in a determined way.

This demand sounded exaggerated to Carter and he lost his patience: "You are sabotaging the peace process and obstructing the negotiations," he said furiously. "The Israelis want a settlement and you are laying obstacles.

At 4:00 p.m. Barak left the cabin. He was exhausted. In four hours he was due to go see Carter again. During this interview he'd been requested to list all the point which Israel accepted and all the points to which it objected. The Israeli delegation convened immediately, called by walkie-talkies. Barak reported and the participants agreed on what should be firmly objected to, and what could not be accepted under any circumstances, even at the cost of the blowing up the conference. Barak made notes on the Israeli position.

The greatest storm erupted when Barak reported on al-Baz's demand to hoist an Arab flag on the Temple mount. Dayan derided it. Begin would not even hear of it. "It is out of the question," they responded.

At the same afternoon hour Sadat and Weizman were meeting. Sadat had already been briefed by al-Baz. "My mood is not optimistic," he told Weizman. "I'll never be able to get acceptance by the Arab world."

Weizman tried to make Sadat soften his demands on the Israeli settlements in Sinai. Sadat retorted: "I will never yield an inch of my land, Mr. Weizman."

It was rumored that the Egyptian delegation had been given instructions to start packing. During the consultation of the Israeli delegation Weizman had said: "We've got no alternative, we have to choose between a peace accord and the Israeli settlements in Sinai."

Toward evening Begin went to the projection room. He had the reputation of being an avid movie fan. Negotiations were still going on in Carter's cabin. Carter became convinced that Israel was ready to make concessions to gain a peace treaty. Carter, Barak, and al-Baz wrote the basis of the formula from which the final form of the peace treaty and the accompanying letters were constructed. "Now," the president told Barak, "I have faith in Israel's sincere desire for peace."

The meeting was over, but Carter pushed on. He wanted achievements and wanted to arrive at decisions that night.

Carter went to look for Begin, and was referred to the projection room. In the darkness he spotted the Israeli prime minister and called him outside. It was evident that

Carter did not want to waste time. The exchange was short. Carter tried again and again to persuade Begin on the subject of the Israeli settlements in Sinai. He realized that on this point the Camp David conference would succeed or fail. Begin was surprised at the support Carter had given to the Egyptian demand for the removal of the settlements.

"It is out of the question," said Begin.

23 THE LONGEST DAY

Heavy gray rain clouds hung over Maryland, adding to the oppressive spirit in Camp David. The members of the delegations did not step out of their cabins or take advantage of the camp's many facilities. The expected rain also created operational problems: in order to avoid being overheard, delegation members had often held consultations while walking through the woods. Some went as far as the heliport, fearing that bugging devices were implanted in the trees. Now there could be no consultations; people crowded in the cabins as waiters served sandwiches and coffee.

Jimmy Carter rose earlier than usual. At 4:30 a.m., he had summoned National Security Assistant Zbigniew Brzezinski, who, half asleep, uncombed, and unshaven, reported to the president within moments. Carter looked deeply worried. During the night he had been informed that Egyptian President Sadat intended to leave the conference during this or at latest the next day. Israeli Foreign Minister Dayan also had hinted that he was heading for home. Carter's fears that the conference would collapse were rapidly materializing.

"We've got to do something," Carter said. Before long,

the other members of the American team were gathered in the cabin. They laid the American document on the desk. Nothing remained of the original; a great many changes had been made since it was submitted to the two parties.

Some of the Israelis were impatient and nervous. "When are we going home?" they asked. "Tonight, tomorrow perhaps?"

"I was foolish to come to Camp David," Defense Minister Ezer Weizman said aloud. He was convinced that the conference was doomed. Deep down, he was prepared to remove the settlements, to pay the heavy price in return for peace. He spoke to Dayan about it but the foreign minister preferred not to clash with Begin on this matter.

Weizman did not keep silent. "The evacuation of the settlements is essential if we want peace," he announced to all present.

"I heard what you said," commented the prime minister angrily. He was adamant about not consenting to removal of the settlements. He noted aloud: "I don't believe a single Arab leader will sign a peace treaty with Israel if he has to give up some of his land."

The phone rang in the Israeli cabin. Samuel Lewis was calling to say that Carter wished to meet Dayan and Barak once more, at 10:30 a.m.

Weizman joined them. Carter, concern evident in his expression, welcomed the Israelis. At the outset he said sharply and plainly: "You must agree to the removal of the Sinai settlements, and that way we will get a peace treaty."

Dayan and Weizman listened intently but did not have the authority to deviate from the official Israeli line. Still, Dayan wished to indicate to Carter that a change had taken place, in his own opinion at least. "That cannot be agreed on here," Dayan said. "It cannot be done without the approval of the entire cabinet and Knesset."

Carter and his aides perceived the modification in Israeli policy. They understood that Weizman was of the same opinion, and it remained only to persuade Begin to concur with his colleagues, the leading ministers in the Israeli government. Carter was not content with that. He urged Dayan and Weizman to agree to refrain from further settlement on the West Bank and in Gaza. Dayan objected strenuously. Weizman did not say a word.

Just as they were about to leave, Carter surprised them with a new Egyptian demand. "He wants an Arab flag to fly over the Muslim holy places in Jerusalem." Carter did not specify which Arab country's flag Sadat had in mind.

Dayan and Weizman did not react. As they closed the door behind them, a sense of frustration assailed them again. The conference would end in resounding failure in a matter of hours.

Hassan Ahmed Kamel contacted Dayan's cabin with an invitation for a meeting with Sadat. A while later, Muhammad Hassan al-Tuhami called with the same invitation. It was the first time Sadat had expressed a desire to meet the Israeli foreign minister.

Sadat spent a great deal of time alone in his cabin: very few members of his delegation knocked at his door. Several times a day he went out for a walk, avoiding running into the Israelis if possible. The only Israeli who spoke with him often was Weizman, but he too was unable to move Sadat from his position.

This morning Carter invited Sadat to join him in a stroll. The U.S. president did not have any good news for him. Sadat told Carter of his intentions to leave Camp David that day, and Carter requested that he not sabotage this last chance for peace. Sadat consented to remain at Camp David as a personal favor to Carter, and succeeded in making Carter beholden to him.

Later in the afternoon, Sadat and Dayan met for the first time with no advisers or aides present. Sadat endeavored to be genial and patient with his guest, who for him as well as for all Egyptians symbolized Israeli military victories and Egyptian defeats. The conversation began with wartime reminiscences and it was Sadat who brought up current matters. "I've asked you to come because we've been sitting here for more than ten days and I see no solution on the horizon. I would like to hear from you what can be done."

"I believe you," Dayan answered. "You have accustomed us to the fact that you are a person with one face. Begin is a strong man, but he cannot oppose the Knesset and the people of Israel, particularly on the matter of settlements. On that question we cannot compromise."

Sadat complained that the Israeli delegation made use of the concessions he gave Carter to speed up normalization and postpone the final status of the West Bank, and then asked for further concessions. "Tell Begin there is no sense in torturing Carter anymore if you are not empowered by Israel to remove the settlements."

Dayan's impression was unequivocal. Sadat's position was extreme, and there was no chance of moving him. Feeling that the end was near, Dayan expressed a hope of coming out with a partial agreement, if a comprehensive one was not possible.

"Absolutely not!" Sadat said.

Dayan was deeply troubled. The son of one of the first Jewish settlers in the country, and himself a man of the soil who had established the settlement city of Yamit, Dayan understood that the time had come for a most painful choice: the Sinai settlements or peace.

Following consultations with his delegation, Begin decided to invite Vance for a final talk. Extremely depressed, Dayan went to his cabin. When Weizman arrived there a few minutes later he found Dayan packing his suitcases.

"Moshe, don't rush. I still have hope," Weizman said to his colleague.

It was early evening when Vance and Begin met. Vance was dejected.

"You disappointed us," Begin said. "You took no account of our elucidations, of our concessions, of our crucial stands."

Begin meant to put a wedge between the Americans and the Egyptians, after learning definitely that Carter and his aides had repeatedly moved closer to the Egyptian positions and succumbed to Sadat's unceasing pressure. That Thursday night Begin knew, as did the others, that time was operating to the disadvantage of all, but no one wanted to be responsible for the collapse of the conference. At night Carter met again with Osama al-Baz, but no progress was made. Sadat let it be known that he meant to order a helicopter to take him to the presidential plane awaiting him at Andrews Air Force Base.

Ezer Weizman was watching a movie, but left before it was over. His thunderous voice frightened the junior members of the delegation as he stormed out. Weizman had heard that high White House officials had briefed some of the media, telling them that the Camp David conference was about to collapse due to Israeli intransigeance. The Israelis were furious.

There was tension and differences of opinion among the Egyptians too. Ibrahim Kamel had been upset from the moment the meetings had begun. At night he would get up and awaken his cabin mate, Boutros Ghali, asking aloud, "Where are we needed? That man Sadat will drive me mad."

From time to time Kamel asked to meet privately with Sadat in order to communicate his reservations. He cautioned Sadat against extensive concessions which would give rise to accusations of treachery and surrender to Israel. Knowing his colleague was nervous and given to outbursts, Sadat tried to persuade him to be more patient.

That night, Kamel's nerves betrayed him. He did not agree with Sadat's last-minute acceptance of the proposal for an exchange of ambassadors nine months after the signing of a peace treaty. He had serious complaints about the settlement provision as well. The conversation was highly emotional.

"There can be no exchange of ambassadors," Kamel said, "until the Israeli flag is removed from all of Sinai. After such an exchange, what guarantee would we have that the withdrawal will be completed in three years? What will happen if there is a demonstration against the Israeli ambassador in Cairo which he considers an aggressive act opposed to the peace treaty, and as a result of this Israel stops the withdrawal?"

"You can't take all Begin's cards away by force," Sadat replied. "You have to get them quietly. It would be a mistake to move away from the American plan that wants to give Israel an exchange in order to bind the peace treaty to Palestinian self-government. Our basic problem in connection with Israel is coordinating our stand with the Americans so as not to give Israel an excuse for avoiding an agreement."

"Self-government is a hollow concept," Kamel said. "The Israeli plan covers self-administration of day-to-day affairs, and that's all. I prefer insisting on the right of Palestinians to self-determination. Self-government can have many interpretations. Even Carter supported self-determination!"

"When we bow to Begin," said Sadat, "in the matter of

names and titles in return for a clear promise he made to end the military government on the West Bank and in Gaza, what obstacle can stand in the way of self-determination for the Palestinians? You yourself always said that if the Palestinians want to get out of the vicious circle of military adventures they must accept the principle of progression—from self-administration to self-government, and from self-government to self-determination. Begin can disregard his promise to end the military government if the Palestinians don't convince the Israelis that their security is not imperiled. Listen, Muhammad. Fear of peace with Israel is unjustified in face of Arab power. We are growing stronger not because we have vision or political ability but because the Arab region is very important. Either we derive some advantage from the importance of our region, or we leave that to Israel, to sell these relations to the United States as it has until now."

The discussion enraged the Egyptian foreign minister. Back in his cabin he tried to sleep but couldn't. After pacing his room for an hour, he awakened Boutros Ghali. "It's finished," he said. "I've decided to resign." He then phoned Sadat and requested an immediate appointment.

Sadat was waiting for Kamel at the door of his cabin. He perceived his foreign minister's agitation. Kamel announced that he had wished to defer his resignation until after the conference but could not hold to that. "I can't anymore," he told Sadat. "My eyes just won't close at night . . ."

"You're right," Sadat answered. "I accept your resignation. Now try to relax."

The two parted friends. Kamel promised to keep his resignation secret until the conference was over. As he led Kamel to the door, Sadat said, "The coming days will prove to you that you made a mistake, *ya* Muhammad. I am no less solicitous than you are of the rights of Egypt and the Palestinians."

To his friends, Sadat said he considered Kamel his son, since they were together in the underground and in prison. "I forgive him. He can't take pressure on his nerves."

Neither the Israelis nor the Americans knew anything of what was taking place in the Egyptian cabins that night.

On Friday morning an atmosphere of a "sad end" surrounded the delegations. Some of the junior staff began to pack documents and files. American Secretary of Defense Harold Brown arrived at Camp David, summoned to help the American team breach the wall of obstinacy put up by the two parties. All the highest officials of the U.S. administration were present: Carter, Mondale, Vance, Brown, and Brzezinski. The prestige of the American president and his administration was in the balance and the scales were tipping in the wrong direction.

Begin passed a tortured night: he hardly slept. He sensed it was necessary to make the most fateful of decisions, and in the morning consultation with the Israeli contingent he hinted at a willingness to reconsider the matter of the Israeli settlements in Sinai. In the absence of a clear statement, however, the Israelis did not perk up.

Dayan left for a meeting with Carter. On his return, he reported that the American president intended to conclude the conference Sunday night. He planned to meet with the two houses of Congress on Monday, and immediately thereafter with the communications media, in order to inform them of the developments at the conference. The implication was clear. The Israeli assessment was that the president would put the blame for the failure of the conference on Israel.

At the same time Weizman was in Sadat's cabin.

"Everything is falling apart," said Sadat.

Weizman attempted to assure him: "Everything will work out in the end," he said.

Sadat was no less pessimistic in a meeting with Vance. He spoke slowly so that his guest would absorb every word and be able to pass it along.

"I want to tell you," Sadat began, "that we have defined our stand. I agreed to several American points, and will not agree to others. I'm afraid that the points I already agreed on will be exploited by the other party in talks that may be held in the future, if Camp David ends in failure. I should therefore like to make clear that I consented to these points only to make things easier for Carter. . . . My consent cannot serve as a basis for future negotiations with the other party. I want this to be absolutely clear, for if no agreement is reached, Egypt is not bound by its commitments to the U.S. if the negotiations begin again."

"I must tell this to President Carter," Vance said.

Vance left, and five minutes later the telephone rang in

Sadat's cabin. It was Carter. He asked Sadat to meet him right away. When they met, Sadat repeated what he had told Vance.

"We've spent ten days here," Sadat said, "and the other party doesn't seem to be agreeing to anything. The gap is widening."

Carter and Vance noticed, and not for the first time, that Sadat would not call Israel by name, preferring to refer to it as "the other party."

"I concur," said Carter. "If the talks are doomed to failure, I shall release the Egyptian stand in full, and the Israeli stand in full. I shall also give our position. Nothing commits you so long as Israel has not come to an agreement with you."

"As to the settlements," Vance added, "I suggest a postponement of forty-eight hours. Today is Friday, and before Sunday I will speak to Dayan."

Sadat answered, "All right."

"You said we've been working together for ten days," Vance said. "Let's add two more."

Sadat agreed. "OK, I'm not afraid."

The president of Egypt escorted the president of the United States back to his cabin, then returned to his own.

Friday was uneventful for the Israeli delegation. Begin was going to attend a concert by the Israeli Philharmonic Orchestra in Washington on Saturday. He decided to invite Sadat to the concert. In the dining room he stopped at the Egyptian table, invited the members to the concert, and asked them to transmit his invitation to the Egyptian president.

Things worked out differently. In the afternoon Mondale called on Begin, bringing a letter from Carter, requesting that the delegations make one further effort and concentrate on the discussions. Begin took the hint. He gave up the idea of attending the concert. The Israeli delegation welcomed the sabbath less festively than they had the week before. No guests were invited this time.

On Saturday regular negotiations were suspended, except for a few reports and conversations. Among others, Barak and Dinitz met with Vance, and succeeded in convincing him that there was no sense in the Egyptian demand that an Arab flag fly over Muslim holy places in Jerusalem.

After sundown Begin and Brzezinski met for a game of chess. This time Begin lost.

At about 8:00 p.m., Begin, Dayan, and Barak set out for a talk with Carter. They had the feeling that the meeting would be crucial. As he left, Begin said, "I have hopes for good news, but wait till I get back."

The meeting with Carter lasted a long time. The other Israelis tried to follow what was going on in Carter's cabin but were unsuccessful. Suddenly the door opened and Mondale and Brzezinski came out. They headed for the dining room, looking benign. In the dining room, they were surrounded by the Egyptians, who were laughing cheerfully.

"If the Egyptians are laughing," said one Israeli, "maybe we should start to worry."

The conversation between Carter and Begin began with an announcement by Begin that turned the Camp David negotiations upside down: "If it is the settlements in Sinai that are the obstacle to peace," Begin said, "I will submit the matter to the Knesset. I will respect the Knesset decision. I will recommend that in the vote on this important and sensitive question party discipline be suspended. That's what I can do, no more."

Carter was both pleased and worried. He was well aware that Begin's recommendation would affect the vote. He was afraid Begin might voice a negative view.

"Mr. Begin," Carter said, "what do you plan to say to the Knesset members?"

"I haven't decided that yet," Begin responded. "I might not say anything. It is a difficult decision."

As the talks continued, Begin realized he had to decide on the spot whether he wanted airfields or peace. Like Dayan and Weizman, the prime minister chose peace, having forgone two out of three airfields in the spring of 1978. He also consented to inclusion in the Camp David framework agreement of a provision that Israel had never before accepted: "recognition of the legitimate rights of the Palestinian people to establish an independent country in the land of Israel." Carter and Begin agreed that the matters which were still at issue should be dealt with in attached letters and not included in the Camp David framework agreement.

The meeting ended after midnight. Carter hastened to

report to Sadat on the latest developments. Begin went to sleep. "To the end of my days," he said later, "I will bear in my heart the painful decision on the evacuation of the Sinai settlements."

The next morning was overcast and rainy, but the Israeli ministers looked serene. Begin, Dayan, Weizman, and their aides had a sense of historic achievement. They felt that peace was at hand. The atmosphere was cheerful. The faces of some of the Egyptians exuded gloom. Ibrahim Kamel was not around. Osama al-Baz stated explicit objections to the agreements that were being typed in the offices of the U.S. delegation.

After an internal consultation among the Israelis, Weizman requested a meeting with Sadat, who agreed immediately. Sadat looked fine that morning and welcomed the Israeli defense minister.

"Within the framework of mutual demilitarization," Weizman said, "it was decided that Israel will also be subject to demilitarization along the border, but the area on our side is very small and it's hard for Israel to consent. We would like to increase the forces permitted in the demilitarized zones."

"How many battalions are we talking about?" Sadat asked.

"Three battalions of the border guard."

"All right, Weizman," Sadat said. "For you, four battalions. Since the October War, I have no more complexes."

The two parted with a warm handshake.

The Americans prepared a letter from the president about Jerusalem. The letter was to be attached to the framework agreement. Begin was told of its contents, but his request to see the actual letter was not answered. As the Americans seemed to be dodging, Begin instructed Rosenne to ask for a copy, but the Americans refused point-blank.

At lunchtime Samuel Lewis arrived for a talk with Begin. He showed a draft of the letter to Begin and Simcha Dinitz. Dinitz was appalled. For the first time at the Camp David meetings, the Americans had submitted a proposal of their own that was not based on anything said by either party. Israel was being asked to agree to an American letter stating explicitly that East Jerusalem was occupied territory. Dinitz called Begin's attention to the wording, which not even the Egyptians had demanded.

Begin studied the letter. He was in a rage. "I will not sign this! Absolutely not! On this point I am prepared to break off everything!" he exclaimed. Israel considered the problem of its capital, Jerusalem, the most sensitive and dearest subject of all. "We're going home," the prime minister declared. Lewis left and quickly made his way to Carter's cabin. His face was ashen.

Outside, Rosenne and Rubinstein, an aide of Dayan's, ran into Hamilton Jordan. "We're warning you," they said, "that everything will break down on this matter."

"I'll talk to Mondale or Carter right away," he replied.

Mondale met with Dayan and Weizman almost immediately. Just a few hours before its conclusion, on the threshold of a great triumph, the Camp David conference was about to break down. The Israeli delegation felt defrauded. The Americans had left the most sensitive subject to the last minute so as to give Israel little choice. The Israelis were dumbfounded. The judgments they voiced against Carter and the American team were harsh. They were sure that this move had been carefully planned in advance in order to take the Old City of Jerusalem out of Israeli hands.

At 3:27 p.m. Carter rapped at Begin's door. He was dressed in sports clothes and carrying a tennis racket. He brought signed pictures of himself as gifts for Begin's granddaughters. Begin was indignant: "My hand will not sign that agreement," he said. "My signature will not appear on an agreement involving a letter that states that Jerusalem is an occupied city."

Carter endeavored to calm him down. "We'll find a way, we'll formulate a paper that won't be an obstacle, we'll try to find a formula you'll accept." His voice, however, betrayed him. His tone indicated that he, too, was in despair. The meeting lasted only a few minutes.

Immediately thereafter Carter joined Mondale's meeting with Dayan and Weizman.

"If you hand us a paper like that," Dayan said, "we're packing up and leaving right away."

Carter explained that he had to write the paper on Jerusalem for Sadat in order to clarify the American position on the matter.

"If that's so, we have a sincere quarrel with you. What do we want? We want to reach an agreement with Egypt and not have to confront an American position. What happened here? For the first time in the negotiations we have a clear American stand. You are intervening in the negotiations between us and the Egyptians. All of a sudden we find ourselves in an argument with the Americans rather than the Egyptians. That's not what we came to Camp David for."

"The Knesset enacted a law annexing Jerusalem," Carter broke in. "As you probably know, the U.S. did not accept the Israeli annexation."

"But we didn't come to Camp David to argue with you about your position on this point," Dayan retorted. "We would not have come here if we had known you intended to announce your position on Jerusalem."

"Sadat is pressing hard on the question of Jerusalem," Mondale said, "and the president promised him a letter clarifying our position."

"Is the Jewish quarter in the Old City occupied territory?" asked Dinitz. "And the university on Mount Scopus? And the Hadassah Hospital?"

Meanwhile, matters became more complicated. Sadat resumed his demand that an Arab flag fly over Muslim holy places in Jerusalem. It was Brzezinski who reported the revived demand. Begin jumped to his feet. "Where does Mr. Sadat want the flag?" he asked in mocking bitterness.

"On an Arab mosque on the Temple mount," Brzezinski answered.

"The Temple mount is the holiest place in Jerusalem. The Israelis don't fly any flag there," Begin said.

"Maybe Sadat wants an Arab flag above the Knesset building too," Dayan said derisively.

"If there is peace in the Middle East," Begin said, "the Arabs will be able to fly flags in Jerusalem." The prime minister paused dramatically and added: "They'll be able to fly a flag on every Arab embassy they open in Jerusalem."

The conversation ended with a compromise proposal. The Israelis were prepared to accept a mention of the U.S. position on Jerusalem as presented at the UN. Carter hoped to persuade Sadat to content himself with that so as not to cause the conference to fail at the last minute.

Carter rushed to see Sadat and report the recent developments. In the course of the conversation, the idea that led to a solution was born. The president of Egypt would write the American president a letter outlining the Egyptian position on Jerusalem. Begin would write a similar letter elucidating the Israeli stand. Carter would reply to the two leaders in letters based on statements about Jerusalem previously made by the two American ambassadors to the United Nations, Arthur Goldberg and Charles Yost. The idea was acceptable to Sadat and Begin, and Vance, Barak, Rosenne, and al-Baz set to work composing the letters.

At 5:32 p.m. the phone rang in Begin's cabin. Barak was on the line. He uttered only two sentences: "Sir, we've tied up the last points. We have an agreement!"

Begin glanced around. In the room with him were his office staff—Kadishai, Poran, Patir, Rubinstein, a press photographer, and two security men.

"Children," he announced gleefully, "we've reached an agreement!"

Begin phoned Yigael Yadin in Israel to tell him the good news. He told the deputy prime minister a number of details and that a peace treaty would be signed within three months, and cautioned him to keep mum.

In Camp David a storm raged. A driving rain beat down on the trees and cabins. Hail fell and thunder and lightning ripped through the air. Begin signed several letters and at 6:40 p.m. telephoned Sadat's cabin. Begin congratulated him on the agreement, and said he wished to call on him.

"Please do," Sadat replied.

Eighteen minutes later, the storm ended. Begin proceeded to Sadat's cabin and shook his hand warmly. It was their first meeting since the trip to Gettysburg ten days earlier. They parted shortly afterward, as though they had never had any differences of opinion.

Later, as personal effects were being packed in Begin's room, Sadat arrived unannounced for a return visit, accompanied only by his servants. Begin quickly summoned his ministers, and Weizman poured wine for them all—including Sadat. In his excitement, Weizman had forgotten that as a faithful Muslim, Sadat never drank alcohol.

"Ezer, I'm not a heretic like you!" Sadat chided him. "I drink fruit juice."

Over wine and juice, the company raised their glasses and congratulated one another. Begin searched through his valise, and returned with a medallion depicting the dream of peace. He presented this as a gift to Sadat.

Night had fallen in the Catoctin Mountains. Before the gathering dispersed, Rosenne and Rubinstein asked all those present to sign a map of Camp David. Only the signatures of the Egyptian foreign ministry officials were missing. Later, Rubinstein and Rosenne met them strolling along a path. Rubinstein asked them to add their signatures.

"Definitely not," they replied. "Until there is peace, we will not sign."

Rubinstein was unable to convince them. He and Rosenne realized that something had happened, and a short time later they were told that there had been a wholesale resignation in the Egyptian delegation—Kamel and two of his aides, Abd a-Rauf Ridi and Nabil al-Arabi. The aides had been tough throughout the negotiations. The foreign ministry men also refused to participate in the signing ceremony scheduled to take place a few hours later in the White House.

It was not a full peace treaty, but two framework agreements that the two parties had to complete within three months—two agreements setting normative directives for the future. But from the outset it was clear that a series of topics had deliberately been left open. The closer the two parties came to the end of the negotiations, the greater became the obscurity. It was clear to both sides that even after the peace agreement was signed, there would be delicate points on which each party would prefer its own interpretation.

The simpler agreement was the framework for a peace treaty between Egypt and Israel. Israel gave up all of Sinai, its settlements and airfields. The United States was helpful here by undertaking to build for Israel two airfields replacing those in the Sinai, and to complete their construction before the Israeli defense forces' withdrawal. But the U.S. would not serve as a referee in the future;

the U.S. early-warning stations in Sinai would be dismantled and reconnaissance flights over Sinai would cease. The UN forces were to remain, and in contrast to the past, would be dismissable only on consent of both parties and the unanimous approval of the Security Council. Sinai would not be demilitarized, as Israel once dreamed—except that no fighter planes or antiaircraft batteries would be allowed—but there would be a large buffer zone between the armies of the two countries. Israel would not maintain any early-warning stations in Sinai.

The Egyptian contribution was the normalization of relations with Israel much earlier than previously suggested; the Suez Canal would be open to Israeli shipping as soon as the peace treaty was signed; nine months later, after the first withdrawal phase had been completed, the two countries would exchange ambassadors.

The more complex document was the framework agreement for peace in the Middle East. It covered peace between Israel and all the Arab countries including Egypt, in the main concerning itself with the West Bank and Gaza. Israel's peace plan was not mentioned in the agreement, but was the basis for it.

With this document, Egypt recognized that Israel had need of guarantees of security in those territories. Israel undertook to allow residents of the West Bank and Gaza full autonomy, agreeing to definitions and expressions never before admitted: that the negotiations should include Palestinian representatives, and not only from the territories, and that negotiations should solve the Palestinian problem in all its aspects. It was even explicitly stated that the solution must recognize the legitimate rights of the Palestinian people and its just demands. The two parties realized that autonomy was good for only a transition period of five years, but Israel retained its veto power in several crucial points, including the right to demand sovereignty over the territory.

More than in the first agreement, this left most of the topics open for future negotiations, and the two parties took leave of each other knowing that they were not likely to agree on a number of the most delicate points, such as the status of Jerusalem and Israeli settlements in the territories.

The leaders and their delegations flew by helicopter to

Washington. From the helicopter Jimmy Carter telephoned his predecessor, Gerald Ford: "I've completed the road you set out on." Ford was the first American president to bring Egyptian and Israeli positions closer, in the interim agreement following the Yom Kippur War in 1973, and later in 1975. An excited Ford congratulated Begin, Sadat, and Carter on their great achievement.

The flags of Israel, Egypt, and the U.S. were already hoisted in the east room of the White House. The Who's Who of Washington gathered that night to celebrate the great triumph in a short, sober ceremony. The leaders were welcomed with loud cheers. Carter was smiling broadly.

At 10:58 p.m. Washington time—about dawn in Cairo and Jerusalem—the framework agreements were laid before Begin and Sadat for signing. Carter was there as witness.

The agreement was a great surprise to everyone. During the conference the press had reported serious crises in the talks. The reporters knew little of what was happening within the electrified fence, and their assessments were that the conference was failing completely. The ultimate success amazed the media along with the rest of the world.

In Tel Aviv and Cairo, telephones rang in many homes before sunrise. The news of the agreement spread like wildfire. Millions of people in the two countries listened to the news on radio and watched the signing on television.

In an exhausted voice Begin said: "Citizens of Israel, as you hear me it is early morning and the sun has risen in the land of our fathers and sons. Will we be able to come to you in a few days and sing together, 'We have brought you peace'? I can tell you this: just as up to now we have made every possible human effort to bring it, so we shall continue until the day comes and each of us can say, 'Peace has come to our people and our land, not just in this generation but also in future generations.'"

Sadat also spoke: "I hope and believe that I will be able to join in the hope and prayer of the prime minister of Israel that we reach the moment of signing full peace between Israel and Egypt. We will forget the past and concentrate on the future."

The ceremony was concluded. White House employees removed the flags, and the participants retired.

277

"In the next few weeks," Moshe Dayan said, "each of us will take stock, will think of himself, of his family, of his children. It will be one of the great moments of the state of Israel, of its self-examination, of its assessment of the future."

24 PEACE. PEACE, BUT THERE IS NO PEACE

SUMMARY OF THE CAMP DAVID ACCORDS

The accords had two parts. The first was a framework for a peace treaty between Egypt and Israel; the second, a framework for peace in the Middle East. The first provided for a complete Israeli withdrawal from the Sinai, including evacuation of settlements and airfields. Sinai would be partly demilitarized, with UN observation forces deployed. Free Israeli passage through the Suez Canal and recognition of the Strait of Tiran as an international waterway were stipulated. The Israeli withdrawal was divided into two main stages, to be completed only three years after ratification. The Egyptians would grant Israel full recognition and establish diplomatic relations after the first stage of withdrawal (nine months after ratification, as the new provisional boundary reaches the Al-'Arish–Ras Muhammad line). Egypt also accepted the obligation to establish economic, cultural, and communications relations with Israel.

The second framework provided guidelines for establishing a self-governing authority in the West Bank and Gaza Strip, calling on Israel, Egypt, and Jordan to agree to the establishment of "full autonomy." Egypt and Jordan would be allowed to include Palestinians in their delegations. This would be a provisional arrangement for a period of not more than five years, during which negotiations would begin concerning the final status of the territories. Israeli troops would be withdrawn and redeployed in certain security areas. In addition, Israeli military administration would be "withdrawn." Elections would be held for a Palestinian administrative council.

The Americans, on their part, promised to assist Israel in constructing two new airfields in the Negev and the new military infrastructure in that region. There was an agreement to disagree over Jerusalem, expressed in an additional exchange of letters. Egypt and the United States did not accept Israeli's annexation of East Jerusalem.

On the whole, Camp David allowed the parties to move forward on the bilateral treaty—to be drafted within ninety days—while leaving the Palestinian issue for a later stage, under more ambiguous terms.

The days after Camp David were difficult for Begin and Sadat.

For many Israelis, withdrawal to the 1967 borders and relinquishing the settlements in the Rafa salient destroyed a myth upon which a generation had been brought up: that secure borders were an essential component of any proposed peace settlement. The demand for safe borders and buffer areas united almost all political streams in Israel.

The idea of dismantling the settlements in the Sinai was particularly painful. For years the inhabitants of the Rafa salient and along the Suez Gulf had been taught to regard themselves as pioneers who had responded to the government's call to sacrifice the comfort of life in the big cities and establish themselves in the sands. In less than ten years astonishingly well-kept townlets and villages had sprung up. The Jews in Palestine had always cultivated the legend of pioneering settlement, so the decision to evacuate the settlements was a shock. The bitter and powerful opposition was headed by some of Begin's best friends and most faithful disciples. Tomatoes and eggs were thrown at him. Open rebellion was discussed in the Rafa salient settlements.

Sadat was not happy either. He flew from the U.S. to Rabat, Morocco, hoping to obtain consolation and support from King Hassan, who, however, was cautious and non-committal, neither supporting nor condemning Sadat in public. Hussein of Jordan was invited to meet Sadat, to receive a report on the Camp David decisions, and consider a proposal to join the upcoming negotiations; but the king refused to come. Sadat contented himself with holding a press conference at which he appeared in splendid isolation. On arriving in Cairo, however, he was given a rapturous welcome by millions of Egyptians, although many of them had been organized to demonstrate their support.

Because of the authoritarian nature of the Egyptian regime, opposition to the agreements was expressed only in whispers. The Muslim Brotherhood publicly opposed the agreement, although cassettes containing sermons condemning peace, made by the popular religious figure Sheikh Kishk, were in Cairo streets. But the opposition remained unorganized.

The more Sadat sought support in the Arab world outside Egypt, the greater his disappointment. King Haled refused to declare his approval of the Camp David agreements in public. Egypt's political situation deteriorated from day to day. The Saudi ruler, King Haled, refused to declare approval of the Camp David agreements in public. Shortly after the Camp David meeting Haled went to a hospital in Cleveland, Ohio, for an open heart operation. After he began recovering, President Carter asked to see him. It was very important for Carter to gain the support of the Saudi king for Sadat and the Camp David agreements. Otherwise the U.S. would have to shoulder the entire financial burden.

Bil Quant, a member of the national security council, phoned one of the king's sons in order to determine the subjects to be discussed by Haled and Carter. The king's son said: "They had better not talk too much about the Camp David agreements. It is not good for the king's health. The less they discuss that topic, the better it will be for the king and the president. It is advisable to talk about other matters."

"Is there any subject which particularly interests the king?" Quant asked.

"Yes, certainly," the king's son replied. "The king loves to talk about hunting quail with kestrels."

Quant was taken aback. He knew nothing about the subject, and he surmised that Carter did not know anything about quail and kestrels either. Before the king reached Washington, one of the NSC officials was sent to the library to do homework on the subject.

On September 27, 1978, after two days of discussions, the Israeli Knesset approved the Camp David agreements: 86 hands were raised in support of the agreement, 19 were raised in opposition. But there was no rejoicing in the Knesset or in Israeli homes; this was the first time since Jews had begun settling the land of Israel in modern times that a decision had been made to uproot settlements.

At Camp David it had been agreed that within three months the two sides would resolve the outstanding issues and sign a peace treaty. Begin and Sadat said immediately on returning home that "only two percent" was left to be resolved, but new problems cropped up every day. A major dispute involved a target date for establishing autonomy in the West Bank and Gaza. Other problems included giving the Israeli-Egyptian treaty priority over defense pacts Egypt had signed with other Arab countries, which Israel regarded as directed against itself; removing the linkage between the Egyptian-Israeli agreement and new arrangements in the West Bank and the Gaza Strip; Egypt's demand that interim stages be fixed for the first pullback from Sinai; and Israel's rights in the oil wells in the Sinai.

The atmosphere in the Middle East grew increasingly turbid. The Israelis learned that the U.S. ambassador to the UN, Andrew Young, had told American reporters off the record that King Haled, who had visited President Carter, had been given assurances that the eastern part of Jerusalem would eventually be under Arab rule again.

The atmosphere was not improved by the visit of American Undersecretary of State Harold Saunders to the Middle East to brief the rulers of Saudi Arabia and Jordan. He was received coldly in Amman and the suggestion that Hussein join the negotiations was negative. In Riyadh, the Saudi leaders told him they wanted a better solution to the Palestinian problem and the return of eastern Jerusalem to Arab rule.

Jerusalem, too, gave him a cool reception, partly because he was remembered as the man who, during Kissinger's heyday, had—to the Israelis' displeasure—stated that the Palestinian problem was at the heart of the Middle East dispute.

Saunders heard some harsh words at a working dinner at the home of the American ambassador, Samuel Lewis. Members of the opposition had been invited to the dinner and Saunders hoped to find succor in that quarter. He was surprised when the opposition leaders attacked the Americans sharply. When former foreign minister Yigal Allon finished listing a series of promises broken by the Americans since 1975, Saunders retorted: "And what about the ten billion dollars' worth of aid Israel has received? Doesn't that count for something?"

Some of the Israelis at the table said it would have been better had Israel conducted the negotiations directly with Egypt, without American intervention.

Ambassador Lewis reacted by saying: "By all means, if you can, go ahead and do it by yourselves!"

Saunders got no relief from his meetings with Palestinians from the occupied territories either. No one dared to commit himself in any way.

"I feel like a dealer trying to sell a used car which has a faulty engine, flat tires, and no buyers," Saunders said, summing up his visit to Israel.

The Israeli cabinet reacted angrily to what appeared to it to be interference in sensitive subjects. Saunders's plane was still on its way to the U.S. when the Israeli cabinet made a dramatic decision to "thicken" Israeli settlements in the West Bank and to move Begin's office to East Jerusalem.

Israeli officials whispered in journalists' ears that this was the reaction to what Saunders told the Jordanians about those parts of East Jerusalem captured in 1967 being considered occupied by the U.S. government.

Without it having been his intention, Saunders had fanned the fires of revolt in the occupied territories. In some places the Palestinian flag was raised. Some Palestinians advocated establishing a state on Israeli territory.

Against this background of general distress, a combined Israel-Egypt-U.S. conference was opened at Blair House in Washington. The object of the meeting was to follow the guidelines of Camp David and mold them into a detailed peace treaty so that the two parties could sign it within three months.

At the beginning of October 1978 Gamassi's position in Egypt was stronger than ever. On October 4, when Sadat was addressing the People's Assembly on Camp David, Gamassi was late in reaching the chamber because of a burst water pipe in the Heliopolis quarter, which had caused an immense traffic jam. On entering the chamber he sat among the delegates and not at the cabinet table. Later on he apologized to Sadat for his late arrival. "Never mind," was the reply, "forget it." When the speech was over, Gamassi invited a group of Israeli journalists to watch the Sixth of October parade. That evening he invited a group of generals to his home. During the conversation he gave his reasons for supporting the Camp David agreements, though he remarked that he had not been consulted before they were signed.

The next morning Sadat summoned Gamassi to his office, where he informed him of his dismissal only minutes before the teleprinters of the Egyptian news service gave the information to the world, together with a biography of the new minister of war, Kamel Hassan Ali.

Gamassi knew nothing of this, yet suggested that Sadat call Ali to him immediately and appoint him. Sadat surprised him again when he answered: "There's no need, he's already sitting in your office."

The Egyptians did not conceal their mistrust of Begin, his government, and his emissaries at Blair House. After their rejoicing over the signing of the Camp David agreements they had had second thoughts; now they tried to raise doubts and find loopholes in the agreements, exposing dangers to be expected. The Egyptians expressed doubt whether the Begin government would in fact implement the full autonomy plan, as agreed at Camp David. This mistrust was nourished by the American decision to link the peace treaty with the autonomy plan. On several occasions the American delegates seemed more extremist than the Egyptians. Things got to the stage where Israeli and

Egyptian delegates hid from the American representatives from time to time so that they could conclude their discussions on certain points undisturbed.

Israel vehemently resisted the attempts made by the Egyptians and the Americans to establish a close link between the agreements in the Sinai and the West Bank. Dayan and Weizman, representing Israel, claimed that peace could not be made dependent on the readiness of others, whether Palestinians or Jordanians, who opposed the peace process and the agreement achieved at Camp David.

"The Palestinians and the Jordanians could deliberately undermine the peace process," Dayan said.

"We do not wish to sell the Palestinians down the river," said Kamel Hassan Ali, who had replaced Gamassi as war minister. "If the Jordanians won't cooperate in establishing autonomy we'll take the responsibility for it ourselves."

"And what if the Palestinians won't come? If they refuse to talk?" Dayan asked.

The Egyptian ambassador to Washington, Ashraf Gorbal, said: "Then they can go to hell."

The possibility was raised that the inhabitants of the West Bank would refuse to cooperate on the autonomy question. The Egyptians proposed sending a delegation of their own to the occupied territories to persuade the inhabitants to seize the opportunity and accept autonomy.

Dayan said: "You are mistaken if you think they'll welcome you with open arms. They'll pelt you with rotten tomatoes, maybe even with stones."

To assure linkage between the two parts of the agreement and to guarantee the implementation of the part dealing with autonomy, Egypt and the U.S. introduced secondary conditions, such as a target date for establishing autonomy. During the days and nights of the meetings the target date wandered from one subject to another: a target date for establishing the autonomy, a target date for holding elections, a target date for concluding negotiations.

The atmosphere was more relaxed in the sessions of a military working group which was attempting to prepare the military appendix to the peace treaty. Under the watchful eye of the American delegate, General Lawrence,

Brigadier Avraham Tamir on the Israeli side and General Taha Magdub on the Egyptian side discussed each detail. One of the points disputed was the amount of weaponry the Egyptians would be permitted to bring into Sinai once the peace treaty had been signed. The Israelis and the Egyptians argued over every cannon and tank. Israel wanted to have as few Egyptian arms allowed in as possible, to create a partly demilitarized zone. The Israelis were concerned primarily with preventing the entry of fighter planes and batteries of antiaircraft missiles like those which had downed many Israeli planes during the Yom Kippur War. The Egyptians insisted on being allowed to introduce antiaircraft missile batteries into the Sinai peninsula.

"Batteries of this kind are part of the equipment of each Egyptian division," General Magdub said.

Brigadier Amos Lapidoth of the Israeli air force replied: "Our intelligence tells us that you do not have those missile batteries in every division."

"But I say that we do," Magdub insisted.

"Up until the day I left Israel this week you did not," Lapidoth replied.

"Well, now we do," Magdub answered.

"You can also add five hundred tanks to your divisions in this way," Lapidoth said.

The American representative, General Lawrence, reported: "After clarification, it was decided that Egyptian divisions do not include batteries of antiaircraft missiles."

While the conference was still underway Sadat had a bitter surprise. The rejectionist states decided to meet in Baghdad to discuss steps to be taken against Egypt and against the peace treaty.

The initiative for the summit conference had come from Iraq, which wanted to end long years of isolation, to become the leader of the Arab world, and to extend its influence to Syria, which had been dealt a severe blow by the Camp David agreement.

Until the last moment Sadat believed that the Saudis would not support a meeting initiated by the radical Iraqis. The Saudis regarded the possibility of a reconciliation between Syria and Iraq as remote; they were confident of their power to prevent isolation and sanctions.

But relations between Sadat and the real leader of Saudi Arabia, Crown Prince Fahd, had deteriorated badly. Egyptian emissaries heard Fahd utter bitter complaints about the concessions Sadat had made about the Palestinians, which had gone far beyond what had been understood between them before the Camp David meeting. The Saudis secretly approved of the agreement, but had urged Sadat to obtain a higher price on the Palestinian issue.

The Baghdad discussions ended with a bitter attack on the Camp David agreements and a call to Egypt to refrain from signing the peace treaty. The conference also demanded complete Israeli withdrawal and decided on certain secret resolutions regarding sanctions to be imposed on Egypt if it signed the peace treaty with Israel, including stopping financial aid to Egypt, cutting off diplomatic ties, removing the Arab League offices from Cairo and suspending Egypt's membership in the League, and placing an embargo on Egyptian firms that traded with Israel. A fund was established to provide financial aid to Syria, Jordan, the PLO, and the occupied territories.

The Arab world had come out in force against Sadat.

This atmosphere influenced the Egyptian man in the street as well as the government in Cairo, which tried to prove it had not made a separate peace with Israel. The events in the Middle East had a serious effect on the discussions in Washington. The Egyptians hardened their stand and were not prepared to give in on anything. Realizing the erosion that was occurring in the Camp David agreements, the Israelis stood firm. Egypt suddenly made the exchange of ambassadors with Israel dependent on steps being taken in the West Bank, claiming that this was the outcome of Israel's refusal to subphase its first withdrawal from Sinai. Israel did not want to agree to linking the exchange of ambassadors with steps in the West Bank. It was also evident that Egypt wanted to achieve quick results which could be displayed before the Egyptian people and the Arab world, including an early Israeli withdrawal from Al-'Arish, the capital of the Sinai peninsula, from the oilfields around the Suez Gulf, and from the ancient monastery of St. Catherine's. Israel refused to comply.

Long discussions were held on the priority to be given

to the Israeli-Egyptian peace treaty over the defense treaties Egypt had made with the other Arab countries. Israel wanted to ensure that Egypt would not take part in a war against Israel initiated by other Arab countries. The Egyptians maintained that their defense pacts with Arab states were intended for other purposes too, and that they would be valid as long as there was no comprehensive settlement in the Middle East. At the end of a long, bitter argument Israel relinquished its demand for the annulment of Egypt's commitments. The Israeli representatives merely asked for a letter stating that Egypt would not attack Israel if Israel had not attacked an Arab country.

The Americans complicated affairs. The opinion of the State Department's legal adviser was that there was nothing to prevent Egypt from coming to the aid of another Arab country with which it had a bilateral or collective defense pact if that country had been the victim of armed aggression.

The discussions in Washington were not made easier by the fact that the two Israeli representatives, Dayan and Weizman, did not have the authority to make even the simplest on-on-spot decisions. They were angry. "If Ben-Gurion were alive," Dayan said to Weizman at one point, "we would have had peace months ago."

It was in effect the cabinet in Jerusalem that conducted the negotiations in Washington. Begin and his ministers received continual reports on the negotiations and proposals. It was easy for the cabinet, thousands of miles away from Washington, to reject American and Egyptian proposals. Begin's leadership was lax at the time. He did not lead the government but allowed it to lead him. The rejection of a number of suggestions aroused fury in Washington. On one occasion, when Weizman flew to Jerusalem to report to the government on the talks in Washington, he was met with the cry: "What have you sold today?" In Egypt the decision-making process was simpler. One man, Sadat, weighed matters and decided. On more than one occasion the American representatives lost all patience with the long, complex, and exhausting democratic process in Israel.

The Blair House conference ended without the sides having reached agreement. Peace seemed far away, and

the treaty would *not* be signed three months after the conclusion of the Camp David meeting. Not even the decision
to award the Nobel peace prize to Begin and Sadat could
sweeten the bitter pill.

25 THE WAY TO PEACE

December 1978 was a black time for the American, Israeli, and Egyptian delegations. Agreement eluded them. Events in Iran were influencing the mood in Jerusalem and Washington, and the impending fall of the shah was forcing all three sides to try to act quickly.

In another attempt to salvage the stalled talks, Cyrus Vance was dispatched to the Middle East. Carter was threatening Israel, while U.S. government officials expressed satisfaction with the Egyptian position.

It had been agreed that after the signing of the Camp David accords the three sides would meet again to sign a peace treaty on December 17, 1978. By December 13, the day of Vance's arrival in Israel, however, it was clear that it would be impossible to make this deadline.

The reception for the secretary of state, who had stopped in Egypt first, was cool. Begin did not intend to give up anything to Vance.

Vance agreed that the Egyptian position had hardened, but he explained this as a result of Sadat's growing fear of the rejection front. Israel should make concessions to make it easier on Sadat, Vance argued, but Begin was not impressed. Vance's mission was a failure. When he flew back to the United States, he left these following problems still unsolved:

• Egypt's demand that the linkage between the Egyptian-Israeli treaty and the implementation of the autonomy plan be made explicit.

• Egypt's demand that it reserve for itself the right to demand changes in the security arrangements in the Sinai after the signing of the treaty.

• Israel's stipulation that ambassadors be exchanged between Egypt and Israel during the first stages of the withdrawal from Sinai.

• Egypt's demand for unilateral symbolic gestures from Israel.

• Egypt's demand for a schedule detailing the various stages of implementation of the autonomy plan.

• Israel's demand that it be clearly stated that the Egyptian-Israeli treaty supersedes all defense treaties between Egypt and other Arab countries.

As expected, Washington blamed Israel for the failure of Vance's mission.

A meeting was planned in Brussels between Dayan and Khalil to revive the negotiations. Vance was invited to participate. Begin made it clear that Dayan was only authorized to negotiate terms of process, not substance.

The Brussels meeting ended without success; disagreement remained over the same issues. The only thing the three could agree on was that the Israeli government would publish a communiqué expressing its desire to continue the negotiations.

In January 1979, Assistant Secretary of State Alfred Atherton arrived in the Middle East for another attempt. Atherton held fourteen meetings with the Israeli negiotiating team, five with Begin, and four with Dayan. He had a seemingly limitless number of phone talks with Vance and his assistants in Washington.

Atherton presented Dayan with the draft of a letter Vance proposed to send him. The letter was intended to allay Israeli fears following the dispatch of a separate letter to Egypt discussing the linkage between the Egyptian-Israeli treaty and the implementation of the autonomy plan, as well as the treaty superseding the treaties between Egypt and other Arab countries. The Israelis immediately perceived a change of tone and position taken by the

Americans, for the letter—only a page and one quarter long—took pains to show support for Israeli positions. In the letter the Americans refrained from using the term "occupied territories," in response to Israel's argument that this term implied that conquered territories could or should be liberated by force. In addition, the letter used the geographic names of the territories: Judea, Samaria, Golan Heights, and the Gaza Strip. Atherton reached a degree of consensus with the Israelis over the common denominator to the conflicting legalistic interpretations held by Egypt and Israel of the unresolved items of the treaty.

But in Cairo, the Egyptians rejected Atherton's proposals.

In February, Egyptian Prime Minister Khalil and Israeli Foreign Minister Dayan were invited to a second Camp David conference. The Americans had another Egyptian proposal in their hands, one that indicated Cairo had hardened its position since Camp David. The Egyptians made the following new demands:

• A clear statement that the Egyptian-Israeli treaty does not supersede other treaties.

• Implementation of the Egyptian-Israeli part of the treaty to be entirely dependent on implementation of the entire autonomy plan.

"We will not budge from these demands," Khalil told Vance and Dayan.

The Americans presented eight new proposals, but none were acceptable to either side.

It was proposed by the United States that Begin meet with Khalil, for only Begin had authority to accept the Egyptian proposals. Begin was offended by the proposal that he meet with an Egyptian of lesser rank who did not have the equivalent authority to make decisions.

The pressure on Begin was intense; at Dayan's request, Begin convened the cabinet. It was clear that the Americans were taking the Egyptian side; there was no doubt that they intended to pressure Israel. Dayan belived that Begin should meet Khalil. "Maybe this is our last chance to reach an agreement," he said. Weizman agreed. "We must do everything to get these negotiations over with," he said impatiently. Begin remained unmoved. "Why should I go?" he asked. "So I can say to the president of the United States, no, no, no, no! Why do I have to be the one to say no to Washington, when I can just as easily do it from Jerusalem?" Begin spoke with great emotion. "Justice will triumph. I am convinced of that. A person could die first, but I have no doubt that justice will triumph."

Begin's statement decided the issue. Before the meeting had started, eight ministers were opposed to Begin's going to Washington; after Begin's speech, the number had risen to fourteen. Begin was greatly encouraged by this show of support; however, the cabinet's announcement at the end of the meeting was designed to leave some narrow room for flexibility. Begin would not meet the Egyptian prime minister, but was willing to meet Carter.

That evening Carter, having been informed of the cabinet's announcement, telephoned Begin at home and asked him to come to a private meeting in Washington.

During his twenty months in office, Begin had visited the United States six times, for a total of forty days in Washington. Setting out on his seventh trip at the beginning of March 1979, Begin said angrily, "We are not a generation that can be pushed around." Landing in Washington, his first public statements were belligerent. He spoke harshly with Carter during their first meeting, telling the president that American mediation had become nothing more than complete support for the Egyptian side. "Is it any wonder that the Egyptian prime minister and other Egyptian politicians are always talking about the consensus of opinion between the U.S. and Egypt if you draw up a document, take it to Egypt, and then tell us that we must accept it without any revision whatever?"

Begin lectured Carter on the sacrifices Israel had already made for peace: removal of the settlements in Sinai, the pain of taking the homes of the Israeli settlers away from them. "And what are you offering us? A peace that is worthless! . . . If you want us to accept the conditions proposed by the Egyptians in the peace treaty it will mean that Egypt will be able to join another war against Israel . . . Do you think that we can agree in advance that a country that signs a treaty with us is allowed to fight against us?"

Begin did not budge from this position, and hardened his demand for guarantees for oil from the Sinai, a claim he justified as a result of the new Iranian government's decision to cease supplying oil to Israel.

Saturday night they talked again. Late that night, Carter made the decision to go to the Middle East. He had nothing to lose.

The next day Carter held a conference with his closest advisers in the oval office. He announced his intention to fly to Egypt and Israel in order to try to bring the peace negotiations to an end. The situation could not have been worse from his point of view. True, the risk was great, but he had no alternative. Hamilton Jordan was the only one of his advisers who supported the idea. The rest were dead set against it, warning him of the tremendous damage his trip would do to his public image if it failed. The president had already made up his mind, however; there was little difference in the damage that could occur if he stayed at the White House or failed in the Middle East.

Begin spent Saturday at Blair House resting and preparing for his appearance before the American media. He decided to attack the American position and to present Carter as being incapable of serving any longer as an honest broker in the Middle East.

Cyrus Vance and his assistants were simultaneously formulating a new proposal for Carter to present to Begin during his Saturday night meeting. The new proposal dropped the previous American support for Sadat's demand on the issue of the Israeli-Egyptian treaty superseding other treaties with Arab states.

After the banquet for Begin, the two leaders left for talks. It was immediately evident that it was not the appropriate time.

New American proposals were shown to Begin the day after. Begin saw immediately that there were three additions to the American position. Within three minutes he agreed to accept the new proposals.

"I can recommend immediately one of the points," he told Carter, "but the other two must be brought to my cabinet."

"Why do you have to do that?" inquired Carter. "At Camp David you were able to make even more important decisions without consulting with the cabinet."

"I have five generals in my cabinet who are used to giving orders," replied Begin.

"I have fifteen members of Congress who are convinced

they should be president of the United States and another fifteen who are convinced they soon will be," said Carter.

The American proposals dealt with the timetable, supersedence of the Israeli-Egyptian treaty over other treaties, and the question of linkage to the treaty and the implementation of the autonomy plan. Carter and Vance suggested reviving the original American position that the negotiations over autonomy should be completed within a year and that elections should be held at an early date. According to the Israeli interpretation, this was something new: the Americans were no longer obligating Israel to complete the negotiations within a year; the term "early" was also considered to add flexibility. The issue of supersedence was to be solved by an accompanying letter that would say, "What it states in the treaty with Israel obligates Egypt without violating Egypt's other treaty obligations." The linkage problem was to be solved by the Americans with a letter which would say that the stipulation of autonomy in the accord was meant to serve as a basis for peace not only between Egypt and Israel but also between Israel and its Arab neighbors.

The cabinet reluctantly approved the new additions and Begin so informed Carter. A few minutes later, Brzezinski invited Begin to the White House for an additional meeting, where Begin learned that Carter was flying to Cairo and Jerusalem.

Before meeting with Begin, Carter had informed Sadat.

Carter was welcomed in Cairo, with great pomp and circumstance, but the reception was contained. There were millions of Egyptians in the streets, but most had come to cheer their own president. The two leaders traveled to Alexandria by train.

Carter presented his new proposals to Sadat, who suggested revision. The changes seemed insignificant to the Americans; when Sadat added some more conditions, they did not seem important either.

Sadat wanted the autonomy plan to be implemented in the Gaza Strip should it be impossible to do so on the West Bank. In addition he wanted to open a liaison office to be manned by Egyptian officers in the Gaza Strip. Sadat refused to grant Israel most-favored-nation status for supply of oil but did agree to treat Israel, which had developed the Sinai oilfields, like any other customer.

On Saturday night, March 10, 1979, Carter arrived in Israel hoping that a treaty might be signed while he was still in the Middle East.

After a private supper, Carter and Begin retired to Begin's home in Jerusalem for talks. Begin noticed Carter's excitement almost immediately. "President Sadat is willing to come to Israel by Tuesday in order to sign, or at least initial, a treaty," Carter told Begin.

"Impossible," replied Begin. "A peace treaty is not that simple. The fate of a nation hangs in the balance. Even if we reach an understanding on all points we cannot sign such an agreement, not with initials or full signature. I promised that I would bring the peace treaty to the Knesset for ratification. I cannot break my promise."

Carter did not give up. He told Begin that he intended to return to the United States before the week was up with a substantial achievement, perhaps even a signed treaty. "There are only a few small things that Sadat is asking from Israel. It would be worthwhile giving them to him," he said.

"This is a matter which involves the life of every person in Israel!" protested Begin. "I will bring the treaty to the Knesset for ratification and if I don't, I will not be prime minister of Israel a second longer."

Carter's irritation was beginning to show. "Mr. Prime Minister, perhaps you might explain to me how you signed the Camp David agreements and then brought them to the Knesset for ratification and now you are telling me that a peace treaty requires ratification of the cabinet, then the Knesset, and only then you can sign it? What kind of way of doing things is this?"

Begin lost his temper. "During Camp David I informed you that I would not initial the peace treaty before it was ratified by the Knesset. My promise was widely noted. Why is this so hard for you to understand? Had you done your homework you would know what I promised, to whom I promised, and you would know how I promised."

To this Carter replied: "I am so personally involved in the peace process that I only want to see it reach a positive end."

Carter showed Begin Sadat's proposals. "What happened to the proposals I received from you last week in Washington, which were approved by the cabinet?" asked Begin. "We are here to consider American proposals and instead you have brought me a new Egyptian proposal that has nothing to do with your proposal last week."

"We will look for words that will express the ideas we discussed between us," replied Carter, "without interfering with fundamentals."

But Begin did not accept this. Several times already, Carter had belittled the value of words.

"If we are talking only of words then why doesn't Sadat make the concessions?" asked Begin.

He had reason to worry. The American proposals that had been accepted by Begin at the White House suddenly disappeared after they were brought to Sadat. Begin realized that Carter was unwilling to influence Sadat to change his position.

"Why should Sadat come to Jerusalem? What will he sign here? A peace treaty dictated by Egyptian demands?" asked Begin. He rejected Sadat's proposals.

"Why does Sadat want to establish a liaison office in the Gaza Strip all of a sudden?" asked Begin. "That is nothing less than a clear violation of the Camp David agreements. What did we sign the Camp David accords for?" Begin had understood the danger implied by Sadat's proposal. Israel's acceptance of a liaison office in the Gaza Strip was likely to be followed by later demands for Egyptian sovereignty over the area, and this was unacceptable to Begin.

"Sadat is a great man and a personal friend of mine. I believe in him and you must trust him," said Carter.

"Impossible," replied Begin.

The next day, after ceremonial events, the cabinet went into special session to meet Carter and his aides, including the secretary of state, members of the White House staff, the defense secretary, and the president's adviser on national security. Begin surprised Carter by suggesting that he serve as chairman of the cabinet meeting, an honor bestowed on no other foreigner in Israel's history.

Carter began simply, telling of his great pleasure at seeing the sunrise from his hotel room that morning. "The president of Israel told me that Jerusalem, the city of peace, had seen more wars than any other city in the world," Carter told the ministers. "I prayed today in church that Jerusalem would not suffer any more wars."

Turning to the agenda before them, Carter repeated his support for Sadat's stance.

"You must consider Sadat's position in the Arab world," Carter said. "On the one hand, the Arab countries have rejected him; on the other, he still does not have peace with Israel. The president of Egypt thinks in terms of global strategy while you think in different terms. You insist on every period, every comma. Every issue is crucial to you. I am not saying that it is not possible to understand this, but the trouble is that there is no trust between you and Sadat. Sadat has no support from the Arab countries, only because of the negotiations he is engaged in with you."

"The one who has to make concessions," replied Begin, "is Sadat. The state of Israel has made great sacrifices. Now it is Egypt's turn. We have reached the bottom line. Mr. President, why are you always telling us Sadat's problems? Why do you not take our problems seriously?"

The meeting was long and hard. "I want to finish the negotiations today, if possible," Carter said.

When the discussion turned to the autonomy plan, Minister of Agriculture Ariel Sharon asked permission to speak. The former military officer, known for his hawkish views, spoke aggressively without any concern for offending President Carter. His remarks were sarcastic and forthright. "I am in favor of the autonomy plan proposed by Mr. Begin, but I am against creation of another Palestinian state between us and Jordan. It will not happen! It is worth telling you that here today, once and for all. Why should a million Jews not live in the West Bank?"

"Why must you talk of a million Jews on the West Bank?" asked Carter. "It belongs to the Arabs."

"There may be one million Jews in the West Bank, even two million," replied Sharon.

"We know exactly what you think on this issue," said Carter. "Let us leave it for now."

"In the framework of autonomy, internal security will remain in Israel's hands," continued Sharon. "It is inconceivable that the Arab residents will handle internal security. This could bring about a war. Mr. President, we have seen many wars and only a person like me who has seen wars can want a real peace. We Israelis can only lose one war. I, personally, am willing to fight another ten wars in order to preserve the existence of the state of Israel."

The conversation turned back to the Egyptian proposals. Harsh words were exchanged, but in the end Carter could have no doubt that Israel was rejecting the Egyptian proposal to open a liaison office in Gaza, that the autonomy plan would begin in Gaza if not on the West Bank. The Israeli ministers also insisted that Israel should have preferential status as a buyer of oil. The chances for peace were slipping away in front of Carter's eyes. Frustration and disappointment were clearly registered on his face. "I cannot return from Israel empty-handed. You must sign," pleaded Carter angrily, as if he were delivering orders from on high. His tone surprised the ministers. There was silence for a second and then Begin spoke. "Mr. President, you will excuse us, but we must tell you that we will only sign what we want to sign and that we will not sign anything we do not want to sign."

Carter then tried to argue the Egyptian claim for opening the liaison office in Gaza. "If Israel and Egypt reach agreement on this issue, it will be a significant achievement," he said.

In the end the Israelis firmly rejected the proposal.

Carter also expressed his support for Egypt's refusal to grant Israel preferential status as a purchaser of oil. "Egypt does not grant such status to any other country in the world, why should it do so for Israel?"

"Because we developed the Sinai oilfields," answered Begin, "and because we must guarantee for ourselves a supply of oil equivalent to that we are extracting today. We will pay in full for this oil."

"What are Israel's oil needs?" asked Carter. "One percent of the U.S. need! I, as president of the United States, am prepared to fulfill your oil needs for ten, even fifteen years, if only someone would promise the U.S. what I am promising you."

"Thank you, Mr. President," replied Begin, "but we are not interested. I do not want an American president to have to face the American public if there is a shortage of oil in the U.S. I do not want any American citizen to be unable to heat his apartment during the winter because oil has been sold to Israel."

The cabinet meeting broke up without agreement. Begin did not want Carter to leave empty-handed. He promised the president and his advisers that after the evening ban-quiet he would convene the cabinet for another meeting, this time without Carter.

The ministers were tired, but spoke nonetheless with a good deal of energy and forcefulness. They accepted the American proposal to change a few words in the sections dealing with the supersedence of the Israeli-Egyptian treaty over other treaties held by Egypt. But then came the difficult part: the opening of the Egyptian liaison office in Gaza, the idea of beginning autonomy in Gaza, and Egypt's refusal to give Israel preferential status as an oil customer.

Begin rejected the proposals to open the liaison office in Gaza and the entire cabinet, except for Weizman and Dayan, supported him. "From such a liaison office a Palestinian state will grow within a month," argued Ariel Sharon.

On the oil issue, Begin revealed the United States had proposed that Israel receive Egyptian oil by way of the United States and that this had been agreed to by Sadat.

"A peace treaty obligates Egypt to maintain good relations with Israel," said Minister of Justice Shmuel Tamir. "Among other things, this means no more boycott. If we agreed to the Egyptian proposal it would mean that we are agreeing to allow them to continue their boycott. We cannot do this. I see this issue as a test of Egypt's intention to establish a real peace with Israel." The ministers agreed with Tamir. The American proposal was rejected and the decision was relayed to the secretary of state.

On the issue of exchange of ambassadors, there was near unanimity. There was no willingness to give in to the Egyptians on this issue; at the same time, however, there was willingness to implement the withdrawal in stages without describing in detail what the stages would consist of. This was not done in order to please the American president, and certainly not Sadat.

The Israeli decision on the principle of supersedence of the Israeli-Egyptian treaty over other treaties encouraged the Americans, who perceived this as a sign of Israeli willingness to make concessions. But the other decisions all rejected the Egyptian-American proposals. When Carter learned of these decisions, he decided to abandon his plan to send Vance to Cairo, since this would only destroy what was left of the peace initiative. The word was being leaked through the many American journalists who had come to the Middle East with Carter that intransigence was leading to disaster.

At 10:00 a.m. a meeting was set up between Carter and his entourage and the Israeli cabinet. Many of the participants had not had any sleep. A tired Begin opened the meeting with a small surprise: a birthday party for the president's secretary. Israelis and Americans burst out singing, "Happy birthday to you." For the first time that day, a smile appeared on Carter's face.

The meeting was relatively short, since everyone was in a hurry to get to the Knesset. The cabinet did not change its mind and was unwilling to make any additional concessions. Carter did not hide his deep disappointment.

From his suite at the King David, Carter spoke with Sadat on the telephone several times. Sadat accepted the Israeli and American decision on the supersedence of the treaty and on the timetable; but on the issue of oil, a liaison office in Gaza, and the start of autonomy in Gaza there was no movement.

As all of Israel watched the events in the Knesset, and Americans were treated to Israeli parliamentary democracy in action for the first time, something happened that only a few people picked up on at the time. Moshe Dayan, who normally sat on the left of Begin, got out of his seat and walked over to the visitors' gallery, pausing to speak to Vance. Since his personal failure during the Yom Kippur War, Dayan had not spared any effort to make himself the hero of the peace. He saw his role as being the one to bring peace. The storm in the Knesset was far from his thoughts at that moment. He was afraid that peace was slipping from his fingers and he sought a solution to the growing crisis. "We must not let the president of the United States leave Israel this way," he said. Dayan feared further deterioration in the relations between the two countries. Although he was close to despair, he was convinced a solution was possible. He spoke with Vance for ten minutes, making an appointment for a later meeting.

At that same moment Ben-Gurion Airport was being prepared for Carter's departure. The honor guard had already arrived.

While Carter was on the way to King David to pack his bags, the Israeli cabinet convened to decide whether or not there was anything to decide. All previous decisions remained unchanged. There was no reason to revise them. The cabinet was in a fighting mood; there was a feeling that a long journey had come to an end. Begin did not appear particularly unhappy, but Weizman was angry. "I am fed up," he said angrily. "Because of all this nonsense we are going to lose the chance for peace." Later, in a statement which reached Begin, he said that "at moments like these one should think about political measures." Some people interpreted this as a threat to resign.

After Begin had gone home, Dayan presented his colleagues with his new proposal. A telephone call to Begin at home made possible an extra meeting with Vance.

In the meantime Vance had reported to Carter on his short conversation with Dayan in the Knesset. Carter decided not to leave empty-handed if possible, and agreed to stay on an extra day. He invited Begin for breakfast the next morning.

"I understand that one of your ministers has raised some new ideas," said Carter to Begin.

"I think, Mr. President, that my ministers' opinions are better shown to you than to me," replied Begin.

Sunday, March 12, was a difficult night. Carter was more irritated than his closest advisers had ever seen him. "We leave tomorrow."

"We have nothing left to do in Jerusalem," said Jody Powell.

Dayan's proposals were simple. The first two problems—Egypt's demand for a liaison office and Israel's demands for oil—were not mentioned in the Camp David accords and need not be included in a peace treaty. Dayan proposed finding a solution to these problems outside of the boundaries of the treaty, perhaps in an accompanying letter, so as not to delay the signing of the treaty. "We should stick to the framework signed at Camp David," explained Dayan. The third problem—establishing the timetable for withdrawals in the Sinai and exchange of ambassadors—was more difficult. Dayan suggested speeding up the withdrawal from Sinai in return for an exchange of ambassadors immediately after the first withdrawal stage. This idea had first been suggested by Weizman at the earlier Blair House talks, but had been rejected by the Israeli cabinet.

Meanwhile, CBS anchorman Walter Cronkite reported from the King David to millions of Americans that Carter's gamble had failed. His colleagues John Chancellor and Barbara Walters gave similar reports. At the same time, in one of the rooms of the King David, Dayan presented his proposals to Vance and Brzezinski in the presence of Tamir. They did not spare any effort to come up with the right formulation to solve the crisis on the basis of Dayan's basic principles. In another room, Weizman was meeting with Brown about the military dimensions of the peace treaty. Carter was at the Israel Museum, accompanied by Yigael Yadin, seeing the Dead Sea scrolls. Upon his return he went straight to Vance's room to find out if there had been any progress in the talks with Dayan. The American staff members promised to contact him as soon as they had finished preparing the final paragraphs.

At 3:00 a.m. Brzezinski and Vance walked into an elevator that took them immediately to Carter's suite. After seventy-two hours of work with little sleep, the two woke up Carter and showed him the new formulations they had worked out with the Israelis. Carter went back to sleep to get some rest for his 8:30 breakfast meeting with Begin.

In the morning the King David was a madhouse. American workers were loading boxes, suitcases, cartons, and clothes into limousines. The president was leaving in a few hours. There was a feeling that the trip had been a failure.

When Menachem and Aliza Begin arrived for breakfast with the Carter family, the prime minister had already been briefed by Dayan. The new proposals appealed to him. Spirits were high; breakfast began and the food even tasted better. The bitterness of the past few days had disappeared.

Carter and Begin reviewed the new proposals:

• Egypt agrees to exchange ambassadors immediately after Israel withdraws to the Al-'Arish–Ras Muhammad line, nine months after the signing of the agreement.

• The question of an Egyptian liaison office will be among the subjects to be negotiated in discussions between Israel and Egypt in the context of the negotiations over the autonomy plan.

• The United States guarantees to supply Israel with oil

for fifteen years if Egypt refuses to sell oil to Israel and if Israel requests the United States to do so.

The moment agreement was reached, the relations between the two men ceased to be cool. Carter was very pleased but he did not say anything as hundreds of journalists continued to report that the talks had failed and that Carter was returning home empty-handed. At Ben-Gurion Airport, very few picked up on the hints given by Begin and Carter in their speeches.

On a rainy day, with gray skies, Jimmy Carter left Israel. Before entering the plane, he shook hands with Avraham Tamir.

"Sir, see those clouds that are blocking the sunlight? Don't worry, behind them the sky is clear blue."

Air Force 1 took off for Cairo. The meeting between Carter and Sadat took place at the International Airport. Egyptian officials told reporters that they did not believe that Carter had brought anything significant with him and that the meeting would last only as long as it took to refuel.

At the same time Carter, Brzezinski, Sadat, Mubarek, and Khalil sat in the reception room of the airport. Sadat immediately gave up his demand for a liaison office in Gaza. Outside, Egyptian officials continued to tell journalists that the talks were going to collapse because of Israel's imperialist designs and inability to trust Egypt.

The talks continued for more than two hours and afterward Carter and Sadat stayed for an additional private meeting. During their talk, Carter telephoned Begin in Jerusalem to inform him of Sadat's acceptance of the new proposal. Photographers were invited in before he could finish his conversation and some of them were able to hear parts of the conversation. They were the first to tell the horde of journalists waiting outside of the impending announcement. Minutes later Carter and Sadat emerged; Carter was smiling broadly.

"There is a treaty," he said.

In the United States, Israel, and Egypt, preparations were quickly made for a signing ceremony. It was decided that the ceremony would take place in Washington. The necessary documents were prepared and government printing offices in the three capitals made the treaty available in Hebrew, English, and Arabic. Some cried; others beamed with happiness; all were excited.

The Governments of the Arab Republic of Egypt and the State of Israel

Desiring to put an end to the state of war between them and to establish a peace which will guarantee living in security;

Desiring similarly to develop relations of friendship and cooperation between them according to the Covenant of the United Nations and the principles of the International Court of Justice which adjudicates international relations during times of peace;

Agree to the above principles, within free exercise of their sovereignty in order to implement the "Framework for the Signings of a Peace Treaty Between Egypt and Israel."

On Monday, March 26, 1979—27th Adar 5739, according to the Hebrew calendar; Rabbiyah Rani, 1399, according to the Muslim calendar—at 2:04 p.m., on the lawn of the White House in Washington, Anwar Sadat and Menachem Begin signed the peace treaty between Egypt and Israel. The president of the U.S., Jimmy Carter, added his signature as witness to the peace document.

INDEX